W9-DDK-569

Stepping Stones

". . . to help future generations learn, achieve and remember the source of their
knowledge so that they will be able to create stepping stones for
future generations."

Morris Silverman '36

Stepping Stones

Marty Silverman

Whitston Publishing Company, Inc.
Albany, New York
2003

Library of Congress Control Number 2003105189

ISBN 0-87875-547-0

Printed in the United States of America by
Boyd Printing Company
Albany, New York

.

Contents

Introduction

by Paul Grondahl

Morris "Marty" Silverman is an American original. If Marty didn't exist on New York state's Capital Region landscape, somebody would have had to invent him. There's nobody quite like Marty. And it's not simply because the Troy, N.Y. native has showered millions of dollars of his philanthropic largess on Albany and its environs. Or, that he is the capital city's most notable master builder in several generations. The $200 million University Heights Association development project, as envisioned and spurred on by Marty, ranks perhaps second only to Governor Nelson Rockefeller's Empire State Plaza in its transformative power and sweeping legacy for the city and region.

Yet, Marty is somehow more than the sum of his parts. There's a quality that's hard to define, an element more profound than the reach of his accumulated wealth. It has to do with an achievement that no amount of money could buy. Even as he was cruising full-speed past his 90th birthday, Marty achieved a kind of communal alchemy more precious than any stock portfolio or vast real estate holdings. Marty Silverman taught the Capital Region to believe in itself. Timing is everything, after all, and Marty came on the scene at a time when it seemed like the citizenry had lost faith in the potential of the place. But along came Marty and he refused to accept the pessimistic notion that Albany's best days were behind it. Instead of bemoaning the city's struggles, Marty set to work convincing everyone to envision a prosperous future along with him.

Marty held the mirror up to the Capital Region and convinced residents that they saw a better self reflected back. "I believe in the future of Albany," he declared in 1997 while announcing his vision for transforming University Heights into a world-class center for the study of law, medicine and higher education. When Albany Law School—Marty's alma mater, Class of 1936—hosted a glitzy Capital Region salute to Marty's philanthropy in the spring of 2001, they had that quote engraved on a thousand silver paperweights. Hey, if Marty says it's true and it's carved into a paperweight, it carries gravitas, right? Who's to argue? The phase continues to have a certain heft to it, now that it's holding down stacks of paper on desks across the region. "I believe in the future of Albany." You can quote Marty on that.

When it comes to promoting Albany as an international center for law and medicine, his pet project, Marty goes at the task like a cross between a Madison Avenue spin doctor and P. T. Barnum. He's the best ambassador the Chamber of Commerce could ever imagine. He calls himself "a cheerleader of the Albany renaissance." What renaissance, a skeptic might wonder? Don't ask. If Marty says it's an Albany renaissance, who's to argue? If you need to have the slogan engraved on a fancy silver paperweight to become a believer in the renaissance along with Marty, that can be arranged.

Marty understands the power of attaching a simple slogan to a complex development idea or a far-fetched dream. He has spread his message of self-reliance to hundreds around the Capital Region by passing out $2 bills bearing a sticker that reads: "If It Is To Be, It Is Up To Me." He likes to print up gag business cards, too, like the one that advertises his own demise. It reads: "You will find Marty at the Riverside Cemetery, Lodi, N.J. He is at Plot 89, corner of Bethel and King David Avenue.

He appreciates your visit and thanks you for coming."

Marty has several of these jokey business cards and delights in passing them out to new acquaintances to gauge their reaction. He's a guy that laughs at his own jokes. As he approaches the punchline, his face lights up, eyes narrowing to a slit, while a wide grin creases his face and he convulses into guffaws just as he finishes the joke. His laughter comes in high, wheezy waves and literally causes his belly to shake. Marty's mirth is a full-body experience. Humor is Marty's fountain of youth. When he's laughing at a joke he's just told, the years melt away, and he's suddenly 91 going on nine.

James Barba, president and CEO of Albany Medical Center, who met Marty in 1994 when he dropped an unrestricted $1 million gift on the hospital, perhaps summed up the essential Marty best: "He's part joker, part visionary, part saint and part sinner in one enormous, glorious package."

Does it really matter, then, that the title of Albany International Airport seemed more than a tad bit hyperbolic for the new name proposed by Marty for an expanded facility that offers nearly all domestic flights—aside from a few charters to Canada?

"We're spending all that money to build a beautiful new airport," he told me when he hatched the idea to add "International" to the airport's name several years back. "Why undersell ourselves? Who wants to fly into Albany County Airport? It sounds like the boondocks. Now, how about Albany *International* Airport?" He has a way of saying "International," which is one of his favorite words, in such a way that he accentuates each syllable and draws it out for several long beats.

When all was said and done, the new signs went up and the official name was changed at highway exits and on maps. Marty had the last laugh on the airport. An *International* belly laugh. And his instincts proved correct. Although it was mostly a cosmetic change, the new name had marketing cachet and did wonders for the region's self-image. Marty worked his name switcheroo behind-the-scenes, with a minimum of fuss or arm-twisting. He didn't take credit publicly. The result was what mattered. He didn't waste time waiting for back pats or thank yous. The name wasn't even dry on the new airport signs when Marty quickly moved on to a half-dozen other ideas and projects continuously churning around in his busy mind.

That's Marty. He's a doer, not an analyst. He combines tenacious business savvy with grandfatherly tenderness. He has a disarming way of making a pitch and refusing to take no for an answer. He uses the fact that he is in his 90s to best advantage. Marty has been know to light a fire under a foot-dragging bureaucrat by reminding the obstructionist fellow that if government can't pick up its pace, he'll be six feet under before the deal is closed. That line usually works. "I'm having a ball in Albany," Marty always says after taking a break from a full slate of meetings during a typical three-day business visit from Manhattan. "I feel like an old grandpa who comes to town to visit, musses up his grandchildren's hair and then is happy to go home."

When Marty burst on the Capital Region scene in 1997—outed publicly by the *Times Union* after giving a few million dollars anonymously to Albany Law School and Albany Medical Center—he was already 85 years old and a philanthropist sitting on a foundation worth some $250 million. Although his hardscrabble upbringing was alluded to in newspaper articles, just how Marty came to be the cheerleader of the Albany renaissance remained a story untold. Until now.

In this delightful memoir, "Stepping Stones," Marty unspools the captivating narrative of his remarkable rise from son of a working-class Troy tailor to decorated World War II combat veteran to business entrepreneur to pioneer of the heavy equipment leasing business to notable philanthropist. The book resonates with Marty's inimitable voice. You can almost hear his infectious cackle cascading down the pages after each paragraph, laughing at his own jokes.

In his telling, Marty's life reads like a Horatio Alger story as scripted by Woody Allen. Shot through with raucous humor, "Stepping Stones" is an unusual hybrid that is part biography and part business primer on the art of the deal. Always entertaining, Marty is a raconteur and enthusiastic storyteller who isn't afraid to be self-deprecating. Marty seems to approach life as if it were a divine comedy. His extraordinary business success, in part, seems directly proportional to his ability to laugh at himself. Even when he's facing the sting of anti-Semitism, struggling academically, being wounded with shrapnel in the war, or hemorrhaging money in business enterprises gone awry, Marty never loses the capacity to shrug it off with humor. Along with a philosophy that laughter is the best medicine, Marty's loose-limbered modesty and utter lack of pretension seems to have a lot to do with how far he rose in business.

For at his core, Marty is a born salesman. He could sell the proverbial Klondike bars to Eskimos. The secret to his success was nothing more profound than hard work and outhustling the competition. "We're not Fords and Rockefellers," Silverman liked to say. "Nobody gave us anything. We just worked hard."

Growing up, his two older sisters worked odd jobs to help support the Silverman family. Marty made deliveries of tailored clothes around Troy for his father, who emigrated from Poland in 1898 and settled in the Collar City near relatives. His dad's tailor shop was located amid Troy's infamous red-light district and Marty tells of his encounters with prostitutes in his memoir with typical humor. During the Depression, Marty worked his way through law school pumping gas at a Standard Oil station he managed in the shadow of the Menands Bridge in South Troy. His anecdotes about early jobs in Manhattan, where the family moved when his father's business faltered in Troy, have the appealing humor and crisp timing of a stand-up comedy routine. The chapters on his experiences during World War II manage at once to be harrowing, moving, profound and as darkly comic about the absurdity of combat as Joseph Heller's anti-war novel, "Catch-22."

After the war, Marty, a decorated officer—and an accidental hero who seemingly bumbled from one unlikely triumph to another—applied that same joyful and open-hearted approach to the business world. With his beloved wife and business partner, Dot, at his side, Marty started hawking surplus Army cars around Albany. Marty succeeded in the used-car business and others like it because he never considered himself too good to undertake the most mundane and unglamorous transaction. As long as it could turn a profit. The product he was peddling might have been warehouses full of odd lot garden hose; or truckloads of military surplus gas masks; or rail cars stuffed with copper wire. He had a knack for being able to sniff out a market for just about any type of goods. He wasn't above pounding the pavement, either, hat in hand, pitching his wares and never giving up after long stretches of rejection. Marty also never forgot the golden rule of the free market. Buy low and sell high. Not that he didn't have an exceptionally brilliant mind for business. He could read all the angles, anticipate problems, think outside the box and stay ahead of the curve. The two big ideas and business innovations that brought Marty his millions were a pioneering application of an innovative leasing plan for the purchase of expensive heavy construction equipment and fronting venture capital to a start-up communications company named MCI.

It's hard to tell from the memoir which side of the business ledger Marty has enjoyed more: chasing down the business deals that earned him his millions or giving those millions away through his family-run philanthropic foundation. Whether amassing his fortune or giving it away, Marty's infectious laughter echoes across each chapter in this memoir recounting his remarkable life that spans most of the 20th century.

Ever the schmaltzy showman, at each one of the numerous groundbreakings and ribbon-cuttings that Marty has
presided over in Albany, he reiterates his noting that he wants
all the church bells in the capital city to ring "to wake up the
city of Albany."

According to Marty, "There is no place in the world that
can offer what the Capital Region can offer. It is two hours
from Boston, two hours from Canada, two hours from New
York City and two hours from Washington, DC." "Albany has
22 colleges surrounding it; it is in the heart of three mountain
ranges and numerous lakes; it has museums and theatres. I
believe it will become the equivalent of the Mayo Clinic in this
century."

After six years of stirring up the pot in the Capital
Region by embarking on a dizzying array of development projects (and some ideas that never saw the light of day), Marty
Silverman has succeeded in rousing Albany. New York's capital city is wide awake now, awaiting word of Marty's next
adventure. He'll never really be finished. In his memoir's final
chapter, he calls his Albany vision a work-in-progress. "I won't
be through until I'm through," he writes. It's the sort of can-do
spirit that belongs on a silver paperweight, words spoken by a
true American original.

Chapter 1

❯❯ ❯❯

STEPPING STONES

Don't Believe Everything You Read

The Bronze Star Medal is hereby presented to Private First Class Morris Silverman of the United States Army for heroic military achievement against the German enemy on November 18, 1944 in the vicinity of Moulins-les-Metz, France.

While participating in the mop-up of German troops, Private First Class Silverman observed unusual movements in the cellar of a nearby building.

Directing two fellow soldiers to provide cover, Private First Class Silverman entered the building alone.

Hearing noises, he descended to the basement, broke open the door, and surprised 24 armed enemy.

Conducting himself with calm confidence, Private First Class Silverman addressed the enemy in German, ordered them to lay down their arms, and although greatly outnumbered, quickly obtained their surrender. His intrepid feat reflects great credit on him and on the military service.

Signed:
THE PRESIDENT OF THE UNITED STATES OF AMERICA

Impressive? Twenty-four enemy with one blow? All by myself, no less. It won me a lot of press, a promotion, some medals.

Very impressive.

The only trouble is, that's not really the way it happened. At least, not as far as I'm concerned.

The *real* event behind the press releases and the decorations is far more interesting than what you've just read. And a good deal more typical of the strange star that has hovered over me since the day I came into this world.

Here's the story.

The Voice from the Blue

At the time this incident took place I was an acting sergeant with a 12-man squad under my command in France. We were prowling around what was left of the country town of Moulins-les-Metz on a mop-up mission when, just as the citation says, I saw something moving through a cellar window.

Now in combat when the shooting begins it's a natural human instinct to *burrow*. Soldiers dig foxholes. Infantry men trench. If they happen to be in a building and can't dig, they do the next best thing; they hide in the basement.

Well aware of this fact, I called over two of my men, ordered them to cover the upper floors of the suspicious building, crept up to the entrance, and walked slowly and silently down the steps to the cellar.

As I neared bottom I heard muffled voices on the other side of the door. I listened carefully. French or German? French or German?

German—bingo!

Now, in a combat situation of this kind the textbook

operating procedure tells us we are to kick open the door, lob in a hand grenade, and enter with weapon blazing before the enemy has time to recover. The idea is to capitalize on the element of surprise. As a military man once remarked, in warfare five seconds of surprise is worth a hundred hours planned.

So I reached down for a grenade from my belt. But to my amazement, all the hooks were empty.

Impossible! I distinctly remembered taking several grenades with me that morning. I must have used them in the clean-up operations and then forgotten.

This lack of fire power threw a completely different light on the situation. I started sweating. No grenades. No way to get help. A roomful of armed enemy. The only thing to do, I decided, is to enter cold, take them by surprise, and hope for the best.

Saying a quick prayer, I leaned back, kicked open the door, and leaped into the room.

Sure enough, inside the rather stuffy chamber it was wall-to-wall Jerry. Most of them were sitting around a wooden farm table, smoking, writing letters, humming to themselves, half asleep, their rifles spread out on the floor in front of them and their gear strewn all around them.

"LAY DOWN YOUR ARMS AND SURRENDER!" I ordered in my most commanding voice, moving to the center of the room and training my weapon everywhere at once, expecting a sudden scramble and the inevitable fire fight. (The command I shouted was in Yiddish, by the way, not in German, an irony that was perhaps not lost to certain of the enemy. They certainly seemed to get the message.)

To my astonishment, instead of lunging for their weapons, this roomful of the flower of brave German soldierhood jumped to attention in unison, dropped their rifles as if they were covered with disease germs, saluted, locked their hands behind their head in orderly German fashion, and began burbling and sputtering: *Nicht shissen, Nicht shissen—*"Don't shoot, don't shoot!" Several of them got down on their knees and started to beg for their lives!

Now you must understand one thing about war: from the hour a combat infantryman enters the military to the hour he's discharged he's taught to do one thing and one thing only: kill. All our training, all our indoctrination, our very reflexes and nervous systems were tuned to this single frequency, to killing. And many of us had been getting straight A's at it since D-Day. In fact, one of the sayings I liked to repeat to the men under my command was: "Never *tell* a German you're going to shoot him—shoot him first, then tell him!"

Now here I was with 24 quacking ducks in Hitler's shooting pond, me with all the bullets, them on their knees, and every inch of my training urging me to perform my patriotic duty and *kill them dead!*

I glanced at my weapon. Seven rounds of ammunition left in the clip. Not enough to do in the whole bunch. Needed more bullets. I moved my hand slowly down to my ammo belt, unsnapped a pocket, and reached for a clip.

It was stuck. Wouldn't budge. I'd never had anything like this happen before in all my months of combat.

So I unsnapped another pocket and reached in. But again the same thing happened, the clip was wedged. It was as if somebody had glued it into the belt.

I looked up in silent panic, expecting the prisoners to note my fumbling attempts and to lunge. Their rifles were still within easy reach.

But no, they still were on the floor, sputtering and whining, so lathered up over their imminent doom that they'd forgotten to keep an eye on the executioner.

What now?

Hell, shoot as many of them as I can anyway, I said to myself. They'd certainly return the favor if they could. I lifted my rifle and took aim.

Then I heard it.

Clearly, distinctly, commandingly. A voice inside my head. It spoke one word only: "DON'T!" At that same moment I heard the safety on my gun click on.

I say "heard" because my fingers hadn't thrown the lever. At least not to my knowledge. There was the unmistakable sound coming out of the weapon—CLICK!—and on went the safety. But who turned it on? I didn't know.

Meanwhile the sight of the raised weapon sent my captives into dithers of terror. Some were hocking and sobbing like seven-year-olds, others were praying aloud, a few were balled up miserably in their chairs waiting for the *coup de grace*.

And here I am, despite my years of combat training and infantry experience, incapable of shooting the bastards!

Several minutes passed.

I stared at them; they stared back at me.

God knows how long this weird peek-a-boo would have gone on if I hadn't come to my senses and shouted for them to march up the stairs in orderly fashion with their hands behind their heads.

At street level I made them line up again the wall. By now others in my company were arriving. Apparently the Germans had made such a ruckus with their crying and slobbering that every American within a quarter-mile had heard the noise and was coming over to investigate.

I mumbled something to my men about covering the prisoners, then turned and slipped away. More men pushed past me and several of them slapped me on the back, congratulating me for single-handedly capturing a roomful of ferocious Huns.

What they didn't understand was that my great act of heroism was actually an unbearable disgrace! At least as far as I was concerned. Here was my opportunity—every soldier's dream—to do my duty as I'd been instructed. To protect my country, guard my people, make the world safe for democracy, vanquish the enemy. Instead I'd stood there with apple strudel on my face and let them cry like babies.

⊷ ⊷

The next day we were given R&R and moved into a safe area behind the lines to clean and repair our equipment and ourselves. But the self-torment continued. I was tired of the killing, the hurt, the blood, the fallen men, the cold, the dirt. Of seeing good boys slaughtered, of hearing the screaming and the praying and then the silence. I had already been given two Purple Hearts. Would the third hang on my tombstone? How could I make it to the end of this war? Especially now that I'd failed my soldier's duty? What else was there for me to do under these hopeless circumstances, I finally told myself, then to end all this misery and disgrace. I would take the only manly way out I knew—I would take a shower.

Don't laugh.

You see, when a soldier is blue, when all seems lost, the one solace he has at his disposal while in camp—sometimes— is a hot dunking and a pair of clean pants. Nothing revives the spirit better than a shower, nothing feeds the soul so well during time of war, nothing gets you so clean, especially if you've been living in a foxhole for a month without a change of clothes.

So off I traipsed. I wanted to cleanse myself physically, mentally, spiritually.

I call them showers now only with reservations, four trailer truck units just brought up and hitched together railroad style like a traveling circus. Inside each was a row of water tanks and a line of nozzles. Shower-takers stripped naked, plopped their clothes into a basket, grabbed a piece of cardboard with a number on it, then marched into a spritz of hot water, soaping up and sponging down for a few blissful minutes until some merciless sergeant blew a whistle. Time's up!

Now you towel off and march yourself out the other side of the truck wagon to an open field where your clothes are waiting for you, neatly folded in a basket with your number on top, all hot and dry.

Doesn't sound like much, maybe. But warm, clean, clothes—well, I don't know a guy in the service who wouldn't have given a month's pay. . .

At any rate, I'm strolling out of the showers feeling a little more human when who should I bump into but my chaplain—a rabbi I knew, a very friendly, wise sort of fellow. Right away it occurred to me that here was an opportunity to talk with an intelligent man of God about the German capture incident, and hopefully get the whole thing off my chest.

I spoke with him for a few minutes about my problem, and just let it all pour out.

He thought about it for a moment. Then he said, "Let's take a walk."

We strolled together along a quiet country road for several minutes while I proceeded to confess to him what a failure I'd been, what a coward I was, what a disgrace to God and country I must be.

In the middle of this tirade the rabbi cut me short. He motioned for us to sit down by the side of the road.

Calmly, simply, on a bombed-out French country lane 6,000 miles from home, he then spoke a few words that have stayed with me all my life.

"You're a hero all right, Marty" he said. "A bigger hero than if you'd gunned down all those poor misguided slobs. They wanted to live, just like you. Wanted to get through this terrible war. Wanted to see their mothers again. Their kids. Wanted to touch a woman again. Sit by the sea. Hear a band play. Smoke a cigarette. Just like you."

"What about the safety on the gun?" I asked. "Why'd it just snap on like that?"

"You did it," he answered quietly. "Or rather, your conscience did it. Maybe you weren't aware of what you were doing the time. You had a lot going on at that moment. But something inside you knew it was the right thing and just went ahead and did it for you."

"That's hard to swallow," I answered.

"Marty," the chaplain said, putting his hand on my shoulder. "Do you know how many lives you saved in that room? Jews have a proverb—remember? 'If you save one life you save the world.'"

"I guess so," I muttered.

"It is so," he continued. "And think of this. Besides the men you spared, how many generations will now be born because you showed mercy that day. Hundreds. Thousands. Era after era, down through the centuries, through the millennia. Picture an endless line of men, women, and children walking towards you from the future, entire family trees, generation after generation—all living and playing and breathing God's air because you had the decency not to pull a trigger on a bunch of helpless men a thousand years before. Seems to me that justifies calling you a hero."

❥ ❥

I've thought about these words many times over the years, and of all those generations escorted into this life by a solitary voice that spoke to me that day through the madness of human warfare.

Having now lived 90 years, having raised a family, spawned children and grandchildren, made a great deal of money and seen many strange and wonderful things, I still find myself harkening back to that conversation on a road outside an ancient French village long ago. There *is* a directing voice in each of us, I hear myself saying. It *can* speak to us, all of us, if we just allow ourselves to listen.

❥ ❥

And so it is, therefore, to these generations born and unborn that I write and dedicate this book. Especially to those generations of my own blood, and of my own people.

My hope and intention is that what I say in these pages will in some small way direct a beam of light onto the road of those who follow — to show what the world was like in an earlier part of the 20th century; to show where the roots of our families and our pasts are planted; and most importantly, to show that behind the confusion and drudgery that sometimes darkens our pleasures there is an array of stepping stones that bridges the stream of our lives. In old age, when we look back at this path of stones we come to realize that they form an entirely purposeful pattern.

And that all of us are here to discover what this purpose is, to cross the bridge of stepping stones that God has laid down for each of us, and along the way — above all other things — to learn.

If asked by the angels and prophets themselves: What is the meaning of this life? I would answer just that — to learn.

Chapter 2

◆→ ◆→

CITY ON THE HILLS

Marty of Troy

For most of my early childhood the town of Troy in upstate New York was home.

We moved away plenty of times, it's true, usually to New York City. But we always seemed to return. I'm reminded of the story of the immigrant who comes to the United States and can't speak a word of English. He has to eat, of course, so his family teaches him to ask for "Apple pie and coffee" whenever he's ordering at a lunch counter. After dining on apple pie and coffee for two straight months, the man becomes sick of the same meal and urges his family to teach him another phrase. So they add "Ham and cheese sandwich, please" to his expanding vocabulary.

Next day the immigrant arrives at the lunch counter, sits down on the stool, and proudly makes his new request: "Ham and cheese sandwich, please."

"What you want that on, Sweetie, white or rye?" the waitress asks.

The immigrant looks around in confusion, sputters for a moment, and then the lights go on. "Apple pie and coffee" he replies with a big smile—proud, no doubt, of his new bilingual skills.

And that was our family's traveling history too—one-track. Every time we moved away from Troy we'd eventually be drawn back to our old security blanket, our "Apple pie and coffee." Here we lived in a warm nest of friends and relatives and caring people. Here we felt secure, blessed, home again.

Today, of course, Troy has lost a great deal of its commercial distinction, but in its time it was a gateway to the world.

We're talking the middle 1920's now, when The City on the Hills was the center of the collar and cuff industry—men's shirts—and the Erie Canal was New York State's major super highway. Many of the engineers who came to build this canal stayed on and settled here, and soon the city became a hub of scientific activity as well. Its legacy lives on royally today in R.P.I., Rensselaer Polytechnic Institute, one of the best engineering school in the country.

The story also goes that during the War of 1812 an inspector of army supplies named Samuel Wilson regularly stamped "U.S." on all goods that passed his muster at military headquarters in Troy. One day someone asked Sam Wilson what the initials U.S. stood for. Wilson shot back that they referred to him—*Uncle Sam*. Thus was born the famous nickname for the United States Government.

Sometimes on warm summer nights my friends and I would stroll down to the Erie Canal—it begins at Troy—and talk to the families who were living there on barges and flatboats. This friendly, fascinating tribe cooked their meals over fires they made right on deck. They had chickens roosting in the hold, arm chairs made from orange crates, flower boxes neatly arranged on the bow, small vegetable gardens on deck, all very comfortable and tidy. We called them the "Barge People." They carried all kinds of cargo up river, and these loads tended to change with the seasons. Corn and wheat in the summer, coal, chemicals, tools, pig iron in the winter.

Livestock and bananas and cotton bales were carried up from the deep South. Gargantuan hunks of steel passed by on their way to factories in New England. Along with these came timber, copper coils, oil drums, machine parts, and, most mysterious of all, huge sealed wooden crates 30 or 40 feet high that we spent hours trying to figure out what was inside.

How did Troy get its strange name?

Some classical wag many years ago noticed that the city sits on lots of hills like the historical Troy of Homer, so he gave it a good Trojan name. Actually, classical titles were fashionable everywhere in the state of New York at that time—Rome, Syracuse, Carthage, Corinth, Phoenicia. I couldn't help wondering, though, when I was a kid studying the map of New York, where names like Schroon Lake, Rosenfield, and Ellisburg slipped in.

At any rate, the English came to Troy first, I believe, followed by the Dutch, Italians, Irish, and God knows who else, then finally a colony of Jewish families, of which the Silvermans were members in good standing.

A Matter of Utility

Our family owned a modest wood frame house in the Jewish section of town perched on one of Troy's highest hills. It was lighted by gas, like all buildings of the day, with brass fixtures that protruded from every wall, displaying white, stocking-like mantles on their spouts.

When you wanted light you'd turn a knob on the fixture, wait till the gas started hissing, and put a match to the mantle. The mantle smoldered for a moment, then burst into a brightly glowing light with an extremely unpleasant smell. During the evening the whole house, the whole city, the whole world, stank of gas.

All you had to do to keep this contraption burning was to maintain a sufficient store of nickels and dimes in the house. When the light suddenly dimmed, as it was likely to do after several hours, you grabbed a coin, ran down to the basement, and dropped it in the meter.

For heat we used coal. My dad ran a tailoring business a few blocks from the house and labored there from seven o'clock in the morning till seven at night. This meant he wasn't home during the day when the coal wagon pulled up in front of our house and unceremoniously dumped its load in our front yard.

It also meant that my mother, my two sisters, Nettie and Toby, and I would spend a good part of the afternoon schlepping the coal inside the house and lugging it into the coal bin.

That's how we stayed warm.

To keep cool we had the iceman. This cheery soul would pull up to our back door once a week. In the back of his horse-drawn wagon he kept a pile of sparkling ice and a pair of tongs. As soon as he arrived we would lower our dumbwaiter down to him on the street where he would place a block of ice into it with his tongs. Then we'd pulley the dumbwaiter up, tote the block of ice to the icebox, and pop it in. You had to work for your refrigeration in those days.

In the depths of winter my friends and I would walk down to the Hudson and watch the iceman saw these huge square hunks from the frozen river, then float them back to land, load them onto his cart, carry them back to his warehouse, and cover them with a blanket of sawdust. When the weather warmed up the sawdust protected the ice from melting—though to this day I don't understand quite why.

Inside *our* icebox it was a different story. After a day or so of our opening and closing the door the ice block would melt, so we kept a tray under it called a "schlissle" to catch the dripping water.

Woe to him or her who didn't empty the schlissle on schedule! Woe, woe!

A flooded kitchen floor was the result, and there would be hell to pay from my mother. So what you had to do to prevent this catastrophe was to open the ice box door as infrequently as possible, do everything at once as fast as you could in a few seconds, taking out the eggs, putting in the milk, holding the meat, grabbing the carrots, spooning out the butter, then close the door and not open it again for the rest of the day. (Lots of luck.)

"Keep the icebox door shut!" was the command heard round the house (and, I imagine, around a million other houses as well). "Keep it shut! The water's going to warp the floor!"

Does water really warp floors? I used to wonder. If it does, why doesn't the floor warp every time we mop it?

Don't ask questions. Just shut the door.

The Conversion

As in many Jewish households, all life, all discipline, all celebration and frenzy centered around our mother. She was a robust and sympathetic woman, small, not more than 100 pounds, full of kindness, worry, jokes, energy, chutzpah. Nothing we kids did escaped her all-seeing eye. She seemed to be everywhere, all the time, picking up, scolding, fixing, cooking, kissing, an early woman's libber. Whenever we needed something big or something small we came to her. When decisions had to be made, money divided, stuff carried, pot roasts basted, math problems factored, feelings soothed, Mother was action central.

My father, of course, was a good man, a gentle, honest and affectionate man. He worked hard all his life to support us and rarely complained. I and my two sisters loved him dearly.

But it was mother, our dearest mother, who ran the family — and who ran our show. My sisters and I worshiped and respected her for the sacrifices she made on our behalf. It would have been inconceivable to hurt her or embarrass her in any way. When life was collapsing around us, when my father was losing his business or the family was going bankrupt, she would simply laugh and say "The Lord will provide." And we never doubted her.

Because of her kindness my sisters and I seldom fought. We shared everything and always gave one another the benefit of the doubt. We knew what she expected of us and didn't waver. (Well, hardly ever.) As a young child I remember how my mother seemed to grow happier and more beautiful every day like a princess in a fairy tale. Her joy made me joyous, and opened me. Like the Jewish proverb goes, "A child without a mother is like a door without a knob."

We were, in short, a thoroughly blessed and contented family, an unusual phenomenon, I'm told, in any age.

I also believe it was mother who one day decided that gas was a lousy, smelly way to light a house, and that if we were going to keep up with the Goldbergs we had to make the switch.

To what? To electricity.

Electricity?

Yes. Believe it or not, electricity was still a novelty 80 years ago, not only in Troy but everywhere in the United States. It was something that big businesses used to run their factories, that drove city trolley cars, something that was found in the mansions of a few families like the Rockefellers.

But in the house? In Troy, New York? This was a thought that simply never crossed any of our minds.

Except mom's.

The day word got out in the neighborhood that we were making the conversion, that we were, as they said then, "electrifying," everybody on the block came over and shook our hands, patted our backs, congratulated us as if we'd just won the lottery.

We waited for our appointment for what seemed an eternity. Finally one day the electricians pulled up in front of our house in their big red truck, and our neighbors appeared from blocks away to ogle the geniuses at work.

I watched in awe as the workmen entered our living room like conquering heros, made grave pronouncements about volts and wall studs, moved from room to room with their important looking tools, drilled into the woodwork, chipped away stucco, stretched wire, stitched cables, left piles of plaster everywhere, installed a single socket on each wall like a little kiss mark along with a single overhead light fixture on every ceiling.

At the end of two days the great work was complete, and father came home early from his shop to celebrate. We stood in the living room drinking tea, everyone talking at once, waiting for it to get dark enough outside so we could put the dynamo through its paces.

Dusk finally came and we crowded into the living room. With great ceremony my father slowly moved his hand toward the switch. He rolled his eyes to heaven, mumbled a silent prayer, stuck out a tentative finger and flicked.

CLICK! On went a single unfrosted overhead bulb, throwing its pale, incandescent light across the room.

Magic! We shouted, hugged, danced, ran from room to room throwing switches like mad worshipers. No more running to the basement to drop a coin in the meter. No more candles and dark rooms. We were liberated.

My mother brought in food and for the first time in my life I dined under the light of a lamp. And for the first time in my life I could really *see* what I was eating. Above all—most of all—for the first time in my life there was no stink of gas while we ate dinner.

What would they think of next!

The Radio Set and Passing Time

Of course, one of the problems with having electricity was figuring out what to do with it.

We had the one bulb hanging over our heads in every room, the one socket on the wall plugged into the one floor lamp. But what else? Appliances didn't exist. You couldn't buy one if you wanted to. Nothing had been invented yet. No electric can openers, no TV's, refrigerators, nothing to plug into.

Thus it was a happy day when the crystal radio set was invented and our father came home one night with a brand new model.

Crystal radio sets were the granddaddies of the modern-day radio, a pretty little stone contraption about the size of a quarter that rests inside a wooden box and somehow—don't ask me the particulars—picks up radio waves. On one side of the stone a pin protrudes with a handle on the end. You jiggle it until it touches j-u-s-t the right spot on the crystal, then a faint radio signal comes through via a set of earphones.

And you listen in.

Doesn't sound like a CD, but what a miracle! Imagine a world without digital readouts or television or power lines. Without computers, radios, tape recorders. Imagine an entirely non-electronic universe. Then picture this tiny, mysterious crystal stone appearing in the middle of your kitchen table one day. You hook it to your ear. You fiddle with the pin. Suddenly you hear Rudy Vallee crooning a love song 150 miles away in New York City.

Talk about magic.

Even then, as a pre-adolescent, as I listened to the sounds flowing out of this primitive gizmo and struggled to keep the headset from slipping off of my ears, I knew we were standing on the brink of strange, brave, stupendous change. I could feel it around me, feel the world shifting on its ends. Undreamed of things were on their way; century-old standbys were passing into oblivion. That very year they were developing a method to manufacture synthetic ice—goodbye ice wagon. And gas heating—gone with the electric wind. Automobiles were replacing trolleys. Horse-drawn carts were being sold in antique shops. Things were moving. Shifting. Merging in and out of existence.

And I realized then, as I do even more today, that everything is passing and impermanent. Nothing stays the same, not even for a minute. Ever.

Why the Women Sit Upstairs in Shul

When I was growing up in Troy there were perhaps 1000 Jewish families living inside the city limits; which meant there were about 3000 to 4000 men, women and children in our community, not a very large number when you think about it.

This sense of smallness was increased by the fact that we rarely associated with people outside our community, at least not on a social level. The Jews owned most of the small stores in Troy, it's true, but when the day's work was over they all sped like locomotives back to the fold, back to the Jewish part of town.

Here we had our own Kosher butchers, our own doctors, lawyers, schools, shoe stores, our own everything. If you wanted a bricklayer you hired a Jewish bricklayer. If you wanted a maid you looked in the papers for a person with a Jewish name. If you needed a prescription drug you bought it from the Jew who ran the drug store. The notion of going outside this charmed circle and fraternizing with the *goyim* on a personal level simply never entered our minds. It was as if we lived on our own shtetl.

One warm and tranquil Troy evening during Yom Kippur a few months before my bar mitzvah, I was walking leisurely with my family past these familiar storefronts on our way to shul.

Now the shul we attended at that time, I should tell you, was not a particularly orthodox establishment (you can always spot a not-so-orthodox shul when their holy books are written in Hebrew *and* English). Certainly it was nothing like the *really* orthodox shul nearby; and *nothing at all* like the infamous German shul.

This peculiar institution was populated entirely by second-generation, *nouveau riche* industrialists whose membership considered themselves to be Germans first and Jews second, and who rarely stooped to associate with the "merchant class" synagogues in town.

On certain high holidays my family might decide to attend the orthodox shul, and this was always a rough assignment for us kids. When the congregation started to pray all of us would be chased outside and told to wait there till it was over. Tradition had it that any young person with living parents who witnessed these sacred events was committing an unforgivable sin.

All of us kids would thus congregate on the steps outside the shul and have long discussions concerning the unspeakable rites that were taking place inside. The mystery was heightened to an almost unbearable degree: when the ceremony was over and we were allowed back inside the room everything there reeked of a strange ammonia-like smell.

We asked ourselves: What pagan sacrament was enacted here; what black magic had generated such a stench?

It was only years later that I discovered the truth about this terrible secret. During the early part of the century it was popular for women to faint whenever they became emotional. I don't know why it was like this; it was simply the fashion. Many women thus carried smelling salts with them wherever they went in case a swoon came on. During ceremonies at the synagogue these women would pray intensely for their departed loved ones, and their memories triggered a bout of faintness. When it happened the victims took a whiff of ammoniated smelling salts.

It was, in short, the smelling salts, not sacrificed babies, that caused the infamous smell.

Now just that week my mother had purchased new clothes for all us kids and we were feeling like little dandies walking along the street, and very affluent.

Then it suddenly occurred to me: we aren't rich. We're poor. Why has mother bought us all these fancy clothes? I asked my sister her opinion.

"Because," she explained to me. "Mother doesn't want us to feel ashamed in front of the other kids. She wants us to feel proud of how we look and who we are."

These words cut through me like a blade.

To my mother and father, clothes meant little. They knew who they were and the community knew who they were. That was sufficient. They didn't need to show off by purchasing new clothes for themselves.

But for their children—ah! that was a different matter entirely. For their children all the world was not good enough. "Mothers have big aprons," goes the saying, "to cover the faults of their sons and daughters."

At that moment I felt incredibly fortunate to have been born a Jew.

While we were strolling along that evening I also overheard my parents talking about how much money they could afford to contribute to the synagogue. They pondered how to shave a few cents off the month's budget, how to cut back a dollar on food that week, so they could maximize their contribution. As usual, my father opted for the more liberal sum and my mother for the conservative.

By the time we'd reached the shul they'd agreed that a donation of $25 was respectable. It was, in fact, a *great* deal of money for them at the time. But it was, after all, Yom Kippur.

We entered the shul. It was ablaze with lights. The rabbi stood at the pulpit dressed in white. He was a handsome old man with a rugged, bearded face, and kindly eyes. He always reminded me of Moses.

My mother and sisters immediately headed upstairs to the area reserved for women — at this time the sexes were segregated in synagogues — and my Dad and I took our seats below with the men.

A long, solemn service began.

I sat there half-listening, dreaming childish fantasies, glancing around at the beautiful lights, the candles, the books, the long-bearded old rabbi. For a moment I felt connected to something very ancient.

At the conclusion of the sermon the rabbi then delivered an eloquent and emotional plea. He told the congregation about the needs of the poor. He talked about disease and misery, and the starving Hindus in India. He explained that in our prayers for the new year, *Tseduka* — charity — must take top priority. Part of being Jewish was being generous and charitable.

Concluding the talk, he called on all members of the synagogue to make a money pledge for the new year, and to open their hearts, and their wallets as best they could.

When this speech was over I glanced at my father. He was very moved by what the rabbi had said and seemed to be searching his soul. When his name was called he pledged $30 instead of the agreed-upon $25. This was a good deal more money than he could afford.

I looked at him and he smiled back at me. Then he nodded his head towards my mother in the women's section above and put his finger to his lips.

He didn't have to say anything after that. I knew what he meant.

◆→ ◆→

Years later I delivered a speech to a room full of Jews.

I told them the story of that evening, than finished my talk by saying that *this* was the reason women sit upstairs in shul.

Because, I explained, if women were allowed to sit downstairs next to their husbands, the synagogue—and the rest of the Jewish world too—would never be the same.

The Rabbi Who Turns Your Knuckles Red

Sometimes it seemed like things *never* changed. Especially the problems.

The biggest of them just then, as I approached my twelfth year, was preparing for my bar mitzvah.

As I told you, the Jewish population in Troy was by no means enormous; which meant, among other things, that there was a scarcity of qualified rabbis to teach Hebrew and to prepare young minds for their bar mitzvah. During this coming-of-age ceremony, participants were called upon to deliver a speech and to recite long, involved passages in Hebrew which had to be committed, letter-perfect, to memory.

Thus every day after school a group of us gathered in a dingy room on the second floor of what must have been the most dilapidated building in downtown Troy. Everything there seemed to be broken down and to smell of cabbage and chemicals. For the next hour we were then subjected to—not taught, I say, but subjected to—Hebrew lessons by the one rabbi in the city qualified to teach us, a despotic little man named Rosenthal.

If I tell you that Rabbi Rosenthal stood over five feet tall and weighed 90 pounds I'd be exaggerating. I might even be lying. Stooped and canny, he had tiny yellow hands that were always fidgeting, and pixie-like eyes that darted around with no affection in them for us 12-year-old boys that I could ever find. I and my friends sat in his classroom straight as poles, laboring away at phonetics, trying to fathom an ancient language that made no sense to us, and that we were asked to memorize but never understand. When he addressed us he never made eye contact, as if a mere boy who knew so little of life and the Torah was not worthy of learning!

Class itself was a bad dream. While we studied and recited, sitting straight in our chairs, Rabbi Rosenthal strolled from desk to desk swinging an eight-inch leather strap. Any boy caught staring out the window or half-asleep was ordered to point to the line in the Hebrew text that we were supposed to be reading. He seemed to have a sixth sense for spotting wandering minds.

"So tell me, little genius" he'd bellow, bending over you with the strap. "Where are we? Show me the line!"

After the boy made a wild guess and missed by six pages, the rabbi commanded him to make a fist and proceeded to smack his knuckles with the strap.

The student was expected to take this blow without flinching. We were in the process of becoming men, after all. If the victim dared yank his hand away before the belt connected this caused the belt (and sometimes the rabbi's hand) to come banging down on the desk, invariably sending the rabbi into a conniption of fury. Lifting the young criminal from his seat by the ear, he would drag him across the room and fling him out the door, into the hall.

Most of us in the class would have found this bit of slapstick bearable and even hilarious had it not been for the fact that at such moments Rabbi Rosenthal also brandished a terrible secret weapon.

"Bring your mother here tomorrow!" he would shout as you flew through the door. "I want to have a talking with her about your behavior in class!"

Our mothers! Turn me on a spit! Skin me like a cat!
But not *that*!

A pain on the knuckles and ear, we knew, was nothing
compared to the hurt this merciless summons would inflict on
our long-suffering mothers. All our mothers, mine being no
exception.

In fact, after my mother was called in by the rabbi for
the tenth time (or somewhere thereabout) causing the joke to be
passed around that she was taking Hebrew lessons with me, she
finally sat me down in the kitchen and poured out a tormented
ultimatum.

"Don't you understand! Don't you get it? *He's the only
rabbi in town who can teach you Hebrew*? If he decides to kick
you out, *you'll never be bar mitzvahed.*"

Exile. Family disgrace. The guillotine.

Rabbi Rosenthal, in other words, was holding all the
cards. No behave, no class—no bar mitzvah.

And so, not wishing to hurt my mother, not wanting to
disgrace 5000 years of Jewish ancestry, against my grain and
my patience, I tried harder. I concentrated more. When the
rabbi caught me napping I accepted my whack without protest.
Will power. Young Nietzsche. When the rabbi called on me in
class to recite, I spoke in a clear and ringing voice. I was polite.
Modest. A model student. I held the door. I brought him presents. I even took lessons home and studied them in my spare
time. All for my mother's good name.

Thus gradually, slowly, class after class, day after day,
against every one of my pre-adolescent impulses *except* my
conscience, I started to learn Hebrew.

Which was a good thing. My bar mitzvah was just
around the corner.

●▸ ●▸ ●▸

Chapter 3

❧ ❧

NOW I AM A MAN

The Big Day Arrives

When a boy reaches the age of 13 he becomes a man. That, at least, is what we believe in the Jewish tradition.

Funny thing was, when my own bar mitzvah service was performed with all due ritual and ceremony I didn't feel an inch closer to manhood. Actually, I didn't notice any difference at all, except perhaps that my collection of fountain pens had multiplied spectacularly. (Pens were such a popular gift that the joke was going around about the boy who started his bar mitzvah speech by announcing "Now I am a fountain pen.")

Looking back over the experience, however, it seems clear to me now that even if a boy doesn't consciously feel any manly advancement after this ceremony there is something deep inside him that hears the message.

"You're now a man," 5000 years of Jewish tradition whispers in his ear during the ritual, and the bell is sounded. Though the hair on his chest is no thicker than it was yesterday, somewhere inside himself he feels an obligation to live up to this new responsibility. Then one day years later he realizes that, no, he didn't become a full-fledged man on the day of his bar mitzvah, but that, yes, because of this ancient ritual the seeds of manhood were planted. Thanks be to God, I say, for the wisdom of our forefathers—who knew what power there can be in a simple, well-timed suggestion.

As for the bar mitzvah party itself, that was a different story entirely. This event left such a deep impression on me that whenever I think back on my youth the memory returns with full force.

The image still lingers, for instance, of my father sitting in the synagogue dressed to the nines, gazing at my pudgy 13-year-old face with such affection! And my mother upstairs with a glow around her. Their beaming was so strong I had to close my eyes for a minute. All around me the shul was jammed with relatives from across the country, along with neighbors, friends, members of the congregation, strays and hangers-on my mother had invited just because she didn't want them to feel left out. It was a strange sensation, really, being the center of the universe for one afternoon. Strange, but very pleasant.

Especially so after I finished making my speech and reciting the Hebrew prayers I'd worked on so hard with Rabbi Rosenthal. The fact that I didn't understand a single word of these prayers seemed to bother no one in the synagogue that day, including me. In fact, the whole thing was more like sweating my way through a tough final exam than undergoing a sacred rite of passage

But I didn't care. I'd made it through without a flub, and my parents were out of their minds with joy. I found myself grasping the two handles of the Torah and looking down at it as it lay beside me, whispering a silent prayer: "Oh Lord! Thank you for this celebration. And thank you for the greatest gift of all, giving my parents the pleasure and *knockus* of this day."

A bar mitzvah boy looks forward to the presents he will receive. For me none was greater than seeing my parents' happiness.

When the ceremony came to a close the guests gathered round me, shaking my hand, patting my head, praising my efforts. In the midst of the hubbub I happened to notice my old nemesis, Rabbi Rosenthal, standing on the edge of the crowd looking meditative and solemn.

I don't know why but the sight of him filled me with sudden emotion. I began thinking of the trouble I'd caused this poor little tired man, of all the efforts he'd made to turn me into a God-fearing Jew. I pictured him bending over me, wagging his finger, rapping my knuckles. "I'll never live to see your bar mitzvah," he would shout in his high-pitched voice, "you'll kill me from aggravation first!"

And now here he was, still aggravated, perhaps, but very much alive.

Suddenly I was seized with the impulse to speak with him, to thank him and to apologize. I started to move in his direction but he disappeared into the crowd. Then he magically reappeared a minute later standing next to me as if he'd read my thoughts. Before I knew what was happening he'd placed his hands over my head in the prayer position and was intoning the following words in a loud, sing-song voice, as if he was reciting scripture: 'It's a miracle! Thank God! It's a miracle! Thank God! It's a miracle! Thank God!"

A number of the guests turned and looked in our direction. A few shrugged, some smiled—but, I daresay, only the rabbi and I fully understood the full meaning of his words. And to tell you the truth, I couldn't have agreed with him more.

Then, he was gone again.

Before I had time to follow him and say my piece the crowd started drifting downstairs in the direction of the food table. Here a prayer was said over the challah and the wine, and everyone headed towards the banquet.

No sooner had I started to cram the chopped liver into my mouth when, sure enough, Rabbi Rosenthal reappeared.

This time I extended my hand to him and he took it. I

told him how happy he had made my parents, how sorry I was
I'd caused him so much *tsuris*. As usual, he looked away while
I spoke. But then, slowly, he made a turn in my direction and,
perhaps for the first time, our eyes met and held. At that
moment I no longer saw old Rabbi Rosenthal the knuckle-beat-
ing dictator but a simple, lonely man, a learned man dedicated
to his ancient books and laws. For a moment I thought I detect-
ed a look in his eyes that pleaded "Don't forget what you've
learned." All he said at this special moment, however, was
"You did good."

That was it. But from him it was the supreme tribute.

As he turned and walked away into the crowd I asked
myself how I could have ever thought him such a monster. He
derived no enjoyment from punishing us—he did it for our
sake, not his. I wondered at the strangeness of life: an enemy
turns out to be a friend all along; our tormenter turns out to be
our helper. It's the Rabbi Rosenthals of the world, with their
straps and insults, who teach us the most. I won't forget him.

◆▸ ◆▸

After the plates were emptied and the glasses drained a
group of friends and relatives came back to our house where my
mother was serving up a massive buffet.

There was another round of congratulations and more
fountain pens were awarded me during lunch. Nine to be exact.
Lucky for me, I thought, I had an uncle in the jewelry business.
Thinking me now a man, I supposed, we did business over the
lunch table as equals and he paid me for eight of them, in cash.
What a day! Trouble was that while blood may be thicker than
water I realized later on that he'd taken me to the cleaners on
this deal and made himself a shameless profit. It was then that
I understood what my parents meant when they told me "You
don't do business with your relatives; with them you go to the
shul."

Finally, all the guests left and I was alone with my family. There were hugs all around, kisses, laughs, tears, rehashings of the day's events; then my mother looked at me and became very pensive. She sighed, raised her eyebrows, and said in a quiet voice "Marty, you will become a lawyer." Evidently she was impressed by the speech I'd made at the bar mitzvah. Since I'd delivered it in a clear, loud voice and had spoken my lines without stuttering or falling off the podium, this meant, in her eyes, that I would make a good advocate of the people. The logic was simple and clear.

Of course, I hadn't even graduated from lower school yet and the idea of going to law school, let alone college, seemed a long way down the road. If the idea made her happy though, why not?

From that day on wherever we went, whatever we did, my mother would declare with enormous pride to anyone who was listening (and a few people who weren't) that "This is my son, Marty. He's going to be a lawyer when he grows up."

Does the idea of a mother choosing a career for her child disturb young people today? I suppose it does. It's no longer the fashion to listen to your parents in much of anything, especially as far as career choice is concerned. It threatens a young person's "independence," I'm told; their "freedom of choice."

In my eyes, however, mother's suggestion was guidance, not coercion, based as it was on her deep and, it seemed to me, infallible knowledge of who I was and what I really needed.

From that time on I knew what was expected of me, both academically and professionally, and this knowledge gave me an enormous sense of inner security throughout the rest of my youth. No agonies of decision now, no floundering around from job to job until I stumbled on "my thing." Law was as good a profession as any. And as it turned out, though I never became a practicing lawyer, the things I learned studying the law would help me in incalculable ways throughout my years in business.

As always, Mom knew best.

Put to the Test

Unfortunately, not everyone in Troy agreed that when a male Jew turns 13 he automatically becomes a man.

The Irish Catholic kids in our neighborhood were especially skeptical. Most of them had been told from the time they rooted at their mother's breast that the Jews killed Christ, and that the Jews deserved every bit of the kicking and pommeling they'd received at the hands of the *goyim* for 20 centuries. It was catechism: God's wrath. They heard it every week in church. The fact that Jesus himself was a Jew who taught the masses at the synagogue didn't play much part in their philosophy.

●◄ ●◄

While walking home from school every day it was, therefore, a frequent event to be accosted by neighborhood bullies, most of them Irish, who charged full steam ahead at us docile young Christ-killers and whacked us to a pulp.

Now one day not long after I'd been bar mitzvahed, I was trudging the familiar route when, sure enough, several of the toughest members of the Irish bully team appeared out of the woodwork and started following me.

"Hey, look who's a man now!" the largest and meanest of them shouted to his friends as I walked along, pretending not to hear him, books dutifully tucked under arm. "Just had his bar shit's fa, I heard! Big boy around town now!"

When I didn't respond to this indignity the ringleader

came up behind me, knocked the books out of my hands, and kicked them across the sidewalk. He was a tall, wiry kid with straw-like blond hair that stuck up at angles all over his head, jug ears, and a big freckled moon face.

"Hey Jew boy, better not walk by too often" he continued. "Your mama's going to have to send your books to the laundry!"

This remark brought cackles of approval from his friends. I could feel the blood lust rising.

Now our usual policy when taunted in this way was to ignore the insults as best we could, just as our parents had ignored them when they were children. Jew-baiting was an ancient sport.

Today, however, things were different.

Instead of pretending that nothing had happened and continuing on my way I stopped, picked up my books, stacked them neatly on the edge of the sidewalk, and turned to face my tormenter.

This was already uncharacteristic behavior on my part, but if it surprised him I could see no indication on his face.

"You're no man!" the moon-faced kid continued, to the delight of his friends who had now gathered around me in a semicircle like wolves sniffing at their kill.

"As a matter of fact"—he drew himself up into his full and imposing height—"You've nothing but a goddamned little yellow kike!"

These words had barely left his lips before I reared back with every ounce of strength I had in me, and unleashed my little fist into his big mouth.

The boy staggered, seemed to sort of swoon for a moment, then straightened himself up, wiped the gore off his face with a handkerchief, spit out a tooth chip, and in a daze mumbled, "Hey, what'd you do that for! I wasn't ready!"

I squared off in front of him with my fists clenched. I was literally seething with hatred. Years of abuse had come to

a head in one burning moment. Centuries. I was no longer
Marty Silverman; I was an avenging angel sent by the Jewish
race to square things off with the *goyim*. My breath came in
short pants.

"Okay," I shouted. "Take a rest. Then we'll see who's
the chicken."

I glowered at him with invulnerability dancing in my
eye, waited a second or two, then sneered, "Finished your rest
yet?"

He glanced away, made a feeble attempt to sneer back,
and made no reply.

I stood there several more minutes, my eyes boring into
him. When he failed to respond I looked at the other kids.

"See!" I shouted. "See how tough your friend is! Tell
him to put his money where his mouth is next time!"

I turned back to the boy. "You ready to fight yet?"

Still no response.

"Come on!" I spurted, anxious to push the envelope as
far as it would go. "Come on, you yellow-bellied, chicken-
assed Mic son-of-a blubber-headed Irish washerwoman! Fight
like a man!"

If this didn't do it nothing would.

It didn't.

He remained there looking pathetic with blood all over
his shirt and confusion in his eyes. More than confusion, really—it was fear.

When it finally became evident to me that I'd made my
point and that my moon-faced friend had exposed his cow-
ardice to all his friends, I picked up my books, dusted myself
off, and made my exit, pushing several of the young Irishmen
out of the way as I went. None of them pushed back.

I learned that day what I'd often been told before but had
never understood from my own experience: call a bully's bluff
and you'll find a frightened nebbish hiding inside him.

Why couldn't I have done this years earlier? I asked myself.

Because I did it now, the answer came back. Because now I am a man.

Then I recalled an old proverb "We get too soon old and too late smart."

Another lesson.

A Test of a Different Sort

Another test of my newfound manhood was to take place not long after this confrontation. This test was of a different sort, and ended on a far less triumphant note. I'll leave it up to you as to whether I passed or failed.

Now as I told you, my father was in the tailoring business, and as fate would have it his shop was located two short blocks from Troy's red-light district.

This red-light district was not just your ordinary sin pit but, as any local connoisseur would inform you, one of the choice establishments of its kind on the East coast—most fascinating women, most accommodating madames, most reasonable prices. I'm told that at the time the citizens of Troy could see cars driving into this neighborhood at all hours of the day and night with the most exotic license plates on their bumpers—Ohio, Maine, Florida, even parts beyond the Mississippi.

The houses themselves were situated along the fabled railroad tracks right across from the station in a row of well-kept redbrick buildings, each with flowered window boxes in front and ornately carved oak doors. To the uninitiated eye it looked like an upper-middle class street on the mainline of Middle America. The only thing that betrayed it were the girls who leaned out the windows all day long, posed provocatively in semi-attire, and called to passers-by in the age old siren song of the whore: "Hi ya', handsome, want to come in and have some fun?"

The traffic from these frolics brought enormous revenues to the town, so no one protested very loudly. Years later when I was traveling around the country as a salesman and happened to mention that I came from Troy, New York, certain of my male clients would give a coy smile and ask if a Madame Ruby, say, or a Candy Louise was still working at such and such a house. Usually I knew the answer.

Why? Because ladies of joy need their clothes dry-cleaned and tailored just like anyone else. Perhaps more. And since my father was known in the area for being honest and reasonable, many of the girls soon became his regular customers.

As it happened, I was the delivery boy at my father's establishment, and every day after school I would make regular runs to the different brothels. Over time a number of the ladies began to know my face and then my name.

Most of them were friendly, pretty, easy-going girls, and I usually enjoyed the assignment. Occasionally I'd screw up my courage at the door and peer inside. The living rooms all looked pretty much the same in each establishment: plush couches, overstuffed chairs, outrageously gaudy satin wallpaper, a bar at the end. Occasionally I'd catch sight of a shadowy figure moving around towards the back of the room in silhouette. Though I had only a schoolboy's notion of what was going on in here I knew certain of the fundamentals. These trips stirred up something very agitating and disturbing in my 13-year-old soul.

❧ ❧

One day my father had an especially hefty order of laundry to deliver to one of the brothels and he sent me to do the job.

I carted the delivery load for the several blocks,

approached one of the larger houses, and knocked at the big red front door. Two scantily clad young ladies named Dolores and Rita met me there with huge smiles. I'd delivered here several times before and we were now on a first-name basis.

Dolores had short red hair done up in ringlets, and long-stemmed legs. Rita was dark, a Latin of some kind, with shiny black hair that reached to her waist. The delivery basket was very heavy, they said. Would I be a big, strong boy and carry it inside for them?

It was three o'clock in the afternoon and business was slow here at the house. Four or five other young women were lounging around the living room in their bras and panties, looking bored. I couldn't help noticing how attractive they all were. I remembered the rumors I'd heard, never substantiated, that local Troy girls worked here in off-hours to finance their educations.

Dolores and Rita rummaged through the laundry and started holding up lace nightgowns and panties, modeling them provocatively in front of me.

"Nice, honey," Rita said to me."Good job. Tell your father he does a great job getting out all those little spots."

I promised I would.

"Hey," Dolores said, holding up a red negligee and looking at me with mischief in her eyes. "We heard you just had your bar mitzvah. You're a man now, right, honey?"

"How—how'd you know that?" I asked.

"We've got spies," Rita answered. "We've been keeping tabs on you, all of us here. Been watching you grow up. Troy's a small town, you know."

She made a sweeping gesture across the room and several of the others nodded in assent. "Handsome man like you," one of them said, then giggled.

A strange emotion began to creep over me, half titillation, half terror. I sensed something tremendous was about to happen.

"How much I owe you for the pressing?" Dolores asked.

"A dollar," I answered in a tiny voice.

Dolores tilted her head back and eyed me for a long moment.

"Tell you what, cutie," she said. "We charge twice that to our customers for some fun. Regular ones included. But for you—'cause you just become a man—it's one dollar. What do you say?"

My mind went blank. I only half understood what she meant—didn't *dare* understand what she meant. My head was spinning. I didn't say yes; but I didn't say no either. Everything started to kind of go blurry and confused. I barely noticed when several of the other girls got off the couch and headed in my direction. Dolores, meanwhile, pressed in for the kill.

"Let's see what kind of a man you *really* are," she said, putting her arms around my neck and pulling me towards her.

I was hideously embarrassed. I didn't know how to respond. I didn't know anything.

But it didn't matter. Because the next minute another set of hands were on my rear end, and another were unhitching my pants. Before I knew it my clothes were on the floor, and four or five girls were standing around me, each stroking or pulling at a different part of my anatomy.

At first, in my innocence I placed my hands over my privates, like Adam. I felt ridiculous and ashamed. One of the girls gently removed my hands and shouted "Wow! Look at that!" The others peered down between my legs and began to *oh* and *ah*.

One of the girls then lay down on the couch next to me, and her gown fell open. The others pushed me on top of her, aiming me in the right direction as if she was playing Pin the Tail on the Donkey. The girl's hips started gyrating beneath me like a dynamo and I could feel her nipples pressing on my chest. I grabbed hold of the arms of the couch. I was afraid I'd fall off.

Everything was going fast around me. I felt like the salad in a mixing bowl.

As my partner drew me further in and sped up the gyrations the other girls stared, spanking my bottom with light little taps. Others laughed and stroked my back. I was bouncing up and down, a wild bull in the rumble seat of a car. Where was I? What was happening? It was terrible; it was sublime.

I rode the roller coaster for I don't know how long—a minute, maybe; an hour, maybe, who knows?—until I felt a strange electric surge in my groin, and then everything felt wet.

As soon as this happened the girl underneath pushed me off, giggling, and the whole group surrounded me. I must have looked like a drunken puppy. The girls were howling. I didn't know what it all meant or what I was supposed to do.

"Now you really are a man!" one of them shouted, and they all clapped. They laughed some more; then I laughed too.

Finally one of the girls brought a pan of warm water and sponged down my privates. Another dried me with a towel, and a third helped me back into my shirt and pants. Before I knew it I was outside on the steps of the house, and Dolores was standing in the entranceway.

"You did great, Marty!" she called to me. "Come back again soon. Even if you don't have any laundry to deliver."

She was about to go inside when she suddenly stopped, turned, and looked at me with a broad smile.

"Mazeltov!" she said.

From inside the house I could hear more clapping.

❧ ❧

Ten minutes later I was back at my father's tailor shop.

He looked at me strangely when I walked through the door but didn't say a thing. He was sewing a garment.

I started folding laundry, trying to look as if nothing had happened. Several silent minutes went by until he finally turned, looked at me in a penetrating way, and asked "You have the money, Marty?"

I froze. My God, the money! In my confusion I'd forgotten all about it. What could I say? I made a feeble pretend-search of my pockets.

"I—I think I must have lost it somewhere, Dad," I finally squeezed out in the limpest voice I ever heard roll off my tongue.

He looked at me for a long moment, nodded his head, then went back to his stitching. A long silence followed in which I died a thousand deaths. He knew what had happened. And I knew he knew. And he knew I knew.

After what seemed like hours, he finally looked at me again and with a sad expression in his eyes said simply, "Don't tell your mother."

We never spoke about the incident again.

And I never told my mother.

◆▶ ◆▶

As to my tutors back at the house of love, they blabbed to the other local talents about our caper, and before long word of my prowess as a lover had spread through the red-light district like brush fire.

From that time on whenever I made a pick up or delivery to one of the houses the girls offered me the same deal, one dollar stead of two, always with the most tempting descriptions of what lay in store. They seemed to enjoy teasing me. Each girl assured me that the others on the block were amateurs. She alone understood what a man *really* wanted; she alone could teach me the fine points that the others knew nothing about.

I smiled sheepishly and stupidly at these offers and said, "My dad is waiting for me. Please, M'am, can I have the dollar?"

But the girls were fun-loving and understanding, and

eventually they helped me see the humor in it. After a couple of weeks I even started to enjoy the teasings. The girls, in turn, made loud laments every time they saw me over the fact that my sexual education was being neglected. "Just as important as what you learn in school, Marty," one of them chided. "Comes in a lot more handy than knowing the capital of Alaska."

Ah life! "Every experience is a good one," my parents used to say, " as long as you don't get hurt." When I was a teenager I had a street full of handmaidens at my disposal. What did I do with them? Nothing. When I became a young man the ladies were still around but I had no money to spend on them. Later, when I had the money, I didn't have the time. Finally, now that I'm an old man, when I have the money *and* the time, I've lost the inclination.

I suppose there's a certain symmetry to it all. Still, it doesn't seem quite fair, does it?

Making Our Move

Now it's a couple of years later.

My oldest sister, Nettie, has married, produced two children, and moved to New York. My other sister, Toby, followed her to the city and landed a job there as model and salesperson in a dress shop.

Naturally my mom missed them both and visited them whenever she could. But traveling was difficult and expensive.

Meanwhile my dad was busy in his tailor shop trying to make ends meet and couldn't accompany my mother on these trips. He missed his girls with a passion. We were rattling around in our house every day, the three of us, and the rooms seemed desperately empty. With the girls gone Mom grew bored and melancholy, and my father seemed to enter a state of permanent mourning.

One night at the dinner table the three of us were sitting there eating our supper under a gloomy cloud and feeling particularly sorry for ourselves. I broke the silence.

"You know, Mom," I said. "Dad could make the same living he does here if we lived in New York City. Maybe better. And we could all be together again."

Mom looked at me, then at my dad, and smiled slightly.

Nothing more was said. But I think we all felt that some important bridge had been crossed that night. Times were tough in Troy just then and New York loomed large as a promised land of jobs and cheap rental apartments.

Thus, not too many months later, we packed up and headed for the big city.

Here we moved into a nice ground-floor apartment—ground floors were the cheapest rentals at the time—in the Dyckman area of upper Manhattan. My sisters lived nearby and everything became tight-knit again. Dad found himself a store location near our apartment and we set up shop. I chipped in by walking around the neighborhood handing out a card that read "New tailor and dry-cleaner. Give us a try. We pick up and deliver." There was no phone number on the card because we couldn't afford a telephone.

Meanwhile I entered the eighth grade. The kids were okay and my teachers decent, but soon I began to feel homesick for Troy.

Mother picked up right away on my long face and took me into her arms. When I told her my problem she answered simply, "Never look back. Look forward."

I don't know why exactly, but those short, plain little phrases had such a profound effect on me that I remembered them all my life. It wasn't so much the words themselves, I suppose, but the sympathy and understanding behind them. It reminds me of the story of the man who gets up in front of an audience and talks brilliantly about the sorrows of life for an hour. When he's finished everyone in the audience is snoring.

Then a second man gets up, walks slowly to the podium, looks out at the people, hangs his head and starts to cry. In a few minutes everyone in the audience is crying too.

No Tickee, No Laundry

Whatever magic it was that my mother packed into her advice, I was soon on my feet and enjoying my new life.

It was during this time also that my training in the subtleties of the business world began. A street-wise friend of mine who worked as a newspaper delivery boy suggested that since I was distributing my father's business card I might as well deliver newspapers around the neighborhood at the same time. This way, he explained, I'd get to know people in the area and could make a few extra bucks in the bargain.

➔ ➔

The next day he introduced me to the head of the newspaper delivery service who explained the whole business to me in five minutes. His company would give me 100 customers to start with, he promised, all of whom lived within six blocks of my dad's store. I could earn as much as five dollars a week, he said—big money for a poor boy. The hitch was that I had to buy the newspapers from his company first, then add my own markup to the cost, deliver them, and collect the fees directly from the customers.

This didn't seem too difficult, so I started immediately. For a few days everything went swimmingly. At the end of the week, however, I was introduced to a side of human nature I'd never encountered: welshing.

One of my customers, for example, told me he didn't have the money just then. He'd have it next week. But next week came and it was the same excuse. And the week after that. When he finally got around to paying I was almost broke.

Another customer made the same excuse. When I told her I needed the money right away because I had to buy the papers myself, she became angry and shouted, "Don't you trust me?"

What could I say? I didn't want her to think I didn't trust her. A nice boy like me. So I waited. And waited. And waited.

Finally in despair, after having been stiffed in this way by one customer after another, I considered quitting the job altogether and finding another line of business. Luckily, I had recently made the acquaintance of an elderly Chinese gentleman who ran the hand laundry next to my dad's store. This venerable man-of-the-old-school lived in the back of his store and seemed to work endless hours washing and scrubbing and ironing — you could see lights on at four in the morning.

We soon became good friends and one day he asked me to deliver an order for him and collect the fees.

Being in the middle of my newspaper dilemma I told him how difficult I'd found it to extract money from customers and how they all seemed to have such airtight excuses.

My friend chuckled and said he would teach me a secret, an old Chinese proverb that I should always remember when I did business: No tickee, no laundry. No joke either — though it's a racist cliche today, this phrase was a legitimate Chinese proverb at the time and the Chinese Americans were proud of it.

Then he gave me another, more modern version of the same tip.

"If customer say 'can't pay today,' you say, 'sorry, must pay now, today. That not mine idea — that company policy.'"

Company policy. I liked the ring of it.

The next day I went back to my first customer. When he told me he'd pay next week I nodded sympathetically but then added politely that we'd have to cut off delivery if he didn't come up with the money immediately.

"Why?" he bellowed. "You've always given me credit!"

"Oh, it's not my idea" I answered. "It's a new rule. Company policy. If I don't do it I'll get canned."

The man coughed up accordingly. So did the next customer. And the next.

The lesson was an important one and I never forgot it: If you make people think some official, unbendable authority is standing behind you they will be far more likely to do what you ask. In other words, in business it all depends on the way you say it.

❧ ❧

This reminds me of another story, this one about a rabbi and a member of his congregation. The member came to the rabbi one day and asked, "Rabbi, is it all right if I smoke while I pray."

"Certainly not!" roared the rabbi. "Who would never tolerate such a disrespectful thing!"

A second member, just as addicted to cigarettes as the first, overheard this conversation and decided to approach the matter in another way.

The next day he came up to the rabbi and asked him the same question, but with a different verbal spin. "Rabbi," he asked, "is it all right if I pray while I smoke?"

"Absolutely, absolutely!" crooned the rabbi, beaming. "I'm delighted to see that you're thinking about the Almighty even out of shul!"

❧ ❧

Our new apartment was loud and open to public view, but living on the ground floor had its advantages. For example, on Sunday mornings I was obliged get up early so that I could cord up the huge Sunday papers before delivering them.

I didn't want to wake myself with an alarm clock; it would disturb my poor dad who was sleeping late on his one day off a week. So I made a deal with my street-wise delivery friend. Every Saturday night before I went to bed I tied a string to my big toe and tossed the string out our first-story window. The next morning my friend came by at 5:30 and gave it a yank, sometimes a pretty serious yank. My toe goes out to this day.

Jolted from my dreams in this way, I dressed hurriedly and joined him on the sidewalk where we set to work making our rounds. The city was remarkably peaceful on these early Sunday mornings and I could look up and down the largest avenues without seeing an automobile. After a while, working hard seven days a week, I began to feel like a true businessman and even squirreled away a few dollars.

Meanwhile, my eighth-grade school year was coming to a close and graduation was upon me. Unlike the hoopla that goes on today at such ceremonies, my "moving up" exercises turned out to be strictly plain vanilla. All I recall of the event was that we were asked to do three things: wear a white shirt, put on a tie—and show up. Diplomas were handed out and the principal made a brief speech to an empty auditorium—almost all our parents were either working or at home with other kids.

That was that.

The question now was: which high school?

A Brief Career Change

At this time in my tender youth I was madly in love with automobiles. I dreamed of developing a super car that ran on nitrogen or orange peels or something, and had an engine the size of a matzo ball.

Both my parents were dismayed at the prospect of their son the auto mechanic and, of course, my mother was still dedicated to my legal career. But they understood things that I didn't, and so after I noodged them for several weeks they gave their permission for me to attend the local vocational school.

I enrolled the next day. To "celebrate" my dad bought me an expensive pair of heavy-duty overalls for bumbling around the school's garage and climbing inside motors.

The first day of class, however, the teacher announced that we wouldn't be going near cars for a while, and that our immediate project was to forge a set of mechanic's tools. He gave me a piece of metal that looked like a *lotki*, and for the next two weeks I heated it and banged it every which way until it resembled something of a wrench. In these two weeks I never saw anything that resembled an automobile, a chassis, or a gasoline motor. I was very disappointed.

One day while sitting in class staring absently out the window and feeling overwhelmingly bored, I saw something from the corner of my eye flying through the air in my direction. Before I could duck it hit me square in the temple.

I looked up in astonishment and saw the teacher standing by the blackboard glowering at me like a judge in the court of last resort. He had just thrown an eraser at my head, presumably to get my attention. It was a kind of vocational variation of Rabbi Rosenthal.

"Wake up, you idiot!" he hollered. "You're in school!"

Now ordinarily I was a polite, compliant student who never gave teachers any trouble. My first impulse was to smile and apologize.

But this time it was different. This time something deep inside my brain, that little voice, started talking again.

And it said: "Throw it back!"

Throw it back? At a teacher? How disrespectful! How criminal! How suicidal!

The next minute I found my hand picking up the eraser and winging it at him with all my might.

I'd never been much of a baseball jockey, and ordinarily couldn't hit the broad side of a barn with a bazooka. Today, however, my throw seemed to be guided by computer control. The eraser whizzed through the air at a sensational speed, flew over the head of the other students, who watched in amazement, and beaned the unsuspecting teacher square on the noggin.

Suddenly the whole class was in an uproar: laughter, shrieks! No one was more surprised than me.

Why'd I do that? I asked myself. It was entirely out of character. The little voice told me to do it, I answered myself.

The little voice? Are you nuts?

I had no time to think the matter over, however, because the teacher was lumbering down the aisle in my direction with blood in his eye.

Illuminated with terror, I leaped from my seat and ran across the room, dodging my way across the maze of desks as I went and knocking several of them over.

The teacher followed close behind, loony with rage, and in the next several minutes the two of us circled the room four or five times like fox and hounds while the other students sat watching, cheering me on loudly, and convulsed with laughter. I couldn't believe what I was actually doing.

Round and round we ran and slowly my irate mentor began to close in. At one point I could feel his breath on my back. He was a big man with a mean face, and his running speed seemed to improve with practice.

❧ ❧

Seeing that my only chance of escape was to leave the premises entirely, I ran towards the classroom door with a magnificent burst of speed, crossed the threshold, and raced down the corridor with my fuming instructor a few paces behind. I reached the main entrance and dashed out of the building, into a nearby park across the street.

I suppose the man knew when he was licked. He stopped at the entrance, watched me tear away into the trees, then turned and moped back inside. I sped on at full throttle, all the way home.

The next obstacle, of course, was informing my parents of what I'd just done. Naturally I was scared out of my wits, as well as totally out of breath, and it took several minutes of coaxing on their part to open me up.

Finally I came clean.

They listened without expression or comment to the whole tale, and when I finished there was a long pause. I could hear the clock ticking in the dining room and our family canary pecking at its seeds.

Finally my mother broke the silence.

"Good," she said. "Now you can go to a real school where you belong and become a lawyer."

"Yes," my father added, barely able to conceal his delight. "And I can get the money back on the pants."

In their heart of hearts, of course, both of them were pleased by my misadventure. And perhaps unsurprised by it as well.

One thing I didn't tell them, however, was about the voice. Not that they would have pooh-poohed it or laughed at me. It was just that there was something very personal about it. Something that was entirely and privately mine. Something, dare I say it, sacred.

❦ ❦

Now the point of this story, besides the fact that even the docile can become lions when it's necessary, is this: If I hadn't heard that voice in my head and thrown the eraser at the teacher, I might have remained in the vocational school for the rest of my academic career. I would then no doubt have become an auto mechanic, and disappeared into the carbon monoxide of life.

Who made me throw that eraser?

Today it seems clear to me. I had wondered off the path of my appointed fate. Auto repair was not my lot in life. I had other fish to fry.

So who made me throw the eraser?

He made me throw it, I firmly believe. *He* was instilling the sense into me of "Don't tread on me," and at the same time was reshaping my destiny. *He* was helping me back to the life I was intended by providence to lead.

❥ ❥ ❥

Chapter 4

❦❦ ❦❦

STORM ON THE RIVER

The Limited Partnership

If I sent you back 75 or 80 years in a time machine to Dyckman Street you probably wouldn't recognize it.

Dyckman's still there, of course, around 207th Street in upper New York City above the George Washington Bridge. In those days a lot of buildings in New York were still made of wood, and piles of dung dropped in the gutters by the iceman's horse was one of the more serious problems faced by local residents.

When you walked due west to the Hudson River and looked out at the water you saw a lighthouse nestled at the foot of the one of the pylons by the bridge. Further across, on the New Jersey shore, it was unbroken forest all the way up north to the bend in the river. To the south where Japanese-built condos now peer down at Manhattan Island like a row of concrete samurai, you mostly saw trees.

I was 17—the year is 1928—and I was jerking chocolate malts and egg creams at the neighborhood pharmacy (we called them "soda fountains" in those days). My father ran a tailor's shop a few blocks away, and our apartment was an easy three-block walk. Most of the inhabitants around the Dyckman area were middle-class Jews. The stores were run by Jews, the street concessions, even the pushcarts—mostly by people who had forsaken the clank and sweat of the Lower East Side and sought greener pastures uptown.

Migrations of this kind were also taking place up to the Bronx and Brooklyn at this time. If you were making a few extra dollars, if you wanted a better neighborhood for your kids, and if you were Jewish, then Dyckman Street, the Grand Army Plaza, Brownsville were *the* places to go. Look around these areas even today. In the cratered ruins and burned-out shells you'll still see handsome hulks of buildings that were once the joy of New York—and the home of a lifestyle that's vanished from the world forever.

When the weather turned warm in our neighborhood my soda jerking partner, Lee Schwartz, and I took a break, strolled over to the river, and watched the Dyckman Street ferryboats cross back and forth from the New Jersey side to New York and back again. They were quaint little tubs, all white and green, with a giant smokestack in the center, potted trees on deck, and a ramp for the lucky ones who owned automobiles.

Even more intriguing was the canoe club perched 100 feet down from the ferryboat terminal. It was a wonderful looking building, a kind of ramshackle pagoda, all wood and slats, with a high peaked roof and a pier that extended into the water on stilts. Inside the club was a locker room where you could change into your bathing suit and an office where you rented canoes.

Summer days found Lee and me hanging around the docks, gazing at the line of sturdy wooden canoes tied up at the pier and fantasizing about what it would be like to own one of these beauties.

One day Lee made an amazing suggestion.

We'd both saved money that summer working at the soda fountain. We should pool our savings, go in as partners, fifty-fifty, and buy our own canoe.

The idea seemed hare-brained. We'd never have enough money for such a thing. But Lee was very persuasive. He showed me impressive looking accounting figures he'd come up with and explained how these numbers *proved* we couldn't lose. Look here: we'd buy the canoe at the beginning of the summer, share it equally for three months, then sell it, perhaps at a profit, to one of the club members. He'd even talked to the club proprietor who'd promised to keep his eye out for one with resale value. The proprietor had also indicated that if we bought one of his craft he might be willing to purchase it back at the end of the season.

It was a no-lose deal.

The next day we approached the proprietor, asked him what was available, and sure enough, a beautiful, solid cedar bark canoe just happened to be on sale today for $20. The price included two seat cushions (which also doubled as life preservers) and a set of paddles.

Now $20, I don't have to tell you, was a great deal of money at that time. Our fathers worked a week to earn $20. At the same time, it was also a reasonable sum for a canoe of this quality. And we knew it.

Trouble was, the proprietor knew it too. He informed us that several other persons, all canoe aficionados, were interested in purchasing this incredible vessel also, and that if we wanted it we'd better cough up a down payment of $5 *right then and there*. Otherwise it would be gone by noon, no doubt, if not to the interested parties then to pirates, sharks, aerial bombardment, who knows?

Now as fate would have it, I'd received my salary that very day and had a $5 bill sitting in my wallet. Lee would be paid at the end of week, he assured me, and would deliver his share of the money on Friday. The proprietor glared at me with X-ray eyes and went into salesman's overdrive:

"Better get it while you can, son."

"Won't have an opportunity like this one in another 50 years."

"Prettiest little thing on the Hudson. . . ."

And so on.

I really did love the canoe, and after all, it would only cost me half of $20. I'd have the fun of owning a real live canoe for the rest of the summer and then get my money back in the fall. What the hell, what's money for?

I pulled the fiver out of my pocket and slammed it down on the table. Lee and I shook hands, partners forever.

It was with this handshake that I received my first lesson in Partnership 101.

◆→ ◆→

The end of the week arrived.

Lee and I rendezvous at the drug store as usual. I'm exuberant—we're going down to the canoe club with the balance of the cash and pick up our investment.

He, however, is distant and withdrawn.

"What's the matter?" I ask. "Listen, schnooky, you're the proud owner of a cedar bark canoe. Why the long face?"

"Well," Lee answers, staring at his shoes. "I told my mother about our deal last night and she, ah, I don't know, she—"

"She what?"

"Well, she thinks it's a *great* idea."

"Swell. What's the problem?"

"The partnership and all. Terrific idea."

"Uh, uh."

"It's just that she doesn't think I should invest any money right now. She says I should put it in the bank. For college."

I stared at him for a long time. "I don't know what you mean," I finally mumbled. "We made a deal. We're partners."

"Absolutely," Lee answered. "And I'd be happy to share the canoe with you. I *want* to share it. It's just that I can't come up with my part of the money just now."

Another silence.

"You see," he continued in an impressively business-like voice. "We'll still be partners in the boat as far as I'm concerned. We made a deal. I'll stick by it. We're just not partners on the money end of things. Until, of course, I can come up with my share when we will be again."

He waited an appropriate length of time for this pronouncement to sink in, then delivered the final bit of chutzpah. "After all, a deal's a deal."

I guess it took several hours for absurdity of his logic to register, and by that time I'd gone home, dug up my savings, and paid off the balance of the bill at the canoe club.

Lee had himself a great summer on the Hudson that year.

My mother once told me it was a good thing I wasn't born a girl. Because I could never say no to anyone.

The Tippy Canoe

Now it's months later. August. I've been giving my canoe a workout on the Hudson all summer, been having a ball, but on this late summer day I'm feeling a strong urge to share these pleasures with someone other than Lee.

So I invited my brother-in-law's sister, Dot, to join me on a trip across the river to New Jersey.

Dot was a pretty young lady and approximately my age. We met once before at my sister's wedding and had gotten along splendidly ever since, like brother and sister. We agreed to meet that Saturday at the dock, pack a picnic lunch, and make a day of it.

Saturday rolled around and we met at the canoe club. Changing into our bathing suits, we loaded baskets of food into the canoe, tossed in some cushions, and pushed off, steering a course for Palisades Park, New Jersey.

Now in those days Palisades Park was a lush riverside playground bordered on the river side by a sandy beach and behind by granite and olivine cliffs that rose up dramatically from the forests below, lining the Hudson River Valley all the way up to West Point. Here visitors barbecued, played baseball, hiked and swam. (Yes, swam. The water on the New Jersey side was unsoiled at this time and you could paddle around in it to your heart's delight.)

That morning the sky was especially clear as we set off and the Hudson calm as a mountain lake. A delicate sprinkling of clouds floated overhead like feathers, and the splashing of water on the side of our canoe produced a deliciously meditative sound as we glided ahead to the Jersey shore where we could already see groves of willow trees and people swimming off the beach.

As we paddled along we giggled and gossiped and sang hit tunes of the day like *Let the Rest of the World Go By*. Dot read in the back of the boat and I paddled. Then Dot paddled and I told her stories. When we passed other canoes we waved and shouted to one another as if we'd all been at sea for a year. The thing was idyllic, a kind of dream.

Finally we reached the Jersey side and pulled the canoe onto the beach. We dashed into the water for a dip, then spread out a blanket, ate our lunch and chatted away. The air off the river was wonderfully fresh and we could smell pine trees and the aroma of steak cooking on nearby barbecues. The hours passed like music.

We chatted so long, in fact, that we didn't notice the black thunderheads moving in from the north. A sudden wind blew down from the Palisades and the temperature dropped ten or fifteen degrees in a few minutes.

The other park visitors fluttered around, packed their boats in a hurry, and paddled away. Dot and I were so absorbed with the joy of the day and with each other's company that by the time we'd gathered our belongings and cast off the water was alarmingly choppy and the wind icy cold.

I was a strong paddler in those days and figured that with a little effort we'd buck the weather and make it back to New York in half-an-hour. But the winds whipped up to an even more ferocious pitch and the waves in front of the boat rose so high they began to look like waterfalls. We huddled low in the canoe to stabilize its weight, and together we started paddling like demons.

For a few minutes we made progress. Then a terrific gust came in from the northwest, blew off the tops of the choppers, and bobbed the canoe so violently that both of us almost went pitching into the river.

We were in big trouble and we both knew it.

The next 45 minutes was one of the most harrowing times I have ever known.

Years later I would be marching off to fight in a foreign war where I would watch as young men died all round me. Yet somehow the fear I felt that afternoon on the river—a fear not just for myself but for Dot and her family—was unlike anything I have ever experienced.

What would I tell her mother and father if anything went wrong? I asked myself. Was it really possible that we wouldn't make it across? Was it actually possible that we were going to die? Could Dot swim?

"Not so good," she answered in a weak voice, and we fell silent.

The gale was breaking hard on our bow, so we turned the canoe directly against the wind and knifed it into the swell, shifting our weight from side to side as we hit the waves to compensate for the pitch and churn. The going was slower this way but the chances of tipping were less.

The problem soon was that the waves started coming in from all sides, and each time we shifted to meet them another hit us from the side or behind. Soon we'd taken on gallons of water and were both becoming disoriented. *Where were we?* The whitecaps were so high and the fog so thick that the shoreline was now entirely obscured. For several panicked moments I thought we'd been washed out to sea. I was navigating by luck and instinct, and I knew it. And Dot knew it.

In the middle of it all I looked skyward and prayed a *big* prayer. "Oh God," I said silently, "I'm sorry I was so arrogant to think I could cross this river by myself in a storm. I'll never do such a dumb thing again. Never. If we make it back in one piece I'll sell this stupid canoe. I'll study hard. I won't do anything bad again!"

After how much time? Who knows? An hour? A year? The fog began to lift, the wind died down, and the New York shoreline shimmered into view. We regained control of the canoe, summoned up second wind, and paddled for all we were worth.

After a few minutes bucking the waves we neared the dock of the canoe club exhausted but strangely exhilarated. We knew we were safe now and everything inside us relaxed. Danger is a terror when it's happening but an adventure when it's past. I even had the fleeting thought that the squall hadn't been all *that* bad, after all. The canoe was none the worse for wear. We were safe. Any good canoeist could have gotten through it. We'd just let our fears get the better of us. Perhaps I shouldn't have made my promise after all.

At that moment several club members came dashing towards us on the pier. They looked pale and frightened.

"For God's sake!" one of them shouted. "Thank heavens you made it! We thought you'd gone down with the others!"

Gone down? With what others?

As it turned out, several canoes had capsized in the storm that afternoon and two people, both expert paddlers, had slipped to the bottom and never come up. The rescue boat was just then bringing in their bodies. Drowning, it turned out, was a common event on this part of the Hudson, especially when the weather took sudden turns.

Dot and I exchanged looks of horror, clambered out of

the canoe, fell into each other's arms and stood hugging each other on the dock like frightened children. All sound, all thought, all motion came to a stop around us. There was only she and I, safe, alive, young, saved for better things by the kindness of a Higher Power.

❧ ❧

A week later, true to my promise, I sold the canoe back to the club proprietor—for half of what I'd paid, incidentally. The proprietor assured me that the drowning of two customers had done nothing for his business or for the canoe's resale price, and I imagine he was telling the truth.

So much for my get-rich schemes.

It was also at that moment, standing on the pier with Dot in our innocent, brotherly-sisterly embrace, that both of us knew intuitively that our fates were intertwined, and that we would somehow, some way, remain together for the rest of our lives.

If the foul weather had not come up on the river that afternoon, would we have been brought together in this way?

I don't think so. I've often wondered: did He create the storm for the two of us? Is that the way things work behind the Big Curtain?

Perhaps.

And it was true too. We were fated for one another. But it would take seven more years before the prophecy came true.

That, however, is another story.

❧ ❧ ❧

Chapter 5

❧ ❧

GETTING MY FEET WET IN THE WORLD

A New Start

With my parents' deepest and most appreciative blessings, I dropped out of vocational school after the eraser incident, gave up my automotive dreams, and began looking around the city for a good education.

As it turned out, most kids in the Washington Heights area near Dyckman Street went to George Washington High School in upper Manhattan or to De Witt Clinton downtown.

Both schools had excellent reputations, so excellent, in fact, that students in these schools were required to study literally day and night with little time off for work or play. This, in a certain way, was a drawback. You see, though the Roaring Twenties were making a lot of people wealthy, my father was not among the lucky ones and our family was feeling the pinch. Wouldn't it be wonderful, I thought to myself, if I could find a real job after school, not just a paper route, earn some hefty money, and thus help out at home as well as get a good education. Yet while times were booming, jobs, oddly enough, were difficult to find. I've never been quite sure why this was so—perhaps because people tended to remain with one employer for long periods of time and not jump around from position to position as they do today. And at any rate, if you're in school you're in school, right? No time to work. So my dreams of extra cash and a big-time career really were pie in the sky.

And yet, we needed the money desperately. *What to do?*

As if in answer to my prayer, someone, somehow, told my family about a new high school in midtown Manhattan on 47th Street between 6th Avenue and Broadway. It was called Haaren High School and it offered a unique "cooperative" learning program to its students, most of whom, it turned out, were from struggling Jewish families like my own.

Haaren's system worked like this: two students were buddied up with one another and were given a paying job somewhere in the city. During one week the first student attended school while the second worked at this job. The next week the order was reversed; the first student worked while the second went to school. This earn-as-you-learn regime continued throughout the entire student year, with both students getting equal time.

It was a great idea, really. Under this system bright, talented kids from poor families like my own could get an education, and at the same time make enough money to help their families. Almost like having your cake and eating it too. In fact, many, many years later I recalled this ingenious system and used it to help some other needy kids.

Here's what happened: One of New York's best social service programs, Meals-on-Wheels (a city project in which wholesome meals are delivered daily to indigent older people in poor areas of the city) was foundering. The workers who delivered the meals each day, it seemed, refused to walk up the three or five or ten flights of stairs necessary to reach the older person's apartments, most of which were located in buildings without elevators or, more likely, in buildings where the elevators were broken. This meant, of course, that if the workers wouldn't go up the stairs the older persons, many of whom were feeble and crippled, had to come down, retrieve their meals, then walk back up again.

Bad, unimaginably so. Several incapacitated clients, I'm told, ended up starving to death because of this bureaucratic snag.

Now it so happened that I was involved in several of the city's social programs at this time, and I couldn't help noticing that the predicament in the Meals-on-Wheels project had what seemed to me a natural and simple solution.

One day I got the ear of my friend, Margaret Seiner, then Commissioner of Aging in New York City. I pointed out that in many areas of the city where poor seniors lived there were also legions of young boys and girls hanging around the streets and store fronts, yakking away, playing their radios, doing nothing in particular. Why not *hire* these kids, I suggested, put them to work delivering Meals-on-Wheels. They're young and healthy, I said, they can easily climb flights of stairs when necessary. Pay them decently, I said, but also make the job contingent on several conditions:

✔ 1) That they stay in school.
✔ 2) That they maintain a decent grade point average.
✔ 3) That they keep their noses clean.

Commissioner Seiner liked the idea and soon the project was in full swing. Sure enough, many youngsters from the streets volunteered for the job, and after the initial shyness wore off between the young people and their aged clients, relationships began to form, some of which literally resulted in lifelong friendships. This blending of age groups was, in fact, so successful that the city eventually pumped millions of dollars into the program. The plan is still going strong today, I'm told, under the title of The Intergenerational Program.

All of this was started, as fate would have it, when the

seeds of the cooperative idea were planted in the mind of a poor student at Haaren High School more than 70 years ago. Which just proves that we don't always know where the moving finger is behind the rolling ball, do we?

At any rate, back to 1926.

My mother and father were told about Haaren High School, they liked what they heard, and so we all went down to check it out.

The school building itself was dilapidated and only half full, and this was discouraging at first. But the closer we looked the more the kids seemed to be having the time of their lives. That got me excited. The cooperative idea was just getting set into place, and my class would be one of the first to try it out. I wanted to be part of the experiment. So, with my parents' permission, I signed on and was immediately given both a partner and a job.

Learning While You're Earning

My partner and I took a liking to one another and for the next four years we did the cooperative learning thing in perfect harmony: I'd go to school one week, he'd work. I'd make sure he got all his homework assignments, he' d do the same for me. Then we'd switch. Back and forth we went year after year without, as I recall, a hitch.

My high school, meanwhile, found me a job at Wanamaker's, which at that time was one of the largest department stores in the world. Located on the lower stretches of Broadway, this famous (and today defunct) emporium spanned two city blocks from 8th street to 9th street, with a panoramic steel and glass bridge connecting the two buildings. Inside the hallowed halls they sold bedding, clothes, furniture, cameras, canaries, the best men's shirt counter, great perfumes and colognes, you name it, all at very reasonable prices.

My job paid 18 dollars a week—not bad—and consisted of carting boxes from one end of the store to the other under the title of "Managerial Assistant"—read: stock boy.

The first floor where the fast-moving merchandise was located—cosmetics, perfume, men's attire, mostly—was my territory and there I was awarded an opportunity to mingle with as wide a variety of human beings as is ever likely to be assembled under one 30-foot ceiling.

Somebody once remarked that an adventure is an inconvenience rightly considered. That's how I looked at my job. The work itself was mostly shlep and fetch, sure, but the opportunity was a pip, and I determined to get the most out of it. In fact, in four years at this remarkable store, I learned about a hundred times more than those kids who simply go to school and never mix it up with the down-and-dirty world of commerce and trade. I was, you might say, attending two institutes of learning simultaneously: the Haaren High School, and the School of Real Life Experience.

What special knowledge did I gain from the latter?

A little about the technical details of merchandising. A whole lot about what makes merchandising really tick: the people who buy the merchandise, and the people who sell it.

Every day, for example, I made a careful study of Wanamaker's customers as they filed into the store through the huge revolving door and turned right, left, center, each one mesmerized, I could plainly see, by a different stimulus: bright colors, flashing signs, photographic advertisements, sexy salesgirls. I watched as they bargained at the counters and made their buying decisions. I studied the reactions of customers. I saw what caused one person to buy and another to walk away; what made one customer choose a red blouse and another a green. I observed how the buying habits of each social group differs: women from men, old from young, rich from poor. I came, I took stock of, I assimilated, until the store itself became my text book, a living study course in human nature, a display case of consuming humanity. I absorbed it all, bit by bit.

And there were things to learn on the other side of the counter too, from the salespersons.

Some said very little, were very low key, yet they sold a king's ransom of goods. Others were heavy on the armtwisting, sometimes too heavy. At first it was difficult to see why one salesperson raked it in while another couldn't get to first. But the more I observed the more I noticed the little things that made a difference—timing, a smile, voice tone, a compliment, affable persistence, playing on a customer's needs and fears and vanities, the exertion of personal will at precisely the right moment; charisma, or lack of it.

Some of the salespersons, I noticed, came to Wanamaker's, stayed a few months, then moved on to better-paying jobs. Others came and stayed—and stayed, and stayed, sometimes for the rest of their lives. These were the good, hardworking souls who over time I came to think of as the drones, men and women who for whatever reasons failed to take advantage of the upward mobility that comes built into our commercial marketplace; people content to remain in their "boxes," afraid to take a chance, to push the envelope.

The more I watched these drones in their department-store hives the stronger my resolve became *to not turn into one of them myself.*

And thus the drones too became my teachers—examples of the very thing I wished to avoid, perhaps, and therefore teachers all the more. As the saying goes: "Your adversary is your helper."

Mixed Emotions

Attending Haaren High and working at Wanamaker's, I ultimately came to think of these two institutions as one, my own private learning laboratory of life. Indeed, the day I graduated from Haaren High School I also worked my last shift at Wanamaker's too. Walking out of the employees' entrance of this great merchandise mart for the last time, having said goodbye to my role models, positive and negative alike, I felt the final paycheck nestled in my pocket and immediately had three conflicting feelings:

- ✔ One, that I'd just been sprung from jail.
- ✔ Two, that I had incurred debt to the sharpies and drones alike at Wanamaker's for giving me such a good education—a debt that I'd never be able to pay off in all my lifetime, even if I one day became a millionaire.
- ✔ Three, that I had my entire life in front of me and was probably the luckiest guy alive.

Indeed, I was so euphoric that I visualized myself climbing the first steps of my own ladder of life, looking up to the next rung and the rung after that, all the way to some top mythical rung in my own personal El Dorado. As I contemplated this image I recalled a passage from a sacred religious book I'd read as a child: "The Lord did a great kindness to man," it said. "He made him unique among *all* living things. All other creatures walk with their eyes directed towards the earth. Man alone walks upright. Therefore, he can direct his eyes upward as well."

I was on the way up, I thought to myself. My eyes were heavenward, just as the scripture said. My only boundary now was the stars.

Or so it seemed at the time.

Miss Putnam High

That was my four year stint at Wanamaker's. What about the other half of my life—high school?

Study, study, study mostly. Nose to the grindstone, fingers to the bone, all that. The school itself was a pleasant and work-a-day kind of place. It grew so rapidly during my four years there that it eventually had to move to the old DeWitt Clinton High School building on 10th Avenue. My teachers at Haaren were, by and large, intelligent, sympathetic, friendly, helpful, and entirely forgettable people—all of them, except for a single special instructor.

Miss Putnam. Bookkeeping teacher *par excellence.*

Ah, Miss Putnam! May you be counted among the immortals! I will never forget you, Miss Putnam.

Indeed, there was so much to remember. Six feet tall, almost as wide, 220 New York Giants pounds of smiling, jiggling, cajoling, browbeating mentor-dom. What other teacher makes you feel special when she scolds you? What other teacher squeezes you like a toothpaste tube and you love her for it? "You're holding back," she hollers at you day and night, knowing you aren't giving it your all. "You can do better! You can do more! Try harder, Marty, give it e-f-f-o-r-t!"

And when I did I could see light in her face. I understood that her joy was for me and for my potential as a man. There was no ax to grind here, no selfish ends, just the love of helping young minds. This made me try even harder. Me, and all the other kids in class as well. I sincerely believe that young students have an innate ability to know when a teacher is really on their side. I believe that when they find such a teacher they will swim to China and back to please her and do well. It's a simple secret—and one that so few teachers ever bother to learn.

Besides her duties as a teacher Miss Putnam also ran the school lunchroom. I came from a struggling family so, naturally, she went out of her way to arrange for me to supervise operations there. In payment I was given a free lunch every afternoon (see — it *does* exist).

I can still imagine her there in the middle of the cafeteria, overseeing the cash register, ladling out food, making sure everyone got fresh vegetables, and most of all, putting us students through our learning paces while we ate and worked: Check in the food supplies, reconcile the checkbook, operate the coin-counting machine, roll coins into packages for deposit, figure out the right amount of change at the register, on and on. For her the whole world was a living bookkeeping lesson.

Meanwhile back in class, Miss Putnam taught accounting shortcuts and arcana that I still use today. She would, for example, dictate a series of numbers and have us write them down on a P&L sheet, then we'd start at the bottom and work our way up, filling in the blanks until we got to, as she called it, the "correct" bottom line, i.e., a bottom line that worked out in our financial favor. Years later, when I went into business for myself, I discovered to my amazement that she had taught us the venerable and time-honored rudiments of "cooking the books." She never gave it this label, of course. She just showed us how it was done and let us make our own future discoveries.

Need I say more? She also passed down her own version of marketing procedure that worked something like this: since every student in the class worked at a different office during the week, examples and assignments were handed out based on the buying and selling practices of that particular job. A student working at a warehouse, for example, was given homework in inventory control. A student working for a wholesaler was told to write up sample spreadsheets. In this way, her students were not only taught bookkeeping fundamentals but were given hands-on training that helped them perform their biweekly job with greater efficiency.

As she tutored us in the ABC's of bookkeeping and business practice, moreover, she kept drumming a single cosmic truth into our noggins:

**THE BOTTOM LINE TELLS THE WHOLE STORY
IT HAS TO BE IN THE BLACK!**

To make certain we caught on, she championed a home-grown pricing formula all her own: If the manufacturing cost of a product is $1, she told us, that product must be sold in the marketplace for $3. After the sale this leaves $1 for other expenses: insurance, taxes, payroll, advertising, plus $1 for profit. Period.

Self-evident, perhaps, but useful, simple and profound. Over the years I applied her formula to many different business situations, and the simple common sense of it was always apparent.

I've heard of many business education classes in my time, really, but none that exposed its students to such brilliant, hands-on learning, and none that gave its graduates such canny and lasting preparation for life in the business world. Long live the memory of Miss Putnam—I see her yet, standing in the lunchroom counting change, rolling coins, barking orders— all with that smile and that rude shout of loving disapproval that made you want to swim to China and back to gain her favor.

The Wet Store

Besides Miss Putnam, high school, Wanamaker's, and my family, there was yet one more episode in my teenage life that remains worth the telling. The soda fountain.

For some reason (I can't say why) the Washington

Heights area had more drug stores per square block than any
other location in the Western Hemisphere—or so it seemed to
anybody gazing down Dyckman Street at the line of corner
drug stores running southward as far as the eye could see.

One of these stores was situated a few blocks from our
apartment, and as it happened the pharmacist who ran it knew
my family. When he learned that I had Sundays off and was
known in the area as a hard worker he offered me a job.

"A job?" my mother screamed. "At the wet store?"

(That's what they were called in those days for some
reason, wet stores.)

"That's right, Mom."

"Take it, Marty, take it! You'll have fun. You'll have ice
cream. You'll have money. The druggist is a nice man."

I couldn't argue with this. I went up the street for an
interview.

The nice druggist made me an offer that was strictly
plain vanilla. He would teach me to become a bona fide soda
jerker, tell me how to prepare malteds and egg creams, show me
the coffee and sandwich ropes, instruct me in the arts of mixing
chocolate with butter pecan so well I'd be a certified snowman
in a week (that's what they called master ice cream cone makers).

At the end of the day he'd pay me $3 in cash. The hours
were 10 to 10 and, if I wanted, there would be a job waiting for
me during the summer. The side benefits included a free lunch
(there you go again), all the ice cream I could steal, and all the
tips I could pocket.

Even though the pay wasn't great and the setting something less than Wanamaker's, the job description dovetailed
with my needs in an amazing way. School would be over at the
end of June, I realized, which meant my job at Wanamaker's
would be over till the fall. The prime time for soda fountains is
in the hot months, June to September, and that's when the tips
are most lavish. I accepted.

Soon I was stuffing cones with the best of them. There's an art to making an ice cream soda, just as there's an art to painting a picture or cooking a good steak. You don't spritz the seltzer over the ice cream in the bottom of the glass. This freezes the cream too quickly, and the drink turns to ice. You put a spoon in the glass, cover the ice cream with syrup, *then* zap the seltzer water over it. The spoon and the syrup keep the ice cream at just the right temperature, and presto, a perfect soda. Little things like that. Tricks. Life is tricks.

I even developed some razz-a-ma-tazz of my own to keep the customers intrigued. I'd seen this stunt first in a Harold Lloyd movie, then practiced it in secret while my boss was out of the shop (costing him at least five bucks a day in ice cream, no doubt). I'd scoop out a ball of ice cream with the metal scooper, play with it till it was baseball round, then toss it over my right shoulder, catch it in the dish or soda glass, and pop the finished product in front of my amazed customer, all in one smooth motion. (The trick? Put the ice cream scooper in hot water first so that the ice cream ball slides off it without getting stuck.)

The customers loved it. I waited for the tips to roll in.

But the money here had square edges .

The blame was not entirely mine. I gave them a pretty good show. It was just that in this era people didn't tip the way they do today. Times were hard, yes, but it was also because goods and services were so cheap, relatively speaking, that there was rarely enough change left over from a cash transaction to add up to a gratuity. A cup of coffee, for example, priced out at a roaring 5 cents. Is the guy going to give you a three cent tip for serving him? It didn't make sense.

So you had to get clever about these things and use the power of suggestion. Recall the way, for example, a bum comes up to you on the sidewalk and holds out his hand. He usually has a few quarters in his palm, right? That's good basic financial psychology: money attracts money, even when it's just small change. Also, the quarters suggest that if you're going to give him something you'd better at least give him a quarter. Why, my good man, I wouldn't think of taking anything smaller! Even dealing with bums, no one wants to look like a cheapskate.

So I made use of the same psychological principle with my own tip bowl. I filled it with nickels and dimes, and let the power of suggestion take care of the rest. It worked—kind of. (I'd make use the same trick later on, by the way, with even better results when I worked at the coat check counter. More on that later.)

A more blatant technique went like this: I'd entertain my counter customers with the ice cream follies, give them some charm and a smile, then, when they were finished and about to get up from the counter I'd take out a nickel, flip it into my tip bowl and look smilingly at them, calling out "Thank you!" The old law of reciprocity: I did this for you, now it's your turn. . . .

Worked wonderfully. Well, sometimes wonderfully.

Then, of course, there were the problem customers.

I remember one old Jewish man, who'd come into the shop every Wednesday at three o'clock sharp. Very elegantly he'd sit down at the counter and order a black and white soda, chocolate and vanilla ice cream mixed with seltzer.

I'd mix it up and hand it to him. He'd take several long glubs on it, then turn to me with an offended look. "Young man, this soda is far too sweet!"

So I'd refill half the glass with seltzer.

He'd take several more mighty pulls, practically drain the thing, then put it down and, would you believe, announce that the drink was still not right. "Needs more seltzer," he'd say with a little sneer.

By the time he had finished sucking down his drink he'd had two sodas for the price of one. I suppose the thing that tickled me most about this was that he thought he was fooling me, and that I was so dumb I didn't know he was a guy who'd take advantage of every situation.

But I did know it. And that was part of the fun—the characters. I especially enjoyed kibitzing with the customers when they came in, teasing them, slipping extra scoops of ice cream into my friends' sodas, waiting for that little man to arrive and order his weekly black and white and a half. Many other kids I knew jerked sodas that same season, and when our work day was over we'd all get together on the corner or in the park and trade counter secrets. It was kind of like a fraternity.

At the end of my first summer I'd worked Mondays through Saturdays and made $18 a week. I was happy as a clam. The next summer, parlaying my counter experience, I worked six days a week and took a job on Sundays as a part-time "relief man" for $5 the day. I soon discovered I could make more money as a relief man working in several pharmacies than staying permanently in one place, so I started going around to different wet shops asking if they needed part-time help. Soon I was working at three different drug stores, pocketing $30 a week, and enjoying a day off on Sundays in the bargain.

My mommy didn't raise a dummy.

Finally, during my last summer of high school a buddy and I teamed up at a drug store on Dyckman Street, took turns managing the fountain for the summer, hired other kids to do the work, split the shifts, and upped our pay to $40 a week.

I was an entrepreneur at last, at least in my own eyes. I had my own "managerial company" with offices at the Dyckman pharmacy. I had employees, a salary, all the ice cream I could eat. In three summers I had, in other words, doubled my salary, become a boss, and learned to make a wicked egg cream.

Not bad for a poor kid from Troy.

Then finally came graduation, 1929: Soda jerking,

Wanamaker's, Haaren High, managerial splendor. Fond early youth, farewell.

I put my head up and glanced at the next rung of my ladder, not knowing whether it would take me up, down, sideways—or a combination of all three.

Why Kids Are So Stressed Out Today

The year was 1929 and the Great Depression was preparing, like a hungry Tyrannosaurus Rex, to pounce on America. Yet for me the central thing, the only thing that year was college.

It was a beautiful Wednesday in New York City. A few blocks from Wanamaker's I'd often walked past an interesting college campus: official red brick buildings with ivy trailing along the sills, lots of determined young academics carrying bookbags, professors importantly striding past in tweeds with briefcase. It was called New York University—NYU—and, I was told, its scholastic reputation was good, especially in business administration.

I, of course, needed an undergraduate degree before I could go to law school, and a B.B.A. would dovetail nicely with law studies. The campus was pretty, the ambiance scholastic. I decided to have a look. So:

Did I make an appointment to speak with an admissions officer? No.

Did I write for an application? No.

Did I choose eleven backup schools, just in case I didn't get in? No.

Did I send in my $150 application fee? No.

Did I take a week off my busy schedule to visit the campus? No.

Did I sit for an interview with a bored

admissions officer and/or a patronizing college dean? No.

Did I spend six months and a thousand dollars taking special courses to prep for my SAT's? No.

Did I even *take* SAT's? No.

Did my family apply for financial aid? No.

Did I trash the coffers of my family's life savings to pay for four years at school? No.

Instead of all this, on this warm, friendly Wednesday I ambled over to Washington Square Park, walked into the NYU admissions office, chatted with the admissions personnel, selected some literature, sat down on a park bench and thumbed through the course-offering catalog—marketing, economics, advertising, financial management. It looked pretty good.

So I walked back to the admissions office, filled out an application form, handed it in—and bingo, I was an NYU matriculate. Period.

And we wonder why our kids are stressed out today.

There were, of course, loose ends to tie up.

First, I had to decide if I'd be taking day or night classes. And second, well, there was an economics to the thing, naturally; in my case, a vital economics. NYU permitted students to take 18 credits per semester at a cost of $10 per credit. That came to $180 per term, not bad as far as college tuition went at the time, but still plenty of dough.

Nor was I alone. Just about every young man and woman I knew at the time faced a similar financial crush, and we all solved the problem the only way we knew how—by working. Stress centers were unheard of in that time. We were all too busy burning off the energy by putting ourselves through school. Think of it: We never had to make big decisions like kids do today; contemporary kids, faced with a hundred options at any given minute and hence with a hundred difficult and stressful choices.   It's overload, really; no wonder they're wrecks.

In my time we never had to make the big life decisions. Fate, our families, the Depression, life as it was, these forces decided things for us. All we had to do was go with the flow.

The Search Begins

Of course, having completed my stay at Haaren High School I could now no longer depend on them for "occupational placement" as the nice people in the employment agencies called it. I was on my own.

How to find a job?

There were three ways:

1) *Answer classified ads in the newspapers.*

Problem was that any job with half a shine to it was noticed by about 5,000 other young newspaper readers. By the time you showed up for the interview a line undulated for three city blocks like a monster snake. It didn't matter how early you arrived, either; there was always a crowd ahead of you. Some of them camped out at the business location the night before. That's how desperate people were for jobs

2) *Visit the employment agencies.*

At first this course of action seemed like a winner.

You'd walk along employment row on 6th Avenue and every agency would have dozens of 3X3 white cards displayed in their windows, each one hyping a terrific job.

Like:

> WANTED: INTELLIGENT, AMBITIOUS
> COLLEGE STUDENT WANTED FOR
> PART TIME WORK AT NEW YORK
> LAW OFFICE. FEE: $2 PER HOUR
> PLUS LIBERAL BENEFITS.

Or

> COLLEGE GUYS AND GALS! LOOK-
> ING FOR EXTRA MONEY TO PUT
> YOURSELF THROUGH SCHOOL? LIKE
> TRAVEL, PRESTIGE, EXTRA MONEY
> ($4 AN HOUR) THEN CALL THE
> ROSENBURG TRAVEL BUREAU FOR
> THE JOB OF A LIFETIME AT BU 7-1221.

Sounded great. Until you walked into the office and were informed that, sorry, that job was just filled an hour ago.

Strange how often you heard this phrase. Was there ever such a job in the first place? Don't ask. And if by chance the job really existed and they sent you for an interview, it was the same story as with the newspaper ad, a line of hopefuls stretching from here to Chicago.

3) Know someone influential who can get you a job.

I didn't.

A trip to the Y

Still, I was young and self-assured, and I figured that if I could just slip past the palace guards at these offices and go directly to the boss my instincts would take over from there and I'd say the right things. The stumper was, how to get a foot in the door?

As it happened, a friend told me that the YMHA on 92nd Street was currently running an employment agency for young Jewish males. Lots of Jewish employers were using their services, my friend said, and the agency didn't charge a fee. Sounded good.

The 92nd Street Y is, of course, still there today, as active as ever with its poetry readings and cardiac swims. Still looks the same, too, even down to the inscriptions in stone over the windows on Lexington Avenue, lines straight from the Old Testament: "Rejoice, young man, in thy youth," and "Remember thy Creator in the days of thy youth," words that tend to resonate in a young man's mind long after he's read them.

So I paid the Y a visit and after a long wait got an appointment with an interviewer. I told him I needed a job that paid enough money to cover my college tuition plus give me a little extra for spending money.

The interviewer was a patient, doleful man who looked like he'd seen it all. He gave a little chuckle at my request, shook his head, rummaged through a pile of papers on his desk for what seemed like hours, and finally pulled out a folder.

"Here's a fur company" he said, sighing. "Downtown, early 30's. A classy operation. They need a stock boy."

"Sounds swell," I said.

"Pay's not bad either."

"What's the hitch?"

"Hitch is getting hired," he said with a tired smile. "I've sent three dozen kids down there so far, a lot of them qualified, and it's always the same bit. The boss's son listens to each one's spiel, says nothing, then shows them the door."

"What's he looking for?" I asked.

The interviewer shrugged. "No one can figure it out. He probably doesn't know himself."

We sat in silence for a moment. "Might be worth the nickel carfare," he finally volunteered. "Want to give it a try?"

I thought about it for a moment, then nodded. Why not?

On the way downtown, with the subway beating in my eardrum and butterflies in my stomach, I kept asking myself the same question over and over, looking for a hint on how to proceed: What had the other candidates already told this guy? Probably a lot of fast talk about what hard workers they were and how much experience they'd had. Then, no doubt, they'd trotted out their resumes and report cards and letters of testimonial, the usual stuff, none of which was interesting to anyone but themselves. All it got them was the door.

As I walked out of the subway at 34th Street I told myself that I had to do something a little different, a little innovative. But what?

The Fine Art of Chutzpah

When I arrived at the fur company's office it was already late in the day. Through the window I could see rows of animal skins hanging on display. Most of them were Park Avenue-style furs, mink and ermine, the big time. The name above the door read:

A. Pines and Son, Fine Furs.

I set my hat on my head to a cocky angle, murmured a little prayer, and walked in.

I was shown into the waiting room and told to sit down. Here, out of the blue, the first bolt of inspiration hit me: Don't talk to the son, talk to the father.

I immediately announced to the secretary that I'd been sent by the 92nd Street Y to see Mr. Pines Senior. That's Senior, not Junior. The secretary thought about this for a moment, got up, disappeared into an adjacent office, and emerged several minutes later.

"Mr. Pines only has a few minutes for you," she said.

"That will be fine, thank you," I answered, all business-like and official.

Mr. Pines was a short, pompous, gray-haired man in his early sixties, stocky, very dapper, but obviously fatigued and out of sorts. No doubt he'd already done a long day's work and was ready to go home. Interviewing a wet behind-the-ears intruder was the last thing on his agenda.

Ha! I thought to myself. That's it! It came to me in a flash as I crossed his office and looked at looked into his weary eyes. Don't waste the man's time. Get d-i-r-e-c-t-l-y to the point.

"I'm here to see Mr. Pines" I announced.

The dapper man nodded noncommittally.

"You sir?—you're Mr. Pines?"

"I am."

"Marty Silverman," I said extending my hand. "The 92nd Y sent me down. I've come for the job you advertised."

I didn't volunteer another word but just looked at him with a confident smile. *Fait accompli.* Your troubles are over. Lafayette, I am here!

He stared at me in a strange way, held my smiling gaze for several minutes, then gave a curt little nod.

"Put your hat in the third locker on the left hand side of the hallway," he said. "Then go up to the office on the balcony and give the girl your name."

I pinched myself. It *worked*?

I recalled an old saying: "To succeed in the world, act as if you're already a success." Telling him that I had come for the job, not asking, not hyping myself, not saying anything at all, really, except that I was here and ready to rhumba, had done the trick. This, and the fact that I happened to show up, I supposed, at that very auspicious moment when Mr. Pines was too tired to protest.

Tricks of the Fur Trade

What I knew about the fur trade you could drop into a mosquito's navel and still have room left over to serve tea. Mink coats? Animal hides? It was about as far from my experience as rowboating in Abyssinia. What did I know for skinning cats? Still, I knew one thing—I'd better look sharp.

I immediately marched myself up to the office on the balcony and found the secretary I indicated to her and several others sitting there staring at me that I'm the new man, just hired by Mr. Pines (you know, ahhhhm, senior) and that I'm not e-n-t-i-r-e-l-y certain yet how everything works around here and could they maybe tell me where to hang my coat.

The secretary yawned, pushed a buzzer on her desk, and motioned for me to sit down. She took my name, blah, blah, and where did I live, blah, blah, blah, told me Pines & Son would pay $18 every Friday afternoon, yawn, yawn; the hours were 9 to 5 with a five-day work week and two weeks' vacation with pay. Any questions? No? Yawn. Yes? Yawn. Well, don't worry, Sylvio will be here in a minute. I've just rung for him. He'll answer all your questions.

A minute later Sylvio himself comes in the door, all energy and impulse, big toothy smile, Italian cheesecake, bone-crunching handshake, handlebar mustache with a permanent wave at the tips, a slap or two of bear grease at the temples.

"Hey, pisano! How ya' doing?"

I liked him instantly. He was dressed in a white coat, the kind doctors and butchers wear to work, and must have been, say, 150 pounds overweight and, say, 35 years old.

"You da' new guy, right?

"That's me."

"What's your name, pal?

"Marty Silverman. But you can call me Marty Silverman."

He laughed and we shook hands.

The next instant he disappeared into a nearby storage closet, burrowed around inside like a rabbit, and reemerged with a white coat similar to the one he was wearing.

"For youse," he said, "Youse'll need it where we're going."

He grabbed my arm and pulled me towards the basement stairs. "Great ta' meet youse, Marty. My name's Sylvio—your boss, you could say."

"Where are we going?" I asked.

"I'm gonna show youse the ups and downs. Come on!"

We descended a dark, odoriferous staircase into the bowels of Gehenna. Sylvio clicked on the lights but this did little to dispel the morgue-like dimness of Mr. Pines' catacomb. Still, there was enough illumination to get the lay of the land, and the sight that greeted me in this grave, cold basement is one I've never forgotten. There were skins everywhere—hanging skins, packing cases of skins, lockers and caddie bags and storage troughs and nesting boxes full of skins, skins piled so high you could sled down the side; skins so dense you'd get lost and never be seen again, skins, skins, more skins, some of them, I would learn later on, among the finest and most expensive of their kind in the world.

"Dis is the place where the raw merchandise arrives," Sylvio announced. "And dis is where we'll be working a lot of the time. The skins are delivered, we lug em' down here. They get graded, we mark em'. Then we send em' out to be dressed."

"Who do you address them to?" I asked.

Sylvio looked up at me with a twinkle, puffed out his cheeks and shook his head. "Na, na, not addressed—*dressed.* Cleaned. Make em' ready to wear—a nice mink coat for the ladies, you understand what I'm saying, pisan?"

I nodded embarrassedly.

"Over here, kid."

A number of neatly wrapped packages were balanced precariously one on top of the other, almost to the ceiling.

"Take a look at dis" he said, pointing to a label on one of the packages.

I read it. The return address was from Whitehorse in the Yukon.

I glanced at another package. This one came from a trading post in Alaska. What a thrill for me, a kid from New York who'd never been further north than the Bronx, seeing all this exotic merchandise from storybook places. I started to visualize bearded hunters and Eskimos, North West Mounted Police and trappers—all somewhere far, far away doing fabled things in the Klondike.

"We start here," Sylvio broke in. "We unwrap the skins and pile em' up nice over in the corner.'"

He carefully pulled one of the packages out from the pile. He placed it on a wooden table, unwrapped it, removed the skin, and spread it out in front of him. Its surface was raw and greasy, and the table beneath it was layered with years of animal fat. I could see why white aprons were the order of the day at Pines & Son.

"Needs marking," he said.

Picking up a hammer and showing me the company insignia, APS, imprinted on the head, he then gave the skin an expert whack, leaving the company's imprint embossed on it for future identification.

"This way anybody got doubts about whose skin this

belongs to, they look for Mr. Pines' mark," he announced. "Think you can do dat?"

Before I could answer he reached out, squeezed my arm, and nodded approvingly. "Youse a good strong boy, you won't have no trouble swinging a hammer. Now come with me upstairs."

We headed back up the dark staircase to the main floor. Here Sylvio led me into what they called a "cold room" (why I don't know, because it was never cold) and here he showed me where the finished skins were graded, sorted, bundled, ticketed and stored. Part of my job, he explained, was to sit at one of the two long tables that comprised the only furnishings in this room, bundle the skins, and put a seal on each of them. Then the skins had to be tagged with the lot number for inventory purposes and a suggested selling price placed on them in code. Finally they were sent to the salesmen for selling and display.

My head was reeling from all this information, and Sylvio must have sensed it because he suddenly announced this was really nonsense, this fur business, and that what I should learn about were the really important things in life—like pasta. Before I knew it I was sitting at a local Italian restaurant with my new friend and mentor, listening to him discourse on the proper way to eat spaghetti.

"You don't need no knife for spaghetti," he explained, emphasizing the "ghetti" like a good Italian. "Just a fork and a big spoon. You pick it up like this"—he demonstrated, never dropping a strand—"and twirl it on the inside of spoon real good. They put a lot of garlic in it so's you shouldn't taste the smell. You try."

I was eating my pasta like a Roman soon enough, much to Sylvio's delight, and wolfing down the garlic bread. He continued to explain the 'ins and outs' of Italian cuisine, how you put parmigiana on some pastas but not on others, how the meat sauce should never be allowed to get too dark, how a ravioli noodle looks different from a tortellini noodle and a fettuccine noodle, and how the bucatini noodle looks different from all three. I was an eager student and he was a great instructor. I asked him to teach me some Italian words so I could handle myself like a man of the world next time I ate in an Italian restaurant (which up till then had been never). He agreed. We shook hands. Friends for life.

I also asked him to tell me how the Pines operation worked, and what was expected of the employees there.

Mr. Pines Senior was the big boss, Sylvio explained, and his son, Mr. Pines Junior, was second in command, heir to the throne, the fair-haired boy. Below him was Mr. Pines' nephew, just off the boat from Russia but with a legendary talent for grading and matching skins.

Next in the pecking order came a small group of salesmen who peddled the skins to department stores and private buyers around the city. Finally there were the assorted secretaries, bookkeepers, stenographers, and warehouse workers.

I myself would technically be known as an "Assistant Salesman," Sylvio explained, though what this meant was that beside the chores he had outlined I would also be responsible for carrying the skins from store to store with the salesmen when they made their calls.

What kind of guy is Mr. Pines? I asked.

Tough, smart, vain, fussy, a crackerjack businessman, Sylvio answered, with a touch of pride in his voice. He'd built a national reputation by dealing fair and square with his customers. In fact, over the years Mr. Pines had conscientiously paid trappers and suppliers the highest possible dollar price for their pelts, so that now, when a really top quality skin came along, the trappers sent it to Pines & Son first before any of the other fur dealers.

I was learning.

After lunch we returned to the office where I suited up in my white jacket and went to work. I could hardly believe that several hours before I'd been just another schmo on the sidewalks looking for a job.

Right away I felt as if I blended into the place, as if I belonged and had been working here all my life. Everyone was helpful and pleasant and considerate. I had never really worked in a real office before; certainly I couldn't consider my escapades delivering papers or jerking sodas comparable to this. And yet, it all seemed very natural and fine.

I started work on a Thursday and as it turned out the next day was pay day. The bookkeeper handed me my first check. It was for $9. I had worked only one-and-a-half days and they paid me for a half-week's work. In the middle of the Depression. What a thrill. What an experience.

I thanked her and went out of my way to find Mr. Pines and tell him how happy I was to be working at his establishment. He received my gratitude with stuffy good will and promised that—ahem, yes, young man—I could expect a future with him and his son here in furs if I worked hard, went regularly to shul, and kept to the straight and narrow. I assured him I intended to do all three.

I walked away feeling very pleased with myself, and with my new situation. If I'd just been a little quicker on my feet, however, I might have paid special attention to the fact that he mentioned himself and his son in the same admiring breath. A crucial point, and one that escaped me entirely.

It was a mistake I would pay for soon enough.

Dot

Getting a nine-to-five job at Pines & Son settled by default the question of whether I would work days or nights. All that remained now vis-a-vis my college arrangements was to make the trip down to NYU and give them my schedule.

Note that I don't speak of *telephoning* NYU. My family had no telephone, nor did most other average citizens in 1929. Phones were still something of a luxury, especially for the middle class, and even many small businesses often operated without one.

Now think about that for a minute. Today we pick up the receiver and do our business in minutes, right? We don't have to actually *show up* to get things done. Electronics take care of all that. In the old days, however, if you were in a hurry, if the mails were too slow, and if you didn't have a telephone on the premises your options were, to say the least, limited. Suppose you needed to make an appointment? Give a co-worker important information? Set a time for a meeting? What else was there to do? You had to climb on the bus or subway and haul yourself there in person. Think of what that meant in terms of time and energy. How many things today that we take so for granted. . .

At any rate, the day I decided to make the trip from Washington Heights to NYU to register I also just happened to call my friend Dot. Remember? The young lady I canoed with across the storming Hudson? It turned out she also would be attending NYU and had, in fact, recently registered. Would I like it if she accompanied me down to the administration building and helped me cut through some of the registration red tape there?

Heart: *thump, thump!* In an hour we were on our way along Fifth Avenue in a double-decker bus gazing at the buildings, chatting about school, making plans to attend the same French class. Occasional coy smiles and diffident looks were also exchanged; and at one point, while congratulating me on my decision to attend NYU, she took held my hand and gave it a squeeze.

Need I say that for those few moments I no longer required mechanical conveyance to move my rear end from one point to another. A cloud did all the work for me just then.

Signing Up

Down at the NYU Admissions Office I signed up to take 12 credits a semester at $10 per credit. Total per term: $120. Thank God for Mr. Pines.

The admissions people also asked me for a $30 registration fee, with the balance payable in one lump sum or over the rest of the term. Dot advised me to take the time-pay option cause, she explained, if I gave them the fee right away they'd be making interest on my money for the next six months.

I was impressed.

After I filled out all the final papers, the two of us strolled around Washington Square for several hours, window shopping and enjoying the park. The place had a feeling of tidy disorderliness to it, a friendly mixture of academia, Bohemia, ethnic family life and local color; the era of drug dealers and graffiti scrawls was still far in the future.

We ate a sandwich at a collegiate hangout and listened wide-eyed as a group of students argued at a neighboring table over class war and Karl Marx and the coming world revolution. One student announced that within five years communism would take over the United States. The other said no, more time was needed, perhaps a decade of two before the bourgeoisie could be crushed and the means of production returned to the working class.

Little did I know as I listened to these strange ravings that I would soon be part and parcel of the same conversations in coffee shops just like this one: Trotsky, the Party, socialism, the workers' revolution—communism was all one heard on campus during the early 1930's; and, oh yes, Sigmund Freud. Somehow these two names were always shouted in the same breath, though what one had to do with the other no one could quite say. I suppose the name Freud lent an air of serious enough intellectualism to the subject of sex to allow men and women to talk about it openly and "objectively," as if discussing just another academic topic, Roman history, say, or comparative philology. A favorite line of students at the time was "If it doesn't concern the dialectic or psychoanalysis it has no relevance!"

Looking back, it *was* a seductive group of ideas, especially the Communist ideology. All would share equally in the wealth. No more poor classes (everyone liked this one). No more rich classes (this one even more). The State will wither away (Hmmmmm . . . people were a little less enthusiastic about this one). Equal distribution of land (terrific if you're a farmer, ho hum if you're not, but what the heck). "From each according to his ability, to each according to his needs" (all right!!—a foretaste of doing your own thing). And so forth.

There was always someone on premises to mouth these catch phrases, and always plenty of heads to nod in agreement. The argument among young people at the time, in fact, was not whether communism was the best form of government. All intellectuals worth our salt knew that capitalism was doomed and exploitative and, worst of all, unfashionable.

The question, was, how could we wake up the benighted proletariat and bring about the revolution in the shortest period of time?

All such conversations were driven partially by conviction, partially by the need to appear brilliant and modern. Sitting around a table at a coffee shop I might hold forth on the rich people who bought furs at Pines & Son—their expensive alligator shoes ($7 a pair), their platinum telephones, their fur-covered toilet seats. Everyone would hiss and shake their heads and announce that time was getting short for the capitalist dogs. Another angry student would then bemoan the workers selling apples on the street. *Tsk, tsk!* Or the bread lines. As if any of us had ever stood on one. Wasn't the State monstrous! Come the Revolution the Rockefellers and the Mellons and the Morgans would all be hung in the square. It was all so clear and plain.

The thing was, though, as with all this high-sounding talk, I never knew a single student who actually *became* a Communist. Somehow it was something you talked about rather than did.

As I got older and matured, as my knowledge of the world increased, as I became a wage earner and raised a family and saw how the things of life are really constructed—human nature, human greed, the natural inequalities of humankind—I began to notice that I and my friends were less eager to give away everything we'd worked to acquire. When we were kids we had nothing, and so we had nothing to lose. Now we were adults, and we had plenty to lose. We'd worked long and hard for our place in the sun. We'd earned it. We didn't want to give it away so soon.

Simple as that. It makes me remember an old Alan Sherman song called "Harvey and Sheila," popular in the 60's and sung to the tune of *Haveh Negila*. The idea—I'm embellishing where memory fails—is that a young Jewish couple, Harvey and Sheila, start out as young flaming liberals. They live together out of wedlock, drive a VW bug, carry placards, go on hunger strikes, belong to radical groups, smoke marijuana. Then one day they marry and settle down. As time passes they become increasingly conservative. Harvey starts to prosper in the business world and Sheila buys a mink coat. No more SDS now. They join the country club instead. By the end of the song Harvey and Sheila are fat, rich, and middle aged; they drive a Cadillac, vote Republican, live in the most expensive part of town, and Harvey smokes Havana cigars instead of pot. Thus it has always been.

At any rate, back to Dot.

We did our rounds on the NYU campus that day, poked around the Village for most of the afternoon, then grabbed the Fifth Avenue double-decker back home. We parted with a promise to see each other soon again.

Thump, thump!

Next morning at the breakfast table—it was a Sunday—
I gave my parents the news that I was now fully and officially
enrolled for my freshman year at New York University, and that
I had the full means to pay for it. Up to that point it had been
nip and tuck. No one was sure if we could afford the luxury of
my education. Now it was official.

"A lawyer!" my mother shouted. "I told you he was
going to become a lawyer! Your eggs are getting cold! The bar
exam! My God!"

As I sat there that lovely Sunday morning surrounded
by a loving family, good food and affection I knew that with the
help of the Good Lord I would indeed become a lawyer some
day. This was a very warm time in my life. I had a paying job.
I was in a fine college. On Saturdays I helped my dad make
deliveries and collections. On Sunday we all relaxed and
counted our blessings. I was learning. I was growing. Many
new facets of life were unfolding in the process.

The only thing I didn't know on that golden Sunday
morning was just how soon the fur rug would be pulled out
from under me.

How to Sell a Mink Coat

Pines & Son ran a busy shop. Buyers and sellers
entered and left at all hours of the day. Salesmen "hondled" in
the corridors. Four secretaries were busy beating up four
Remingtons from sunrise to dusk. New shipments arrived continuously by post, some from places as far away as Siberia.

My own schedule was divided between sorting and tag-
ging the skins in the basement, and accompanying the salesmen
on their rounds. My job during these excursions was to pack up
the skins before we left, carry them to the meeting place, unload
them, pack them up again when the meeting was over, then

carry them back to the store at the end of the day.

One of the interesting things about this business was the chain of buying and bargaining that took place before the fur actually reached the back of a customer.

This requires a bit of explanation.

Remember, the Depression was beginning, and even the ritzy department stores like Bergdorf Goodman and Saks Fifth Avenue were loath to spend their money unless they had a guaranteed return. Most of the skins they handled were thus on consignment rather than directly for sale. The store didn't really own the skins. They just put them on display and waited for a rich taker.

That was one way of doing it. Another was to pre-sell the goods to the customer.

Here's a typical scenario. One day a salesman from Pines & Son named Sid grabbed me in the hallway. We had a meeting that afternoon, he said excitedly, with a big buyer at Altman's department store, Nathan Petiker.

Mr. Petiker, it seemed, had a client who wanted to see only the finest mink skins available, a French diplomat's wife who had just sailed into town, was on a mad shopping tear, and was determined to return home with an expensive souvenir from New York.

Sid chose a selection of skins from Pines' basement, I packed them up in cartons, and together we hustled over to Altman's on 34th Street to meet the buyer and his rich customer.

The customer, it turned out—I caught sight of her for just a moment—was a shockingly elegant woman in her late 50's, svelte, with a long French face, million-dollar coiffure, nervous, pursed lips, heavy-lidded, heavily mascaraed eyes, a $300 hat and veil from Charpentier, a lace-fitted, peppered silk chemise that even I knew was to drop dead over.

The buyer met us at the entrance to Altman's viewing room. I unpacked the skins and he snatched them from my hands.

"It's Madame Trosceau-Douce" he whispered collusively, as if we were supposed to recognize the name. Then he darted back to his customer.

Sid and I sat down in the next room and for 45 minutes listened in through the wall as Mr. Petiker sang the salesman's ancient mating song, coaxing, charming, creaming, maneuvering, stroking, shaming, soft-soaping, buttering up, decoying down, massaging, entrapping, tempting, schmeering, wheedling his patron into buying the most expensive fur. She, in turn, sat in regal silence before this multi-media selling blitz, smoking one perfumed cigarette after another (the smoke from which choked us even in the next room), and letting out a jaded "*oui*" or "*non, non*" every few minutes.

Finally, after a good deal of unrolling and unfurling of fur skins, the mysterious Madame le Diplomat voiced her approval of one item, then stood up abruptly, walked towards the door, and was immediately met there by a chauffeur and valet who escorted her downstairs to a waiting limousine.

Mr. Petiker marked the chosen skin, then hustled after Madame le Diplomat, presumably to bid his loving goodbyes and, ahem, oh by the way, to make sure Madame knew the price of the skin and how much it would cost to make into a mink coat.

He then rejoined us in the viewing room where he and Sid bargained for an hour over the wholesale price of the fur.

◆→ ◆→

This was a typical sales event for Pines & Son. After the skin was paid for by the department store, I also learned, the store had it tailored into a custom fur coat and sold it to the Madame le Diplomats of the world who could afford such extravagances, even during the Depression. Everyone thus got their jollies, or at least made their day's buck, even those at the bottom of the eating chain—me.

Which, apropos of the Depression and starvation, reminds me of a joke that was going around at the time. A dowager millionairess is sitting in the back of her limousine at a traffic light when a bedraggled beggar comes up to her with palm outstretched.

"Please, lady," he says. "I ain't eaten for three whole days."

The woman looks him up and down scornfully for several moments, puts her lorgnette to her eyes, and answers sharply, "Then for God's sake, man, force yourself!"

Too True to Be Good

A year and some went by at Pines & Son, and gradually I came to be accepted by the staff and even by staid Mr. Pines himself. At the end of each week I'd peep into my pay envelope and there I'd find an extra two or three dollars, compliments of, hmmmm . . . the boss? One of the salesmen? The house? I never knew for sure, but either way it was all from the same horn of plenty. Occasionally I even had the forbidden thought that being a fur magnate might be just as rewarding as being, well, as being a lawyer. . . .

I got to know all the salesmen intimately at Pines & Son as time passed, all, that is, except for the boss's son, Mr. Pines Junior, a sullen little chap who kept himself removed from the rest of the staff.

He, it turned out, besides being the heir apparent and the golden boy around the office was also a superstar salesman. This was not due to nepotism but to talent pure and simple—or so it appeared. More fur sales were written up each month by this nebbishy little fellow than by all the other salesmen combined.

Mr. Pines Senior touted him accordingly as a kind of

Einstein of salesmanship. No one, including myself, could understood how he did it. How he outsold all the other seasoned fur pros. Until one day I was sent out with young Prince Pines on a sales call, and there I learned his secret.

It happened like this. Our assignment that day was to bring a selection of skins to a salesman named Schwartzman who represented a small, struggling fur salon on the outskirts of the fur district. During the meeting, after several hours of selection, Schwartzman picked out an enormous pile of particularly beautiful furs and placed the rejects in a nearby heap. How, I asked myself, was the buyer at this small establishment going to afford to pay for so many top-of-the-line skins?

Then the moment of truth arrived. The two men had obviously worked together many times. They cut right to the chase.

"This one's a beauty," Schwartzman said, picking up a skin and glancing at the price tag. "Says $100."

"How much do you want to pay?" Junior asked.

"Fifty," came the reply.

"Deal," said Junior.

He walked over to the reject pile, delved through it till he found a skin with a $50 price tag, snipped the tag off, and tied it onto the $100 skin.

Simple as that. Boss's son's prerogative, after all. Who among us is going to argue? I suppose he assumed I would keep my mouth shut to the other salesmen about this interesting transaction, and/or that since I was such a lowly worm in the firm no one would believe me if I blabbed.

Junior and Mr. Schwartzman then proceeded to go through the rest of the selected skins in this same way, Schwartzman quoting the price he wanted to pay and Junior switching the tags.

Live and learn. Anyway, it wasn't my concern. I knew enough to keep my mouth shut and my eyes ahead, just as Junior wished.

Several weeks later, however, I was invited to attend one of Pines & Son's monthly sales meeting. I'd been allowed to sit in on these sessions several times before, and each time, being young and green and wanting to show how brilliant I was, I'd made occasional comments, mostly naive, that the company members including my friend Sylvio and Mr. Pines himself had listened to with good-natured forbearance. By now I figured I was one of the boys.

This particular meeting was not a sunny one. Mr. Pines paced back and forth in front of the room, chewing out one employee after the other for not generating enough sales and for goofing off. First he castigated Sylvio until Sylvio was ready to break into tears. Then Sid was put on the pillory, and others in turn. Knowing how hard these guys actually worked, and how much of themselves they gave each day to the company, I found myself getting angrier and angrier as Pines' tirade thundered on. Finally came the last straw.

"Why don't you fellows wise up!" he hollered at everybody in the room at once. "Look at my son. He goes out in the field every day with the same furs as you. He goes to the same department stores as you. Same buyers as you. Everything, just like you. But does he sell like you! Heavens to Bets, no! He sells twice as many furs! *T-w-i-c-e* as many! What's the matter with you, you can't keep up!"

Despite all my better instincts, I cleared my throat and raised my hand.

"Yes?" said Mr. Pines, stopping in the middle of his speech, amazed that I had the chutzpah to interrupt him at such a critical moment.

"Mr. Pines," I said. "Anyone can sell like your son."

He took a step back. "Really? And how did you come to that conclusion?"

"Well," I continued, warming to the task, assured that everyone at the firm would think me a hero from now on for being so forthright. "Your son visits a buyer. After a bit of chit-chat the buyer announces that he wants to buy the skins in the expensive bundle at the same price as the skins in the cheaper bundle. Your son says fine, and he switches the price tags. Seems to me anyone can make a deal that way."

Silence.

More silence.

Everywhere silence. Silence across Manhattan. Silence in Amarillo. Silence among the walruses in Antarctica. Silence on the planet Uranus. Silence from floor to ceiling at Pines & Son.

Mr. Pines seemed to sort of faint inside himself for a minute. Then his eyes narrowed and he stared at me, then at his son across the room who had turned a deep vermillion. Then back at me. Then at his son. Then at me. Not a word was spoken.

Finally Mr. Pines Senior coughed into his handkerchief and announced that the meeting was over. He and his son then hastily left the room, and were followed quickly by the others. No one looked at me. No one said anything to me. I had been turned invisible.

And so it was when I walked out of the conference room into the hall. Lena, the bookkeeper, was standing there holding something in her hand, a funereal look on her face. It was an envelope. She handed it to me, then walked away without saying a word. I opened it. Inside was a week's salary plus a few extra dollars severance pay. No note, no explanation.

Invisible.

I'd been—yes, the F word.

Numb and wounded and silly, I looked around the office for an ally, an explanation—or at least a kindly goodbye. If only I hadn't. . . . If only I could have. . . .

But I had. And I couldn't. The arrow had left the bow and there was no calling it back. I caught sight of Sid walking down the hall and waved to him. He looked back at me blankly and continued on.

Invisible.

The real test would be Sylvio. I opened the door to the basement storage room and looked down into the gloomy piles of furs I'd come to know so intimately. He was there, all right, piling skins.

"Hey, Syl," I called out, trying to sound casual. "I just wanted to tell you good—"

"Uh, uh," he said, not even turning to look at me.

I stood on the steps for a long moment gazing down at him until the picture got through my thick skull that there was no way on earth he was going to look up or say a word. He had a job, after all, a family, a career to protect in these hard times. He couldn't take the chance of fraternizing with me after I'd disgraced Mr. Pines and his son in front of the whole staff.

I turned around, picked up my hat in the main office, put it on my head at the same cocky angle I'd worn it the day I entered this place two years ago, and walked out the door of Pines & Son for the last time, devastated, furious at myself, hurt beyond words by people who had been my friends a half-hour earlier.

Out on the pavement. Traffic, noise, concrete, reality. Unemployed. I looked up and down the street in a daze. Then I remembered: What would I tell my folks?

Dad was the first to hear. I could see the sadness well up in his eyes, not because I lost the job but because he felt my hurt.

Then I told the same story to my mother. Her reaction was less sympathetic.

"Who asked for your opinion anyway!" she shouted in the same voice she used when the teachers sent me home with a reproachful note. "You got just what was coming to you. Open your big mouth. And now where are you going to find a job, huh, Mr. Big Shot? In the middle of a Depression?"

I agreed. *Nolo contendere.*

Then she threw her arms around me. "I didn't want a furrier in the family anyway."

I felt better instantly. How did she know I was thinking of joining the fur business?

"Things will work out," she continued, still squeezing. "You'll see. They always do for you. For you, things always do."

I Make a Sentimental Journey

As I write this story so many years later, I'd like to include this addendum. I recently made a sentimental journey back to what was once the Manhattan fur district. I wanted to relive my youth and to look at the Pines & Son building once again.

But it's all gone today—the stores, the buildings, the busy shops once so full of sewing machines, fur notions, buttons, linings, trimmings. All gone, wiped out, they tell me, by a group of activists who insist it is a mortal sin to wear the skin of a domestically raised animal.

Perhaps. But then, tell this to the people who made a living from these skins Many have never found work again. I think of the trapper and trader and the trading posts in far away places. They are gone. I think of the dressers who dressed the skins. They are gone. The graders who handled the skins— gone. The ranchers who raised the animals for their pelts. They are all gone. Even the animals themselves. Many were freed, then left in the wilds, half domesticated, to be eaten by other animals or to starve. So they vanished too. Now the industry is wiped out, and the one-time thriving fur district is a war zone of graffiti-covered storefronts and empty lofts.

Despite what the activists may say, this makes me sad.

Meanwhile, it's been over 70 years since I walked out of

A. Pines fur emporium that morning with hot tears choking in my throat. Seventy years, and yet that moment is as real to me today as if it happened an hour ago, or two. Betrayal, shock, the enormous price we sometimes pay for a single foolish mistake—how the lessons poured in on my young head that terrible day.

Afterward, I would go on to spend years in colleges, in graduate schools and universities. There I discovered that what you get from books and classrooms, what we call education, does indeed prepare you for your life to come. But the act of learning itself, real experiential learning in the gaming fields of the world, is not simply a preparation for life—it is *life itself*.

●▸ ●▸ ●▸

Chapter 6

◆→ ◆→

I LEARNED MORE ABOUT LIFE IN THE CHECKROOM THAN IN THE BOARDROOM

Pavement Pounding Once Again

No job. Not enough money for my college education. Nothing to bring home to my family each week. Pie on my face from the Pines debacle.

What now?

Hit the road and look for another job, which, as I've told you, wasn't all that easy during the Depression.

I wasn't worried, but at the same time I was worried as hell, if you get my drift. I was approaching my 20th birthday. No longer a teenager. College was half-way through, and I was just finishing up the semester. There wouldn't be a new semester if I didn't land gainful employment.

I wasn't worried, okay? but, well, it seemed like the end of the line. There was only one alternative that I could see: rejoin the neighborhood workforce and jerk sodas for the months of June, July and August, then try to parlay my earnings into bigger profits. This way I could probably scratch together enough to pay for college.

But then there was my family to consider. Whatever

cash could be found in the Silverman coffers was dwindling like sand in an hourglass. Business was especially slow for my father and getting slower; in the middle of the Depression people had more important things to spend money on than having their trousers pressed. Every night at 8 o'clock he'd traipse home from work completely exhausted and half asleep. He'd been sequestered all day long in his tiny tailor shop with a fleet of steam irons sizzling near his head and clouds of steam roaring out from the pressing machines. I imagine during July and August this inferno heated up to 110, 115 degrees, perhaps higher.

And yet I never heard the man complain. Not once. His joy was simply to know that his son was going to college and was becoming an educated man. You can't begin to know how important that was to him, and to my mother. They had their boy in school. A good school, a fine school. He'd be a lawyer some day, get a degree, help others, make a name for himself, earn enough money so that he wouldn't have to worry himself to death over the bills. What more could a person ask for? My well-being was what counted.

Theirs? No matter—they had a boy in college. *That* was their well-being.

I knew all of this, of course, and the reality of it became the cornerstone of my young life. If the Good Lord would just spare me, I promised myself each day, and grant me good luck in this world, I would make it up to them some day a thousand times.

"Please, Lord," I whispered every night as I climbed into bed. "Please, Lord: How about tomorrow?"

But though I was unworried, tomorrow wasn't soon enough. I needed a job *today*.

An Old Friend and a New Friend

And so day after day I read the want ads, visited the employment agencies, pounded the pavement, pestered friends and enemies alike. I even went back to the 92nd Street Y to visit my agency ally.

But no soap. Everyone had plenty of suggestions, lots of advice, opinions, theories, recommendations, leads. But nobody would say the enchanted words: "You're hired." During this time, by the way, I did hear one term a lot, "net working." Most people think it's a new word. Actually, plenty of us poor, out-of-work souls talked about "net working" our way to jobs more than half a century ago. Since there were no electronic communications or TV "networks" at the time, we used the word in a somewhat different way; something like: "Toss your net into the job market and haul in a catch." It was even spelled differently, with a space between the "net" and the "work." But the essential meaning was the same.

One day, as luck would have it, I was walking down a street in Washington Heights when I bumped into an old high school fraternity brother, Steve Cohen. We were delighted to see one another again and immediately began to reminisce about what already for me had become "the old days." I recalled how, after coming to New York, I'd missed my Troy fraternity so much, Alpha Beta Gamma, that with the help of frat brothers in Troy, I'd managed to start a chapter here in New York City. I knew a lot of kids in the neighborhood at the time, and had met others at the synagogue. Soon I'd talked a bunch of them into joining ABG. With a bit of organization, some bartering and arguing, we soon had our own meeting place (a room in the Washington Heights synagogue), banners, a pin, a handshake, a logo (we were the Theta Chapter), and a steadily growing membership which prided itself in helping out in local civic affairs and in performing works of charity.

As Steve and I talked it all came back to me: the trips to

the Yankees games with frat brothers, the conventions, the dances, the feeling of belonging, of being part of something larger than myself, a fellowship forever. I felt particularly friendly towards him as we talked, so friendly, in fact, that I decided to test the limits of our brotherhood.

"What does your father do?" I suddenly asked.

He looked at me puzzled. "What do you mean?"

"For a living. What's his job?"

Something in my gut told me to push for an answer.

"Well, he runs a coat and hat check concession. How come?"

"Just curious. How's it work?"

Steve had to think about this for a minute. He was a pre-med student at City College and, I guess, any other profession was beyond his concern.

"Well, let me see. He goes to a restaurant or nightclub and offers to set up a check room free of cost to the management. Then he hires a group of college kids to take the coats and hats. He pays them a flat fee and keeps the tips for himself. Something like that."

"Do you think he might want to hire me?"

There was a long pause.

"No harm in asking. . . ."

"No harm at all—brother."

Next evening, Friday night, our phone rang. Steve Cohen on the line. Come over after dinner. About 8 o'clock. Father's anxious to talk to you. Might be a place for you in the organization. You never know."

Brother.

Quain (As in Cohen)

Steve met me at the door at 8 sharp. He ushered me into his apartment, through a high-ceilinged foyer, down a long marble hall, into a mahogany-paneled dining room. Here I was warmly greeted by members of his family seated around a baronial dining table. They were just finishing their Shabbus dinner.

An older man at the head of the table stood up, cleared his throat as if about to give a speech, and extended his hand in my direction. He was a short, friendly looking man with a clipped waxed mustache that sprouted from beneath a shiny bulbous nose, merry eyes, and a sweating, balding head. Even at home he dressed in a beautifully tailored three-piece suit with a fresh carnation tucked into the lapel. Steve told me later that he changed the flower at least three times a day.

When addressing anyone within a 180-degree radius this formidable gentleman first pivoted in his or her direction, made a short bow, and took hold of one of his lapels, as if about to give his opinion on the international question before Congress. Only after he had a commanding grip on this lapel did he seem able to speak. I liked him immediately.

"This is my father," Steve announced as we shook hands. "Mr. Quain."

"Mr. Quain?" I thought. "That's strange! I thought their name was Cohen."

He shook my hand warmly and motioned for me to sit down. The rest of the evening I dutifully Mr. Quained him this and Mr. Quained him that, wondering why I was using this odd name when my old friend Steve had always been Cohen. It was only some time later that I learned the facts about doing business when you have an obviously Jewish name, and how Jewish businessmen must from time to time nimbly bend the Yiddish tongue in order to stay afloat on the goyish sea.

After I'd downed the mandatory cup of tea and a honey

cake, and made the appropriate small talk, Mr. Quain motioned me into the living room for a private chat.

"So what can I do for you, young man?" he asked settling into his easy chair, lighting up a cigar as long as his arm and hooking a free thumb onto his lapel.

I told him that I was looking for a job, was willing to work any hours necessary, that my family needed the money, and that I'd be putting myself through NYU on my earnings.

He listened attentively, then asked me a series of staccato questions: Where did my family come from? What did my father do? How did I manage my time in school? What was I majoring in? What were my plans for the future?

After 15 minutes of this interrogation he suddenly fell silent, puffed ruminatively on his cigar (which seemed not to have burned down one micrometer since our conversation began), and finally looked up, smiling paternalistically in the way a person does when he's about to do you a favor.

"When can you start?"

"Soon as possible, Mr. Quain," I almost shouted, about to bust my buttons.

He patted his stomach, blew a smoke ring, and proceeded to explain what my job duties would entail

The Quain "industry," as he called it, maintained coat and hat concessions in the fanciest clubs and restaurants in New York City, including places like the Stork Club and the Copacabana. I would be working nights at the Hotel St. George in Brooklyn, he explained. The salary was a flat $7 a day, paid in cash at the end of each evening. All tips and other incoming monies went directly to him. I'd be taking coats, hats, furs, umbrellas, hanging them up, retrieving them, the usual thing. I would work three nights a week, Friday, Saturday, Sunday plus certain holidays—Christmas, New Year's and Thanksgiving. I was to wear black trousers every night, a white shirt, and a dark tie. The hotel would supply a jacket.

Was all this acceptable? Were there any questions?

Inside I'm thinking, I just got fired from a full-time job paying 18 dollars a week and here this guy's offering me $21 for three nights a week. That means I can have my days free, spend the time studying, going to class, helping my father make neighborhood deliveries.

"Yes, sir," I said, trying not to look as if I was about to swoon with delight. "That's acceptable."

"Are you prepared to start tomorrow night? Saturday?"

"Absolutely ready to start whenever you want, Mr. Quain," I answered instantly. "Whenever Quain Industries needs me."

"Fine," he replied, his eyes twinkling. He knew exactly what was going on inside me. "I'll call the manager at the hotel and tell him you're coming tomorrow evening, St. George Hotel, 6 o'clock sharp."

The rest, he announced, taking a long puff on his never-dwindling cigar and holding his lapel, was up to me.

Working the Inside

Today the Hotel St. George is a forgotten piece of New Yorkiana. I'm not sure if the grand old building is even still standing, or whether it's been eaten by the bulldozer. In its time though this austere edifice was one of the city's most elegant landmarks. Certainly it was the swankiest hotel in Brooklyn, and some said in all the five boroughs. Most old-timers shake their heads when you mention it today, get a starry-eyed look, and recall the hotel's most famous delight, its—gasp!—indoor swimming pool, an unimaginable luxury in the middle of the Depression, affordable only to the likes of the Fords, Mellons, and Capones.

But there were a thousand other amenities here too, of course—high-ceilinged rooms, fine dining, celebrity night-clubs, superb service. Most impressive, in my eyes at any rate, was the Grand Ballroom. I oh'ed and ah'ed as the manager showed me through it, pointing out the revolving bandstand, the giant dance floor, the ladies' checkroom on the right and the men's on the left, educating me how things worked in Mr. Quain's coat-and-hat-check world.

One man works the "outside," the manager explained as he handed me my checkroom jacket. He greets the customers at the counter window, takes their wraps, gives them a ticket, and helps them on with their coats when they leave. The second man stays on the "inside," behind the counter. He hangs up the coats, keeps track of the tickets, and delivers them on call.

"What's that?" I asked, "nodding towards a large copper plate perched conspicuously on the counter.

"You ask the right questions. That's for the tips. Mr. Quain stops by every night to collect them."

"But he's got concessions all over the city," I said. "He goes to each one himself? Every night?"

"You bet," the manager said with a touch of pride. "With special bags to carry the money in. Mr. Quain doesn't miss a trick."

Several of the other checkroom workers now arrived, and the manager introduced me around. All of them were college kids my age, very warm and chummy; in ten minutes I felt like one of the gang.

After my tour of the hotel was over the manager led me to the men's coat room and I went right to work. The job was straightforward. You hang up the coats, arrange them according to the ticket number, and retrieve them when the outside man calls out the number. The first night I checked exactly 251 coats—I counted—and met more people in eight hours than in two years of college. Before I knew it the clock was striking 3 and the musicians were starting to pack up their instruments.

Mr. Quain then magically appeared at 3:30, a big smile on his face and a fresh carnation. He patted me on the shoul-

der, told me I was born to the job, and handed me seven brand
new dollar bills.

I grabbed the subway home. It was a 70-minute ride
back to Washington Heights and the hour was so late, or so
early I should say, that I saw people on the train *going* to work.
But I didn't mind. I had just spent a fascinating evening, met a
group of terrific guys, seen the cream of cafe society strut their
stuff, and received seven dollars for the pleasure. Not a bad
day's work for a poor college kid.

Next day, Sunday, I arrived bright-eyed at the hotel,
already feeling like an experienced inside man. Another stage
of my education had begun.

Real Life À La Mode

It's no exaggeration to say that I learned more about life
and people and, well, things in general working at the Hotel St.
George than I did in four years of college plus three at law.

Sound strange?

Maybe. But think about it. From that little cubbyhole
of a checkroom we could observe all the fine points of the fast
lane in a fish bowl—people of all shapes and sizes and axes to
grind come to sample the cakes and ale of a ritzy New York
cabaret; the waxed parquet dance floor with the most fantastic
bands in the US of A, the Dorseys, the Jameses, the Goodmans,
blowing their hot horns over silhouettes of dancing men and
women in a smoky Jericho, watching them melt and flash and
collide into one great rhythm of the Jazz Age. Here they come,
here they come, like silver bullets on gold brocade, strutting up
to our counter with their fox furs and camel's hair coats, husbands with their wives and without their wives, tycoons,
Broadway idols, has-beens trying to get back in their agent's
good graces; cigar girls, call girls, marathon dancers, piano

tuners from Omaha and hog salesmen from Pelahatchie, deal makers and deal breakers, Prohibition teetotalers and sssssshloosing down drunks, sugar-woogas from Harlem with their white millionaire escorts, beautiful women leeching after everything that glitters, dowager heiresses bored with it all; bright, brash, secretly broke young men with their hair Brillianteened, climbing towards the top; tired, rich, aging plutocrats trying not to fall, or be pulled down by the younger competition.

These four-star dramas stopped off for a brief moment at our check counter each night and deposited their wrappings with us on trust, all against the backdrop of the big city, behind the big bands and the phosphor floodlights crisscrossing in the sky, the fabric of the excitement, the money, the pizzaz. It was like watching an endless play. I was actor as well as audience. I relished the roles.

Tricks of the Checkroom Trade

The first thing I learned about the checkroom at the St. George Hotel was that as far as our revered boss, Mr. Quain, was concerned, the world revolved around one thing and one thing only—*the tip plate*.

The tip plate was the final score, the big enchilada, the *raison d'etre* for the whole operation. The more coins we gathered each night the more we made Mr. Quain smile.

He had rigged up a neat little box under the checkroom counter with a slot on top and bottom to automate the collection process. When enough coins accumulated on the tray we would drop them through the slot like a piggy bank. Later on, sure enough, Mr. Quain appeared, just as the manager said, carrying an assortment of account books and money bags. He'd empty the contents of the night's take into one of the bags. He had an uncanny ability to tell how much change was collected each night simply by lifting the box. He'd compliment us if the take was good, or make a sour face and leave without a word if it wasn't.

It also became apparent that Mr. Quain had a definite method to his hiring madness, that he employed only college boys like me to run his concessions. This was a smart piece of business. We looked good, had lots of enthusiasm, energy, humor, and since we came from good homes, we were honest as well. That was the most important thing in Mr. Quain's eyes. It would have been awfully easy to steal those tips.

There was another reason for his hiring practices that didn't dawn on me till some years later. One of the finest things about Mr. Quain, we all agreed, was that he gave poor college kids like us a chance to make some money and advance our chances of success. Milk of human kindness. Later on, as I did some business myself and learned how things work, I came to understand that since all of us were planning to become professionals, lawyers, doctors and the like, there was little chance we'd steal his secrets and open a competing checkroom business. We were safe that way. So he may have been a philanthropist of sorts, old Mr. Quain, but he was also a *finanthropist,* and a darned cagy one.

Despite such hidden agendas, all of us at the hotel knew what a good deal we had going here at Mr. Quain's house of coats, and we liked the man immensely. We worked hard to make him smile.

But one pesky problem continually got in our way. Technically, you see, customers were not charged for using the check room. It was a "free" service offered by the establishment. House rules solemnly forbid any of the hotel workers to solicit a tip.

This meant, in turn, that we had to develop a regimen of strategies to "suggest" to customers that they should cough up, and to "suggest" that if they didn't cough up something not so nice might happen to their hats and coats.

All this, what's more, had to be communicated with looks, gestures, oblique references and body language alone. Not a word could be said directly.

Sounds impossible, perhaps. But there were ways.

Here, for instance, is a typical scenario.

A customer comes into the Grand Ballroom. The outside man at the checkroom takes his coat and hat, and hands him a ticket. If the customer doesn't leave a tip at this point the outside man then signals the inside man—that's me—and I hang up his wraps in a certain way, with the check ticket set at a cockeyed angle. This tells us that the customer is in arrears.

Now it's 2 o'clock in the morning, and the guy returns for his coat and hat (in those days men always wore hats, usually a dark blue felt model).

I take his ticket, locate his belongings, and notice that the angle of his ticket is crooked. By previous arrangement I shout out the number of the ticket (if the customer had tipped us already I'd remain silent). This is the signal to the outside man that the customer owes us.

Now the fantastic part begins: It's up to the outside man to use all his brains and wiles to hustle the customer into forking up. There are an infinite number of ways this can be done.

One, for instance, is to keep four quarters prominently displayed on the tip plate. This tells customers that tips are welcome—expected, is a better word. The sight of the money also loosens people's purse strings. Power of suggestion again, just like back at the wet store.

Another less subtle ploy: suppose the customer checks a topcoat. When he returns for it you help him on, then lightly grip the lining of his suit jacket, holding it in a casual kind of way until the guy figures what's up and reaches into his pocket for a coin. It takes practice to get this one right. You can't pull too hard on the lining, but then you can't be a wimp about it either. Same with a hat—you hand it to him and hold on to the rim for a few extra beats until he gets the point. Like I said, an art.

Occasionally a customer might play dumb, acting like he doesn't know a tip is expected or pretending not to see the coin plate.

To improve his grasp of the situation you plop his coat directly on top of the plate. When he picks it up there's the bottom line staring him in the eye. The customer now knows that you know that he knows he has to ante up. Embarrassment is a heck of a way to hustle tips.

At still other times a customer will saunter up to the check window and ask you point-blank: "How much tip should I leave?"

This puts you in a real bind, since technically the service is free.

To cover your flank you say casually, "Same as last year, Sir, " as if you know the guy. Naturally the customer wants to appear hip and in the know, like he's a regular customer here at the fashionable St. George Hotel ballroom, especially if he's with his girlfriend or wife. He comes up with a bunch of money without further delay, usually more than he'd have given if he hadn't asked the question.

Then there's the hard-ass customer, the who won't play ball no matter what hints you drop. While this type is always a problem, there are a number of ways to loosen him up Sometimes our guys will stand in front of a character like this, pretending to brush his coat off with a whisk broom but actually blocking his way. Then they step back, point to the plate, and exclaim, "How's that for service, Sir?"

Your hard case might then declare, "I paid on the way in."

The kid replies that to the best of his knowledge no monies were received, and he takes out an official-looking list kept for just such a contingency. He pretends to read it over carefully, puts it back in his pocket, and shakes his head solemnly.

"We have no record of such a transaction, Sir," he announces in an official voice. This little ploy makes even the toughest customers cave in.

At other times shame is the best medicine. Some of the more aggressive guys would tap the tip plate persistently, or wiggle their eyebrows Groucho Marx style, wink, go *tsk tsk*, ask, "How about it?" Some would even pick up the plate and stare at it with a look of mock sadness, as if about to break into tears. One of our real fire-eaters followed customers who stiffed him out of the club door rattling coins in his pocket. Another had a favorite song he'd bellow out for everyone in the vicinity of the deadbeat to hear:

"I ain't got no money today,
no right to be gay
no lettuce, no hay;
I ain't got no money today
Cause my man says no way,
will he pay!"

There were dozens of variations on the theme. I watched them all, and I learned. I learned how to handle people, how to soothe them, anger them, excite them, placate them. Human Nature 1A again, just like in Wanamaker's. To this very day the lessons from the checkroom remain fresh in my brain.

Then, finally, there was a situation that really made life interesting at the Grand Ballroom: the lost check ticket.

This fascinating event was linked to one of our favorite pastimes, philosophizing on human foibles. Having seen literally thousands of people come and go over the days and months, and having carefully observed their behavior, we were unanimous in our opinion that there are no more than ten different types of people in the entire world.

Yes, ten. We all agreed. Each of us had our theories concerning what these ten might be.

One very obvious type, we all decided, was the nebbish. Another was the authoritarian boss type. There was the servile follower, the hostile dyspeptic, the aloof observer, and so on down the list. We even assigned each of these types a number. The boss type was, say, a 6; the dyspeptic a 3.

One of the people we encountered especially often was a type we dubbed the "Cloud Head"—the confused, the absent-minded, the fumbler and bumbler who forgets what his coat looks like or whether he's wearing a hat. Nine times out of ten this guy loses his check ticket within the first hour of his arrival, along, perhaps, with his wallet or glasses. He has a very recognizable look to him, sort of flustered and all thumbs; of all the types on our list he was the easiest to spot.

It got so that we even turned Cloud Head watching into a kind of science. Whenever a customer arrived at the checkroom who fit the profile one of our guys would shout out the Cloud Head number—8, in this case—and everybody studied him silently for a minute. When we all agreed that yes, this was a Cloud Head, a betting spree would begin among the employees, nickel ante mostly, based on how many times this character would return to the checkroom window for his cigarettes, his lighter, his handkerchief, his umbrella; or even more commonly, whether or not he would lose his coat check that night.

This game not only helped pass the evening but sharpened our observation skills. Later in life it helped me recognize different types of persons while doing business and showed me how to deal with them according to their needs and temperaments. All from this little game.

Say, for instance, that the Cloud Head loses his ticket and comes up to the counter, fumbling pathetically in every crease of his pants and jacket. No ticket. What now?

If the man is a decent and reasonable chap we help him out.

But if he's difficult, stubborn, mean drunk, well, woe betide him!

The charade was simple and highly entertaining. First we'd ask, "How do you know you lost your check?"

"I can't find it anywhere," he'd reply, very sheepish and distressed.

Next question: "Did you look in all your pockets?"

Yes, he had.

So we told him to take everything out of his pockets and spread the contents on the counter.

To our utter amazement, he always obeyed, even if he was a big shot or the world's meanest grouch. We discovered a lot of interesting things about what a man carries in his pockets this way.

What the poor customer didn't know at this point was that by now we usually knew exactly where his coat was and could find it in a minute if we so wished. Sometimes we even knew where his coat was at the beginning of the side-show, when he first reported his lost ticket. But we didn't let on. We were kids having fun. And besides, we had to draw the process out, make it look like we were knocking ourselves out or we might not get that extra tip.

And so the game continued. A quiz would now follow:

What time did you come in?

Who did you come in with?

What part of the room did you sit in tonight?

How long were you there?

Did you search the area thoroughly?

What's the color of your hat?

Of your coat?

Of your scarf and umbrella, of that package you were carrying?

◆▸ ◆▸

The beleaguered customer had to answer this barrage of questions as if he was a prisoner of the Inquisition, which in a manner of speaking, he was. We had his topcoat, after all. We had his hat. We had his gloves, his scarf. It was 20 degrees outside. Maybe colder. What would you do?

After the body search and interrogation were then completed, and everyone agreed that his check was actually lost, several options lay open to us.

If the fellow was a pleasant Cloud Head, if he was grateful for our help, and if he seemed inclined to reward, one of us would walk back to the coat aisle, spend a long time rummaging around there as if battling hell hounds to find the coat, and finally emerge triumphantly with the goods, to the ecstasy of the Cloud Head, his girlfriend, his boss, his mother. . . .

If the customer was a nasty drunk or just plain rude, this was a different story entirely and, for many of us, the highlight of the week.

The first thing we all agreed was that the nasty ticket-loser was entirely predictable, that his behavior fell into a pat routine of demands and explosions that could be known ahead of time and prepared for in advance. The stages of the scenario went something as follows.

First, the customer shows up at the checkroom window and announces in an angry voice that his ticket is lost, as if the whole thing is our fault. When we tell him no tickee, no laundry he immediately gets incensed and announces that we'd better come up with that coat immediately *or else!*

This is stage one.

We inform him that there were thousands of coats in the cloakroom at the present moment, Sir, and that without a ticket, finding his particular wrap is impossible.

Stage two. Like clockwork, he then demands to go into the back room himself and identify his garment.

"Sorry, Sir," we explain. "That's against hotel rules. Without a check ticket we're not allowed to give out a hat and coat, even if a customer can identify it."

"That's ridiculous!" the man bellows back. "It's *my* coat!"

"I understand," one of us says, wide-eyed. "But if we disregard regulations and gave you the coat, and the coat doesn't really belong to you — nothing personal, of course, Sir — we'll lose our jobs."

This makes him even madder, naturally, and at this point he demands to see the manager. Stage three.

"Right away, Sir."

One of us runs out of the room directly, and in a minute returns with a uniformed member of the staff. Now the fun really begins.

"I'm sorry, Sir," the official representative of Mr. Quain's coat and hat world says, "but the manager has left for the evening. I'm the assistant manager. What's the problem?"

This forces the irate customer to go through his entire spiel again: lost his ticket; nitwits at the counter won't let him into the cloak room; he is personal friends with the owner of the hotel, with the Mayor, with the President; he's going to make terrible trouble for us if we don't find his coat immediately, blah, blah, blah, blah, blah.

The "assistant manager" (who is just another one of Mr. Quain's young employees), listens to all this, nods his head, wrings his hands, then patiently explains that it's against "state regulations" to give a customer his coat without a check — pause — but that *in this particular case* he'll make an exception.

Pow! Bingo! The customer's lights go on. He thinks his threats have cowed us into submission. He hangs there, tough.

"But, " the assistant manager adds, as if by afterthought, "for the hotel's protection we must ask that you to wait here until the club closes and all the customers have gone home. Then, if there's a coat left that you can identify, it's yours."

Stage four: The customer hits the roof, shouting, fist-pounding: an outrage, a disgrace, he's a busy man, it's already past midnight, how dare we, we'll pay for all his, blah, blah, blah, blah, blah.

"I'm sorry," the assistant manager replies, unruffled, "but we're making an exception in your case anyway. That's the best we can do."

Now the guy, who by now is slavering from fury, frustration and helplessness, has three choices:

> ✔ 1) He can pull out a wad of dollars and suggest that we "speed up the process." Fine. That's what we're here for, we tell him cheerfully—to help out.
> ✔ 2) He can sit down, twiddle his thumbs, count the threads in the carpet, and wait until 3:30 in the morning to get his coat.
> ✔ 3) He can storm out of the club coatless and hatless into the 20-degree weather, burbling revenge and litigation. Then he can come back the next day when he's calmed down and/or sobered up and get his coat.

Much as part of us wanted him to choose the first alternative, and thus increase our net worth, another part hoped he'd choose the third alternative, that he'd stomp out in a huff.

Because, you see, we knew something he didn't know.

We knew that the next day when he returned to claim his belongings, the full-time manager, by now informed of the previous night's festivities, would be waiting for him with a bill— five dollars hotel charge for overnight hat and coat storage. The manager would inform the customer that until the bill was paid regulations required that he not "release" the coat.

"Sorry, Sir," he would say, smiling ingratiatingly at the honored guest who by now was apoplectic, "House rules, you know."

Stage five.

I remember when I was a kid my folks told me many a time: "Always take care of the cop on the beat. He's the man who can help you—or do you in."

Now 70 years later I offer these illustrations an example to my children and grandchildren of how useful this saying can be. May they learn from its wisdom and closely follow its counsel: "Pay a penny today, save a dollar tomorrow."

PS: *All Good Things Come to an End*

The easiest and most rewarding part of the coat-check business was counter work. But in the two years I was at the hotel I never got a chance to work that coveted outside position. Mr. Quain knew instinctively, I guess, that I was a pussycat, and that I didn't have the nerve to con his clientele into big tips. Hustling was an art that had passed me by. Mr. Quain knew this—as he seemed to know everything about his boys—and acted accordingly.

And anyway, in my heart of hearts I would have paid *him* for this job. Not only did it give me a degree in human psychology but also a darned good time. The fellows I worked with were a great bunch; we learned from one another. I listened to their trials, their dreams, their hopes and tribulations, and they listened to mine. Not one of them felt deprived, I discovered, though all were poor, and each was deeply grateful for this job that fate, luck or God had handed him.

The job also offered lots of interesting perks. After the first stampede of people arrived each night and we checked them in, break time came. We'd go for a quick swim (for free) in the hotel pool. Listen to one of the big bands. Go into the hotel kitchen and schmickle some snacks from the chef. Or just sit and shoot the breeze. Back home in Washington Heights my friends were amazed to hear me talk about how much I loved this job, and how much fun I was having. Hanging coats was the most boring thing imaginable, they assured me.

I shook my head—no: hanging coats was half the world.

They thought I was nuts. I told them you had to be there.

Besides my friendship with the workers I also maintained a kind of special relationship with Mr. Quain himself who, for a while, treated me like a son.

I say for a while, cause our friendship ended on a sour note.

Here's what happened.

I'd been working at the checkroom for three or four weeks minding my own business and learning the job, when one evening during my break Mr. Quain invited me to share a meal with him at the downstairs coffee shop.

We sat down at the counter and he proceeded to order a tuna fish sandwich, a cup of coffee, and a piece of apple pie. To be polite, I asked the waitress for the same. When the bill came Mr. Quain gave me a wink. "My pleasure," he said, taking out his wallet.

"And mine," I laughed.

A few days later Mr. Quain invited me to eat with him again. Once more it was a tuna fish sandwich at the coffee shop with apple pie and coffee.

Soon this meal became a kind of ritual between us: we'd take the same seat at the same counter, chat about the coat-check business for a few minutes, then order the standard fare. He'd pick up the tab, I'd be grateful, and we'd have a grand old time. Why he chose me as his regular dining mate rather than one of the other employees I have no clue. After some time we became rather good friends.

Then one evening about a year after I'd started work at the checkroom we visited the coffee shop together and for some reason, why I'm not sure, I decided to break precedent, and instead of the tuna, pie and coffee I ordered a ham and cheese sandwich.

As I gave the waitress my order I noticed a kind of shadow pass over Mr. Quain's face. I didn't think much of it at the time. But the next night when he arrived no invitation was forthcoming. Same thing the next night, and the night after that.

Soon it became apparent that our tete-a-tete days were over, and that I had somehow offended him. But how?

I didn't know. And still don't know to this day. Was it because I ordered ham? Mr. Quain was an observant Jew, I knew, but not all *that* observant. At least that's what I thought. Maybe I was wrong.

Or another theory: we always ordered the same meal every night, almost like a religious rite. Then I changed the menu. Perhaps he took this as a slur. Who can say? The human heart is unknowable.

Once again, however, a lesson emerged. From this time on whenever I ate with another person, high or low, rich or poor, I tried never to do anything that would in any way embarrass them. If my eating mate ordered beef I'd order the same; if he ordered stuffed nightingale tongues, why, nightingale tongues it was! It was more important, I decided, to please my friend than to give myself pleasure. The lesson behind it was a simple one: *never give offense if you can possibly avoid it.*

I continued to work at the checkroom for another year at least, but my relationship was Mr. Quain, née Cohen, was forever changed. By the time I'd graduated from college and entered law school we'd become strangers.

Still, I remember the man today with great affection. He was a brilliant business head, a kind father, a good man. His son Steve couldn't make the grade as a doctor, by the way, so he became a dentist instead; and his daughter ran off with the doorman. But that's another story. At the time, with brains and guts he fine-tuned what would have been a puny little business in the hands of a less talented man into a kind of mini empire—and he did it, what's more, during the worst years of the Depression. In those desperate dog-down days, when a man might give a finger off his good right hand for a job, Mr. Q. had the decency to pay his employees handsomely and to treat them like people.

New York cafe society, in turn, paid him back for his kindness in spades—or perhaps I should say in diamonds. He went on to become the owner of two large hotels, one of which still has a portrait of him hanging in the lobby today, holding his lapels. All of this, we can say, for the privilege of hanging up someone's winter coat and checking their blue felt hat. God bless him.

❧ ❧ ❧

Chapter 7

◆→ ◆→

THE GAS STATION ERA

But Life Had Different Plans

Much to the delight of my mother and all concerned, I continued at my studies and my job in the checkroom, finished college, graduated with a BBA, and began studying for a degree in law at Brooklyn Law School, the next step in my lifetime agenda of stepping stones. The year was 1932.

During my college days I had imbibed many facts. I learned the names of all the 9th century conquerors of Bulgaria, how to parse a verb (I think), how to keep an account book and find the sense in nonsense. What I *didn't* learn much about in college was human nature. That part of my education was provided for in a different sector, in the checkroom. Here I learned a more essential set of facts: the facts of life.

I now understand, therefore, that subjects like accounting and geography and administrative management are tools for daily living, okay in their place. But that being in the trenches, seeing, hearing, tasting, smelling life as it is lived, well, this is education with a capital D—for DIRECT. It taught me that the real process of learning is composed of two things: how the world works, and how I work in it. During this period of my life I learned a great deal about both. Now here I was in law school, looking forward to whatever new lessons were on the way.

Then a strange thing happened.

I'm a full-blown graduate student, at least nine-tenths of a grownup, my own man. Studying to be a barrister. Yet the only thing that seemed different was that I was going to school via the Borough Street subway stop in Brooklyn rather than on the Fifth Avenue bus.

Besides that, my graduate degree experience was a kind of *déjà vu*. Brooklyn Law, it quickly became apparent, was the same impersonal, factory-like place as NYU, only more so; because now we were all a step closer to having to make a living, and thus a step farther away from collegiate fun and games.

The kids at Brooklyn Law were just like the kids at NYU. They looked the same, expressed the same opinions; some of them even *were* the same. The campus was a staid clone of NYU's, so much so that I'd sometimes forget whether I was in Brooklyn or Washington Square. There was very little competition among students here, which was a relief. (I'd heard that at the Harvard or Yale Law School you never leave your notes around: another law student might steal them.) But then there was very little school spirit too. I rarely met anyone who was interested in writing for the law review or clerking in a high court. Most of my classmates were intent simply on getting through their courses, passing the bar, and finding a job that paid enough to buy groceries. It was a typical Depression mentality. The moment classes ended in the afternoon the campus emptied out as if someone had shouted "Fire!" or "Bubonic plague!" Instantly. Ghost city. There were no after-school activities, no political discussions in the school lounge, no cafe arguments over the latest manifesto, no clubs, sports—zip. Even the Borough Hall campus cafeterias became sleepy affairs after 2 o'clock.

My first year at law school thus passed with very little

incident. I finished the second semester with a solid C average, no stars and stripes but good enough to get by. I looked forward to two more boring years of studies and then my law degree.

Once again life had different plans.

Our Caravan Heads North

As the Depression deepened business drifted downhill for my father's tailoring establishment; worse upon worse. One day my parents decided that the battle could simply not be won in New York City, and that it was time for a change. To what? Only one choice, really. Move back to Troy.

At first we were all resistant to this notion. We'd lived in New York City for enough years now to feel comfortable and ensconced. My sisters were settled in Washington Heights, as were their kids. If we moved it would mean they might also have to move.

On the other hand, Troy was home. Really home. And deep down inside us we all knew it.

So in the summer of 1933 my father took down his shingle, packed up home and hearth, and we moved upstate. Traveling members included my mother, my father, me, sister Toby, her child and husband Mel and, most intriguing of all, Mel's sister (and present business partner) Dot.

❖ ❖

Once back in Troy we rented a house. My father opened a shop not far from the old location, and before long it was as if we'd never left Troy.

❖ ❖

By now, I should tell you, my relationship with Dot had gone far beyond the brother-sister stage, so much so that it was a foregone conclusion among her family and mine, linked already by the marriage of my sister and Mel, that as soon as I earned my law degree and found a job the two of us would tie the knot. This was terrific as far as I was concerned, but right now the immediate issues were how to find a job, help my family, and learn.

Trying not to be discouraged, I was soon cheered to learn that Albany Law School was just a hop down the river from Troy, no more than an half-hour's drive.

Trouble was, Albany Law was considered to be one of the best law schools in the country, an elite, restricted little lawyers' enclave famous for being highly selective in its admissions, for flunking out 5 percent of its student body every six months, for loading students down with so much work that extracurricular activities (such as a job) seemed out of the question, and for *rarely* accepting transfer students.

To make matters worse, the quota admissions system was in full swing at this time, meaning that only a tiny percent of non-Anglos and non-Saxons—read Jews—were accepted. This was true no matter what the Jewish student's grades happened to be, and mine weren't all that terrific. (Rumor had it at the time that Jewish students were so driven to get the best higher education that without a quota system all the colleges in the country would soon become schuls.)

On top of all this, the whole notion of my continuing law school was a bit of a bird-brained scheme anyway, because without a steady job I couldn't afford the tuition.

The prospects for the continuance of my law education were, at best, small.

Simpatico Days

I was tempted to forget about law and look for a regular job. I had never been that enamored of a legal career in the first place, truth to tell, and there were hopefully other opportunities I could pursue

Then I remembered my mother's dream. Her son the lawyer. Did I want to disappoint her? After having come this far?

And my dad? That proud look in his eye. That extra note of self-respect in his voice when he told friends and relatives that his son was becoming a lawyer.

What to do?

Everyone I knew was living hand to mouth. Yet at the same time there was something unique in the air during these down-and-out days, a kind of community simpatico, a feeling that we were all in the same boat, and that if we didn't pitch in and row in unison we'd all go down together.

In a more affluent and alienated era like today this seems a strange notion. But you can ask anyone who lived through this difficult Depression period and they'll tell you: If you could assist a relative, a friend, even a stranger, you just didn't hesitate. Nobody had very much, but you always tried to help if you could. As we looked around us we saw many people who were even worse off than ourselves. So we felt grateful for what we had, and we tried to make our neighbor's lot easier. What a joy that was for us, and how we appreciated the fact that we help.

And that's why I decided to take a chance.

You see, I knew that if I applied directly to Albany Law through the registrar my transcript would be thrown out with all the other transfer requests. On the other hand, if I took the same tack I did at the Pines company and spoke directly to someone higher up this might improve the odds. My father always told me, "If it works once try it twice. If it works twice, marry it."

So with my heart in my throat I telephoned the Dean's office at Albany Law School, and asked to make an appointment with Dean Alexander, the head man.

To my utter amazement, the Dean's secretary matter-of-factly told me that Dean Alexander had a few minutes free next Wednesday. Could I come by at half-past one?

I could.

A Fated Meeting

The Dean was a distinguished looking man, in his early 50's and graying at the temples. He met me at the door of his office with a firm handshake, motioned me inside, and sat down behind his huge wooden desk. At that moment I felt like Tom Thumb: the desk seemed to be about seven miles away, and the Dean about 122 feet tall.

"So what can I do for you, Mr. Silverman?" he asked in a flat voice.

"I'm interested in continuing my graduate studies here at Albany Law," I said, and handed him my transcript.

He glanced at it for a moment or two, then looked at me curiously.

"Why do you want to go to Albany Law?"

I proceeded to launch into my family history, how I'd worked my way through high school and college, how my mother had a dream of seeing her son become a lawyer, and how I absolutely had to make it come true, etc., etc.

Dean Alexander listened to all this with admirable patience, then leaned back in his chair, lit a cigarette, and fell silent. He held his cigarette European style, I remember, with the burning end pointing upwards. Each time he puffed he closed his eyes as if about to fall asleep. He was obviously trying to figure out how to soften the blow.

But no. A new barrage of questions followed. Did I have any idea what a difficult undertaking it was to study law during the day and hold a job at night?

I shrugged, not knowing whether to answer yes or no.

There are four hours of classes every day here at Albany Law, he explained slowly, then four hours of homework. The assignments are all casework, which means they're done here on the premises, at the library. That doesn't leave much time left over for a job, does it?

What's more, he continued, times being what they are, it's next to impossible to find a nighttime job around the Capital District. Albany is not New York City, he emphasized, blowing out a thin line of smoke and looking at me, I thought, in a not unkindly way. Everything closes down at 6 o'clock.

And even if I do perchance find an after-hours job, he went on, did I intend to stay up all night, then attend law school during the day? When, pray tell, did I intend to sleep?

I took his last question as a rhetorical one and remained silent.

He snuffed out his cigarette and looked at me with a faint twinkle. "How then, may I ask, will you handle all these many activities, Mr. Silverman? I'm interested to know."

I could only think of one answer. It seemed goofy to me at the time but somehow, well, honest.

"Sir," I said, without missing a beat. "The Good Lord will provide me with that answer."

A look of curious interest crossed the Dean's face for a moment. Whether he was a religious man, or whether he was simply amazed at the naiveté of my answer I didn't know.

Almost instantly he stood up and held out his hand without saying a word.

The meeting was apparently over and I had apparently flubbed it. In fact, my credibility was so low I was being given the hook without the courtesy of a formal dismissal. A handshake and shuffle job.

Oh well, I thought, taking his hand, hurt to the quick: I've done my best. I've tried hard. I've explored every avenue.

"Let's give it a try," he said, still shaking my hand and half-smiling.

"A try?" I answered, instantly frazzled. My mouth seemed to have become rubberized. The words oozed out at 33 and a third. "Well, yeees. I mean, well, yes, Sir. Let's doooo—let's do that. I—I completely agree."

"Fine," he said briskly. "Get your full record and transcript to us and we'll start the registration process right away."

"Oh. Okay. Thooonk—I, eh, thank you, Sir."

I thanked him several more times, six to be exact, then made the appropriate leaving noises and sort of backed out of the room, almost dragging an end table with me.   Outside in the hallway a kind of euphoria immediately came over me. The realization dawned on me that I'd just been admitted to one of the most competitive, most exclusive, most impossible- to-get-into law schools in the country, all on the grounds of a single sentence—"The Good Lord will provide."

Was it possible? Does the Good Lord provide *that* fast?

A Funny Thing Happened to Me on the Way to Troy

I floated out of the admissions building, sailed down the stairs, swam across the parking lot, levitated into my car seat. I sat in a state of suspended animation for several minutes, carefully reviewing the events of the last hour. Did he really say what I think he'd said? Was I really accepted so easily? Was I dreaming?

I then started the drive back to Troy to tell my parents. For a few minutes I felt totally at peace with the world and everything in it. All my problems had disappeared.

No sooner had I started down the highway, however, when a realization hit me. Those delicate matters the Dean had brought up—about going to law school days and working nights at the same time? How, *indeed,* could I keep two enormous balls in the air simultaneously? At Brooklyn Law School the homework load had been moderate, yet I'd had trouble keeping up. And then I was only working weekends helping my dad deliver and collect. Now we're talking all day at law school *plus* a full-time night job which I probably can't find anyway, in which case I won't be able to afford the law school career which I wouldn't have time for if I was working in the first place!

These thoughts circled disturbingly through my mind as I tooled along the road to Troy, and the more I considered the shakiness of my situation the more anxious I became.

The distance between Albany to Troy is around six miles, and I'd covered about half of it when I reached the Menands Bridge. Construction on this impressive structure had just recently been completed, linking Albany to Troy. As I neared the approach my eyes fell on a stretch of farmland along the side of the road.

Suddenly I heard it: that voice again.

"Build a gas station here!" it said.

What? A gas station? Me? A student of the law? Surely I was hearing things.

Still, it was the voice. *The* voice, and by now I'd learned to give it the proper respect.

So I made a U-turn, looped around and doubled back. Passing the same stretch of land I heard the identical words in my head. *"Build a gas station here!"*

I took a third turn around and again: *build it here.* Almost biblical.

By now I was beginning to think that I'd better pay attention. The location was a dandy all right, situated along a well traveled road and easy to get to when pulling off. Plus there wasn't another service station around. Automobiles were becoming common in these days and just about everybody owned one by now. Yet the gasoline industry hadn't tooled up to its full glory yet, and service stations were in short supply. Interesting.

The next morning I telephoned the Standard Oil Company's offices in Albany. I explained that I'd found an excellent site for a service station just off the new bridge. I said I'd like to speak with them about putting up a structure on that spot.

Fine, they said. An appointment was arranged.

The next day the Standard Oil representative met me on the site and I showed him around as if I already owned the joint, pointing out the location's logistic virtues, explaining how easy it was for trucks and cars to pull in, how it would be the only gas station for miles around in a heavily trafficked area.

Before long he began to see the advantages, and he agreed that yes, this was an excellent site, and that yes, Standard Oil might possibly be interested in bankrolling the project. If so, would I be willing to manage it?

I explained that since I was a law student I wouldn't be able to work full time as manager, that I would hire people to run the station during the week, then I'd take over at night and on the weekends.

They agreed, and within a week Standard Oil made an offer: they would loan me $6,500 to build a station plus furnish the fuel tanks, the gasoline and the pumps. This loan would then be repaid by charging me two cents tariff on every gallon of gas I pumped.

I, in turn, was to buy the land, run the station, and hire whatever help was required.

With a modest loan from a relative I purchased the property from a local farmer, and construction began immediately. A few months later the station was up and running in all its brick and concrete glory, just in time for opening day at Albany Law.

To make sure the station ran smoothly while I was in class I made an arrangement with Dot and my brother-in-law, Mel; at this time they were running a company together that bought and sold used machinery and equipment in Troy. Mel had worked for his uncle in this same business in New Jersey, and was now trying to make a go of it with his sister. Trouble was he didn't have enough money to rent an office.

So I made them an offer. We'll make part of the gas station your office, and in return you keep an eye on the station while I'm at school, and pump gas when we're short of help.

What about a telephone? they asked. It was essential to their business, but they couldn't afford the cost.

Use the phone booth that's already at the station I suggested. The booth had a listed number, and when they called clients would never know they were talking to a gas station. Hence, the station would receive a commission on the calls they made instead of us having to pay for a separate phone! We called that making a liability into an asset.

They liked the idea.

And so we agreed. Mel and Dot moved into their new "offices" within the week and before long their business was off the ground. Not many inches off the ground, mind you, but it was a start. From then on when ever I was busy during the day with my law studies and the regular employees were tied up, Dot or Mel covered the pumps.

It was the beginning of a three-way partnership that would last without a break for the rest of our lives.

Manning the Pumps

The station was an immediate success.

People had a penchant for helping one another in these days, as I've said, and for going out of their way to do you a favor. Simpatico everywhere.

So when word got around that a young college kid was putting himself through law school by managing a neighborhood station, the citizenry rallied. The local papers picked up the story and ran an article on me. Soon people started going out of their way just to buy my gasoline.

And I mean *way* out of their way. On Saturday and Sunday nights friends and relatives and distant acquaintances arrived from Troy, Albany, Schenectady, a dozen towns in between simply to tank up their guzzlers. There were other stations closer by, some of them bigger and cheaper than mine. They knew this and I knew this. But they wanted to help.

Most amazing were the strangers, anonymous men and women who didn't know me from Johesephat but who had heard about this cheeky kid trying to put himself through school, and who wanted to lend a hand.

One time, I remember, a green sedan pulled into the station and up to the pumps. As I was cleaning the windshield I overheard a child talking to his father inside the car. They didn't know I could hear.

"Why'd we have to drive so far just to get gas?" the child asked in a petulant voice.

"Because," the father answered, "we're helping the young man who runs this station go to college."

That was all, just a quick two-liner. But I never forgot these kind words and, I hope, the kid never forgot them either.

At Albany Law

Albany Law School was located smack in the center of the city surrounded everywhere by government buildings and conspicuously minus a campus, a gym, a tennis courts, and anything fun; just classrooms, libraries, hard work, brick. Enrollment was around 200 students, several of whom went on to great achievements. One of the alumni, Robert H. Jackson, became Chief United States Prosecutor at the Nuremberg Trials. He had already become a Supreme Court justice by appointment of F.D.R.

Mostly, though, the student body was made up of methodical, determined, uninspired young persons, just like at Brooklyn Law, all of whom hoped to get their degree, return to their home town, and find a decent job in their new profession. Extracurricular life was nil. The most fraternizing we ever did was to sit around the smoking room after class fantasizing over how much money we'd earn someday. Interestingly enough, we all agreed that if we found a job that paid $10,000 a year we'd be in clover for the rest of our lives. Ten thousand dollars at the time was the equivalent of a million dollars today, and maybe two.

There wasn't a student in the room who actually thought he'd ever *make* that much money, understand. We simply used the $10,000 figure to symbolize the impossible dream, the pot of gold at the end of the rainbow. Little did any of us realize that someday members of our class would be making that much money or more *in a month*.

New Gas in Old Bottles

Things went well with my studies and at the station, and before long, thanks to the compassion of friends and local patrons, I was ringing up enough gas to pay my tuition *and* supplement the family income. I attended classes in the morning, ripped through my casework in the afternoon, rushed home at 100 m.p.h., wolfed down supper, visited briefly with the family. When it got dark I shot off to the station and pumped gas to 11 or perhaps midnight, chatted with Mel and Dot, and finished up my homework. Full day.

The three of us kept busy in other ways too, especially when a side opportunity presented itself.

I remember once, for instance, Mel had to travel to the Bayer Aspirin plant in nearby Rensselaer to look at some surplus machinery, and he took Dot and me along for company.

Mel negotiated with the manager for what seemed like hours while Dot and I wandered around, killing time. When the bargaining was over and we were ready to leave Mel happened to notice a pile of large greenish-blue bottles stacked up against a wall.

Mel had a great gift, something I've never known or understood: he could see beauty where others saw only junk.

"It's a pile of junk," I said. "Let's get home."

"No, wait, " he shot back. "I'm not so sure it's junk. Let's give it a quick look."

We strolled over to this mountain of bottles, and sure enough, they were all hand-blown beauties, each about three feet long and two feet wide—you still seem them occasionally in antique stores today. Each bottle was nested in a finely woven wicker basket that was a kind of treasure itself.

"What's the story with these old bottles?" Mel asked the manager.

"Oh, those," he replied. "German factories use them to send us their chemicals."

"How come you've got them all piled up like this?"

"Well," the manager answered. "It turns out—don't ask me why—the Interstate Commerce Commission has decided you can't ship chemicals in bottles shaped like these any more.

Your bottles must have straight sides now. New rule. And no more wicker containers either. Boxes have to be made of wood."

"I see," said Mel. "So how much you want for the whole shebang?"

Dot and I looked at him in horror. There must have been 400 or 500 bottles in the pile.

"Eh!" the guy answered. "Give me a quarter apiece and get them out of here for me."

"Done," said Mel before we could object and proceeded to fork out the money from his wallet.

Next day we hired a truck and toted the entire collection back to the gas station.

"So what's your plan?" I asked him when we had them stacked up.

"No plan," Mel answered. "But you never know. Someone might come along tomorrow who needs 500 hand-blown glass bottles."

I shook my head in bewilderment and started to walk away. He grabbed my arm. "And anyway, you and Dot wanted to take a vacation, didn't you? I thought this might be your chance. Why don't you take a bottle as a sample, drive to New England where you've always liked to go, and peddle them to the antique dealers. It's their high season right now and antique collectors love this kind of thing. When you get an order write it up and tell them you'll send the bottles to them COD. What do you have to lose?"

That was Mel. We called him our "Angel."

I ran the idea by Dot and she became very excited. She even added a twist to the plan. Why not fill the sample bottles with gasoline and bring along a piece of rubber hose as a siphon—that way we can travel across New England without spending a penny on gas.

The next week we took off in my Essex Terraplane, one round, hand-blown German bottle sitting in my rumble seat like a fat little Kaiser, capped and filled with distilled petroleum.

We drove across four New England states, visited dozens of antique stores, and with a lump in our throats, remembering what we'd paid for the lot of them, quoted a price of $5 a bottle.

To our surprise, a majority of the dealers were receptive, and by the end of the trip we'd unloaded our entire inventory. This, of course, made us feel like big time entrepreneurs, and very clever. It was easy to ship the bottles via truck because each bottle was surrounded by straw and embedded in a wicker basket.

But P.S. There's an aftershock to the story.

After we'd sold all the bottles Dot decided to keep the last two for decoration and for planting flowers. No problem. I'd even come to like the things. A few weekends later she then traveled to New York City to visit relatives and I was left working the station alone.

Late in the afternoon a guy pulled up in a limousine. He took one look at the two bottles out front with the flowers in them and his eyes practically exploded.

"How much do you want for those bottles?" he asked with poorly concealed excitement.

"Sorry, sir," I answered, remembering how much Dot enjoyed her little planter gardens. "They're not for sale."

He responded: "Everything is for sale. I'll give you 20 dollars apiece for them."

I looked to see if he was smiling, and he wasn't. This was a different story entirely, garden or no.

I responded: "They are for sale."

And we made a deal.

I then got to talking with this man who, it turned out, was a dealer. He informed me that our bottles were especially hot items these days in the antique market, and that no one could find them anymore, let alone keep them in stock.

Exactly how rare are they, I asked.

"Heaven's sake," he said, climbing into his car with his two new treasures. "Any antique dealer in the world would give you at least fifteen, twenty bucks apiece for them. Anything lower and you'd be gipped. Heck, I'd have taken the whole collection off your hands at that price if I'd have known. So long now."

The Eleventh Hour

Business was bad everywhere but especially in the used equipment field. Despite gallant efforts and help from Dot, Mel's enterprise began to founder after about a year, and he talked more and more about closing up shop and moving back to New York City with Dot and his family.

This was, of course, the last thing in the world I wanted to see happen, and I tried to help him out as best I could. Trouble was, after I'd paid my tuition and contributed money at home for food and rent, there was nothing left over for any other purpose. Meanwhile, my father was having a deuce of a time making his monthly nut at the tailor shop and there were bills everywhere. The Silverman economic ship was, in short, starting to go down.

One rainy Saturday afternoon Mel confided in me that he had just written a slough of bad checks. He'd never done anything like this before, he said, and was filled with fear and remorse. How else could he stall off his creditors? he asked. What else could he do?

It was a rule among our family *never* to talk about financial issues in front of my parents. Never. Since everyone in the family pooled their money into one big pot, and since nobody was doing a great deal of pooling just then, these discussions invariably ended up depressing and scaring them both. (There was, I should also mention, a kind of family joke among us at the time: my father had a habit of saying in perfect seriousness that if he didn't have to pay for the rent, the car, the heat, the electric, the clothes, the groceries, and all the bills at his tailor shop he'd be making a darn good living. I often think of that phrase today when check-writing time comes around each month, and I tell myself the same thing with a chuckle: My gosh, if I didn't have to pay any of these bills I'd be a darn wealthy man.)

We thus made it a point to discuss money matters far, far from home, in this instance in the gas station office. Tonight, of course, the matter was an especially serious one, so we agreed to meet right away. A few hours later, Mel, Dot, and I gathered at the station to discuss our options.

We talked and talked. But nothing added up. None of us had the vaguest idea how to cover the bad checks, or how to make good on the bills. Mel worried over how long he could stall the creditors off. He was going back to New York City, he announced, back to work at his uncle's used equipment company in New Jersey for $35 a week—if the law didn't deport him to San Quentin first.

We tried to calm him down but there wasn't a lot we could say. The three of us sat there as close to despair as I ever remember.

Then suddenly, at 11 o'clock, the phone in our phone booth rang.

I glanced up at the clock, then looked at Mel and Dot. Eleven o'clock? Saturday night? Who in tarnation was calling us this late?

I answered. A gruff voice on the other end asked if this was the Constructor's Equipment Company, and could he speak to Mel Rosen right away?

Mel got on the line and talked with the mystery voice for 10 or 15 minutes, looking over at us excitedly several times during the conversation, widening his eyes in disbelief and shrugging.

Finally he placed the receiver down and sort of rubbed his head. The call, he explained, was from the owner of a granite quarry in Barre, Vermont. How the man got Mel's name is still a mystery. There had been a washout in his quarry, the man told him, and to fix it he needed three loads of galvanized pipe by Monday morning at the latest. Price was no object. Could Mel deliver?

Realize now we're talking about finding three truckloads of galvanized pipe in the middle of the night on a weekend during the Depression, then hiring three truckers to pick up this pipe and deliver it to a location hundreds of miles away in New England, all in less than 36 hours.

The whole thing was so unexpected, so ridiculous, so miraculous, how could we say no? If we pulled it off the profits would be enormous, the answer to our prayers. What, we asked ourselves, were the chances of someone finding us in our office at 11 o'clock Saturday night? It was a miracle.

So we set to work. Mel woke up his uncle in New Jersey, explained the situation, and as luck would have it the pipe was sitting there available in his supply yard.

Next the pickup. A gypsy trucker had stopped by our station a week ago and left his card. He'd boasted that he and his crew worked any kind of job at any hour of the day or night. Let's let him put his money where his mouth is, we said.

So Mel phoned him up—remember, it's late Saturday night—and told him that we needed three trucks right away, this very minute, and that they would have to leave for New Jersey within the next two hours if they wanted the job (in the days before superhighways it took approximately six hours to drive from Troy to New York). Mel explained that his uncle would be there at his supply yard to meet them with men to help load the pipe. From there they'd have to take off for Vermont, drive all night, and reach their destination by Monday morning at the latest.

Amazingly, the trucker agreed. We negotiated a price,

and he and two other trucks took off within the hour. Mel left immediately for New Jersey. That's how hungry everyone was for work at this time.

◆→ ◆→

Sunday morning Mel called from New Jersey. The trucks had arrived and were loading.

Three o'clock in the afternoon. The pipe is still being loaded. Progress is slow.

Seven o'clock. Still loading.

Eleven o'clock in the evening. The trucks leave for Vermont many hours behind schedule.

Three o'clock in the morning. They've been driving like banshees, hoping they can get there in time.

Seven o'clock Monday morning. Arrive in Barre with the rising sun. Three truck loads of galvanized pipe, as requested. The quarry owner is there to meet them. He's amazed and ecstatic.

That afternoon the quarry guy calls Mel. Praises, raves, thank you's!

The next day a check arrives from Vermont, Special Delivery, for $6,000. Exactly $3,400 goes to Mel's uncle for the pipe, and $2,000 to Mel. Jackpot—more than enough to cover the bad checks, pay the bills, buy a whole lot of groceries. The last $600 belongs to the truckers.

But where are they? Shouldn't they be back by now?

So we wait around the station for them all day Tuesday with a $600 check. Then Wednesday. Then Thursday and Friday. No show. We call their telephone number several times but there is never any answer. We continued to call sporadically until we learn that the number has been disconnected.

A week passes. Two. Then a month. Then more. They simply never came back.

Many months later someone filled us in on the mystery

of their disappearance. After dropping off their loads in Vermont they decided to make a quick run across the Canadian border and bring back an illegal load of whiskey. A truckload of Canada's finest brought a bundle. Trouble was, they were caught at the border returning to the States and were promptly dispatched to jail.

So that was that, and we ended up keeping the extra $600 since we never could locate them.

Many years later, we still joked about how those three truckers were still going to show up at our front door someday and demand their pay. I just hope that if they do they won't insist on getting interest on the money along with their $600 fee.

Down by the Station Early in the Morning

After the pipe deal was successfully concluded and word got out in the trade that Mel's company could work miracles, things began to improve for him in leaps and bounds. I, meanwhile, continued to study torts, pump gas, and watch the world go by— until before I knew it graduation day had rolled around. I'd received my diploma, and had taken the final and biggest step of them all, the bar exam.

The only thing left to do now was to wait for the results, and hope.

Late one Saturday night about a month after I'd taken the bar exam a car pulled into the station.

The driver, it turned out, was the father of one of my classmates and a member of the Board of Regents. He was also a genuinely nice man who had often gone out of his way to patronize our station. We cleaned his windshield and filled his tank. I came over to collect the money and he was smiling at me.

"Marty," he said in a collusive voice. "If I were you I'd get a copy of tomorrow's Sunday *New York Times* as fast as you can."

Then he drove away into the night, leaving me frozen in my tracks. Would this man go out of his way to drive to my station at 11 p.m. on a Saturday night just to tell me to read tomorrow's *New York Times*? I asked myself.

Then I remembered: the names of law students who had recently passed the bar exam were always published in the *Times*, though nobody knew exactly when they would appear. Could it be that my name was among them?

I closed up for the night and headed directly to the Albany railroad station where I found myself a bench and prepared to sweat it out until the Sunday morning edition of the *Times* came rolling in on the 3:06 a.m train. In those days one could pass one part of the bar exam (which was given in two parts) and fail the second part. Did I pass one part or both parts?

As I sat in the station I thought back to what would soon prove a significant event.

A month earlier my mother had visited my older sister, and together they made a daring excursion to the local tea parlor to have their tea leaves read, a practice that was much in fashion at the time.

When it came time to decipher my mother's leaves the in-house swami studied the cup with great ceremony, then told my Mom that, "You will receive some very good news at the end of the month. But you will not believe it until you see it written down in black and white."

My mother returned from her trip shortly thereafter, told us about their little adventure, and we were all duly amused. The incident was promptly forgotten.

Now it's four weeks later and here I am in the Albany train station, waiting for the 3:06, and remembering the gypsy's prediction.

Finally, after hours of torture sitting on the hard station bench the whistle blew and around the bend she came, puffing up to the station in a cloud of sparks and steam. Piles of bundled Sunday papers from New York were tossed off from one of the cars. I bought a copy as fast as I could, opened to the back section, and started thumbing through the pages, my fingers trembling.

Where was it, where was it? Ah! Here! The list; *the* list. I scan up and down the rows of names. Not here . . . not here . . . not here. Do I have the right section? Of course I do. All law students know this section intimately. Wait!—Yes! Here. The name: My name! Marty Silverman. Bar exam. Monday, the 30th.

Passed!!!

Suddenly I was transported back ten years to my bar mitzvah. My family and friends were all around. Relatives I had never seen before and would probably never see again. Here's Rabbi Rosenthal. Here are my uncles, my sisters, my father. And most of all, my mother. I hear her voice over the crowd. "Marty," she's saying, "you give such a good speech. When you grow up you're going to be a lawyer someday. Mark my words—a lawyer."

Now here I am a decade later, and here's my name on the bar exam list, just like she said. I have a sudden impulse to call her immediately, but it's 3 o'clock in the morning and everybody is asleep. And anyway, there was that gypsy's prediction.

So I drive home, go to bed, and the next morning we're all up and at the breakfast table. I wait until there's a lull in the conversation.

"Mom," I say almost under my breath. "I passed the bar exam."

She continues eating and doesn't even look up. "I won't believe it until I see it in print," she says.

"Okay," I say, "take a look," still very low key. I hand

her the section from the *Times*.

She reads it, lets out a shriek, and bedlam breaks out. My dad takes down our only bottle of wine and makes a toast: "To the next Max Steuer" (a famous litigator, now forgotten).

More bedlam, more kisses and shrieks. Then I quiet them down and raise my glass.

"To the one person in the world who knew all about my passing the bar well in advance of everyone else." I looked at mom, and paused for effect. "The one person: my mother's gypsy tea leaf reader!"

I waited for a moment, got my laughs, then winked. "And also to my mother—who knew it long before that, and who hasn't stopped telling us about it since." We all howled, shouted, drank.

There wasn't a dry eye in the house.

Postscript

I'm tempted to conclude this chapter on the gas station era right here because this is where it all began and all ended, with my family. But there's an addendum to the story, and an amusing one, so I'd like to, well, get it down in black and white.

As I told you, one of the most wonderful things about this period of time was seeing how friends and neighbors went out of their way to help me out and purchase gas at my station. All very kind, very simpatico.

But when word got out that I'd *passed* the bar exam and that I was about to become a bona fide lawyer everything changed. No need to support the local boy any longer, folks agreed. He's already made good.

So they stopped buying my gas.

Within a week profits were off 25 percent. In two weeks they were down 50 percent. In three weeks, 75.

Business got so lousy, in fact, that the good folks at Standard Oil began to think something was fishy out my way, that I was neglecting the station or worse, pumping someone else's gas through their pumps.

Finally they sent a representative to investigate.

I explained the situation to him as best I could but he was dubious. He started prowling around the station suspiciously, checking inside the pumps, peeking under the storage tanks, looking for God knows what. An argument finally ensued between us, and the upshot was an ultimatum: We buy you out, said the guy, or you buy us out.

Talk about turning a liability into an asset. This was a better deal than *anything* I could have ever dreamed up on my own. Here was a major oil company offering to take this albatross off my neck and pay me for it in the bargain. I had no deep hankering for the gas business now that I'd finished law school; I had, in fact, been trying to figure out how to unload it. What kind of credibility, after all, would a lawyer have if he was also running a gas station on the side? Not much. The gas station era was thus coming to a close and once again providence stepped in and arranged everything for me.

Several rounds of discussion then followed and finally we came up with a mutually agreeable solution: Standard Oil would cancel the remainder of my debt, pay me a couple of thousand dollars for the land, and take over the station. I, in turn, would relinquish all rights to the property and forfeit all future interests.

Agreed.

And oh yes, one more thing the man added as we were drafting the papers. Something very important. I must sign a non-compete clause with Standard Oil certifying that I *will never again open up a gas business*.

I pretended to give the matter some deep thought, then I shrugged with a serious look on my face, and finally agreed.

We signed.

❥ ❥

And so I was free. And now many years later I am here to testify before you under oath that in all the years since I signed that clause I have honored my promise not to open another gas station.

I have never broken this agreement at any time no matter how great the temptation may have been. Not even once.

God bless us all.

❥ ❥ ❥

Chapter 8

❧ ❧

ON THE ROAD

It's 1936

It's 1936. Big rumblings and lots of grumblings.

The Depression plods on, and despite the New Deal and the big plans of the newly reelected F.D.R., there are few signs of economic improvement.

Still, things are changing.

New York City's streetcars are converted to all-bus service. Sulfa drugs are invented. Joe DiMaggio signs with the Yankees. Pan Am initiates Clipper flights, serving hot meals for the first time in the air. Campbell starts selling soup in a can, a daring marketing ploy. The BBC establishes the world's first TV station, and *Life Magazine* begins weekly publication, changing from a humor format to picture news. This year the *Ziegfeld Follies* will star a rising young comedian named Bob Hope along with Josephine Baker and Fanny Brice (with music by George Gershwin).

Meanwhile, across the sea:

Japan signs the anti-Comintern Pact with Germany and by the next year will invade China. Hitler denounces the Locarno Pacts, reoccupies the Rhineland, and the Rome-Berlin axis is formed. France's Laval government tumbles. Joseph Stalin purges eight million enemies of the state inside the Soviet Union. In the midst of this turmoil Ethiopian emperor Haile Selassie addresses the League of Nations, begging them to stop the slaughter of his people by Mussolini. As he steps down from the podium someone hears him mumble under his breath "It is us today. It will be you tomorrow."

In retrospect, the moving finger was writing but only a few people were listening. Still, when you were there, when you were a poor guy in 1936 with a family to support and an empty belly, these things were secondary to what seemed like the *real* concerns of life: finding a job and putting food on the table.

In my own sphere—and thanks to my mother's vision—I was a full-fledged lawyer by now, and with a little luck could make my way in these hard times.

And since I'd earned my law degree, it also meant I could marry Dot.

We tied the knot in a quiet, private ceremony in the home of Rabbi Rosen, a cousin of Dot's. The ceremony was attended by family and close friends, most of whom kept telling us that it was about time. We had planned our wedding for Friday afternoon so we could honeymoon for the weekend in Atlantic City. Years later when people asked about our wedding day we'd tell them only that, well, we got married by a cousin of Dot's because he did it for us wholesale, and even threw in the reception.

The Firm

So I entered the field of law.

Now in 1936 the legal profession was considerably different than it is today. Lawyers were respected members of the community, it's true, probably a good deal more respected than they are in our time. It was just that, like doctors and other hard working service-oriented professionals, they made the same salaries as, say, the owner of a retail store or an accountant. No big deal.

At the same time, they were as much in demand then as now, and before long I'd landed a position as clerk with an Albany firm known as Williams and Williams. The pay was miserable, ten bucks a week, less than what I'd made as a soda jerker and coat and hat check boy. But I didn't mind too much. Low starting wages were part of the deal in a system that was built on 300 years of English law—you begin as a lowly clerk, serve the other lawyers, and work your way up. (Recall the Gilbert and Sullivan song about the "office boy at the attorney's firm" who polished up the handle of the firm's front door so carefully he was made ruler of the navy.)

I remained at Williams and Williams about a year processing negligence cases, then moved on to the Legal Aid Society of Albany. Here one day I was given a minor case revolving around a Workmen's Compensation issue. I argued the case, won, and as sometimes happens in small communities, a local reporter who had no bigger news to cover stopped off in the court and watched the daily proceedings. Next day, still having nothing of significance to report, he wrote up the case on the front page, manufacturing a big deal out of my "crusading spirit," and making me seem like a new Clarence Darrow.

From then on I was typed as a champion of negligence law with a specialization in Workmen's Comp. This was fine except for the fact that Albany was a small, white collar, government town and basically non-litigious. Which meant that compensation cases were about as common there as two-headed policemen. "If you want compensation," one of my coworkers informed me after six months of twiddling my thumbs, "better move to an industrial town where people get mashed up in machines all the time."

I didn't move, and my law career soon painted itself into an unglamorous corner with few options to choose from, and ten dollars a week to live on.

Then one day I needed an automobile.

Cars Again

I guess you could say I've had a romance with automobiles most of my life.

At first, you will recall, I wanted to be a mechanic and even spent a few minutes in occupational school. Then I went into the gas station business. Now I needed an auto to get to work.

I looked around for an affordable heap until one day I noticed an ad on the bulletin board at the post office. The Department of Agriculture in downtown Albany was selling three used 1934 Pontiacs.

With high hopes I headed to the third floor of the Department of Agriculture and presented myself to the man behind the desk. His name, a sign informed me, was Bud Quigley.

"I saw your ad at the post office, Mr. Quigley," I said. "The one for the Pontiac."

"Good cars," he said. "Government takes care of their vehicles."

"How'd the Department of Agriculture end up in the used car business?" I asked.

"Simple," said Quigley. He was a nervous, friendly man with tousled hair and a firm gaze. I thought of him as an older man at the time, though looking back through the filter of 50 years he was no more than 40.

"The government buys them new for our department," Quigley explained. "We use them for two years. Then we sell them off in sealed bids to the highest bidder."

"You mean I have to *bid* on the car? Like at an auction?"

"Not on *the* car" he said. "On all three cars. You have to buy them all together in one lot."

The wind went out of my sails instantly. All I wanted was one car, not three. So much for my high hopes.

Quigley saw the disappointment on my face. He looked at me for a moment, then asked me what I did for a living.

"I'm a lawyer?" I replied.

"Big time?"

"Little time. A clerk. Ten dollars a week."

"How much money do you have on you right now?" he asked.

I was taken back by this rather intimate question, but figured I might as well go along with the program and see where it took me.

"You mean for a car?"

"Yep."

"Around 50 bucks."

"Good. Here's what you do. Put in a bid right now for all three of the Pontiacs. At 50 dollars apiece."

"But I—"

"Just do what I say," he interrupted in a friendly voice. "I think I can help you out and maybe see that you make something extra on the side."

"What do you get on your end of the deal?" I asked.

He looked at me in surprise and shrugged. "Nothing. You're a young guy, just starting out. Thought I'd just give you a hand."

Like I told you, it was the age of simpatico.

So I wrote up the bid for the three Pontiacs, just as he told me, and dropped it off at the post office.

The government then had a policy of purchasing large lots of new cars from the automobile factories for the discount price of $450 (retail was around $650, including the dealer's 15 percent commission). The workers in their various agencies used them for two years or 40,000 miles, whichever came first, then sold them off cheaply to the highest bidder. This plan was designed to make sure government employees drove decent cars and, in Depression times, to help keep the automobile factories at work.

A couple of weeks passed. Then one day I received a phone call: Your bid has been accepted. You are now the proud owner of three 1934 Pontiac automobiles.

I sped down to Quigley's office and showed him the form.

"Okay," he said. "Here's what you do now. Go down to the post office, buy a money order for 50 dollars, and make it payable to the Department of Agriculture. Then come back here and give it to me."

I did as he said.

When I returned he took the money order (in these days most people paid their bills with money orders, not checks; nobody had enough money in the bank to have a checking account). Then he rummaged through a drawer in his desk, emerging with a car key.

"Here's your first car," he said. "Go downstairs, pick out one of the Pontiacs on the lot, and go out and sell it. Make sure you get more than 50 bucks for it, of course. Then come back, buy another money order, and get your second car. Whatever extra you make on all this is gravy."

Now understand that I'm supposed to be the lawyer and the brains of the operation. But here he is calling the shots, and I'm listening, following his instructions to the T, and basically liking what I'm hearing. The whole thing is beginning to look like a rather interesting game.

So I go down to the parking lot and inspect my new vehicle.

Sure enough, it's just as the auction flyer promised, shiny on the outside, clean on the inside, and mounted with all the basic necessities. There is no radio, clock, or heater. These items were considered extras, and you had to buy them separately from a store like Montgomery Ward, then install them yourself. So I climb into the front seat, start it up, and drive directly to an area of town known as "automobile row" on Central Avenue.

I pull up to the first used car dealer I find, introduce myself, and show him the car.

When the dealer sees what I'm offering him his eyes light up.

"How much do you want for it, sonny?"

"Seventy-five dollars." That's the first figure that pops into my mind.

"Okay," he says without hesitation. "Got yourself a deal."

Now part of me is elated. I've just made a quick, easy sale, and earned 25 dollars in an hour (remember, I'm making ten dollars a week at the firm). But another part of me is upset. I can tell from the dealer's quick response that I sold the car too cheaply.

I handwrite a bill of sale for him and he pays me in cash. In those days you didn't bother with certificates of sale, taxes, inspection forms, registration. The government didn't even require license plates. A sign on the side of the car simply said: "US Government—Official Use Only." All you needed was an informal bill of sale telling the world that for a dollar and other valuable considerations you'd just purchased or sold a such-and-such. End of story.

Now this whole deal, I'm realizing, is a very easy, very clean way to make money.

So the next morning I return to my friend at the Department of Agriculture with another postal money order for $50 taken from my earnings of the previous day, and he gives me the keys to the second car.

This time I decide to be a little cagey.

Driving directly to Central Avenue, I pull up at a different used car lot, show the dealer the my shiny new Pontiac, and when he gets around to asking me the price I tell him $100.

He replies that he'll give me $90 for it. Already I know I'm going to make more on this deal than on the one yesterday. I'm also starting to get a realistic picture of what these cars are really worth.

We haggle for a few minutes, then he says, "tell you what I'll do, we'll toss a coin. You win, you get the $100, I win, I get the car for $90."

Not being a gambling man I tell him to forget the casino stuff and just split the difference. Give me $95 and call it a deal. I also hint mysteriously that there are many more bright, shiny, cheap autos where this one came from. We shook hands and he handed me the money.

So I take the bus home again, this time $45 richer. I've just earned as much in three hours as I take home at the law firm in an entire month!

Next day I return to Quigley's office for the third car.

"How long has this thing been going on?" I ask him. "It's like shooting ducks in a barrel."

He explains that in Albany the Department of Agriculture only sells off vehicles now and then, but that there's an office in Washington, DC, called the General Services Administration that sells used cars from every government agency including the FBI, Secret Service, Department of Indian Affairs, Department of Forestry, the Border Patrol, the Department of State, and all the rest.

Quigley suggests that I write the General Services Administration, and ask them to put my name on their bidders list. Every time a new batch of cars come up for sale they'll automatically let me know.

"And speaking of cars," he says. "Take a glance down there."

I look down at the parking lot and there by the side of the building I see four shiny Ford automobiles lined up in a row, handsome four-door jobs with sparkling chrome and scarcely a nick on them.

"Just came in today," Quigley says. "They were traded back to the Ford Motor Company at $40 apiece against the purchase of four new cars. Representative from Ford's coming up from New York City in a week to arrange a pickup. If you happen to be in my office when he arrives maybe you can persuade him to sell you all four cars directly."

"Sounds great," I said.

Ten days later Quigley rings me up: Be here in my office tomorrow in the late afternoon, he says. And bring cash.

Next day I show up in his office with bells on at 4 o'clock and the Ford representative is already there. He's a tall, aristocratic guy, almost movie-star handsome, and on his arm is the most beautiful girl I'd ever seen. Quigley and I shoot looks of envy back and forth at one another, both knowing we're thinking the same thing: *ba-va-voooooom*!

We introduce ourselves all around, and in the next few moments it becomes obvious that this guy couldn't care less about the four cars down on the parking lot, and that his only concern right now is being alone with his luscious lady friend who's clinging to him like a love-sick octopus, laughing at everything he says, smiling, blushing, preening, the whole nine yards.

"Mr. Silverman here is interested in buying those four used Fords we have for you downstairs," Quigley says to the man after we talk for a while.

"Yes," I added. "I'm ready to take them off your hands for $40 apiece. If you're interested, which is what Ford allows on a trade-in."

The representative, I can see, is only half-interested in the deal.

"Ah, yeah," he finally says. "No, I don't think so. . . . Well, um, listen, do either of you know anything about this Albany Night Boat?"

The Albany Night Boat was one of the town's most famous attractions, a souped-up Mississippi steamer that made a regular run down the Hudson from Albany to New York City, offering passengers a long list of amenities—a bar, a first-rate jazz orchestra, dancing, gourmet dining, lots of plush cabins for the night, and, of course, total anonymity, a kind of floating motel.

"Um, what time does it leave exactly, do you know?" he asks, trying to maintain a professional tone.

"Six-thirty every evening," Quigley replies. "And it arrives in New York City at eight. The dock is a bit of a distance from here by cab so you should leave pretty soon if you want to book yourself a cabin."

At this point I picked up the ball.

"If you were to let me take those four Fords off your hands right now you could be out of here and down at the dock in less than an hour. That gives you plenty of time to get settled in."

I could see the guy's mind racing a thousand miles an hour. He had obviously planned to make the best of a bad thing here in the boonies, staying the night in a hotel with his girl friend, then spending the next day arranging car shipping details—a major pain in the neck. Now I come along and offer to make his life a good deal easier, both the business end and the pleasure end. Mr. Quigley added than I'm an attorney but have very little cash. Quigley offers to draw four $40 money orders and mail them in a self-addressed envelope to Ford in New York. Then, he says, he'll release the cars to me as they are paid for.

"Of course," I added, "if the deal's not possible I'll be on my way. You and Mr. Quigley are probably going to be staying up pretty late tonight discussing shipping problems, locating drivers at the last minute, filling out the forms for tomorrow. I don't want to bog you down."

That did the trick. He promptly agreed that Mr. Quigley's plan would be satisfactory.

Next day I returned to Quigley's office with the first money order payable for $40 to the Ford Motor Company. Quigley gave me a lecherous wink.

"I wonder if our friends got a restful night's sleep on the boat?" he said.

Then I drove Ford number one to my dealer on Central Avenue and promptly sold it for $95. I explained to the dealer that I had three more cars like it. He replied that he couldn't afford any more cars right now, but that he'd help me sell them to other dealers he knew.

With his help I sold the other three cars within a week at $95 apiece.

Clearly, I was on to something interesting.

A New Business Dawns

By now, as you can imagine, I'm asking myself: does it make any sense to go on practicing law? Why not throw my hat into the used car ring instead? I've already made $200 profit in a couple of weeks doing nothing more than driving an automobile from downtown Albany to uptown Albany. And apparently there's no end to the source. It's that, versus $10 a week pleading Workmen's Comp cases.

As far as law school goes, I tell myself, I proved I could do it. Everybody's happy. I have a law degree now, I've done my duty. Mother's pleased, father's pleased. And wouldn't they be even more pleased if I was earning $200 a month instead of $40? Or $300 a month? Or $400?

Of course they would. And if worst comes to worst, I always have the law to fall back on.

So I run the idea past Dot and she thinks it's worth a try.

Next I go to Mel and tell him about this bed of roses I've tumbled into. After a bit of hemming and hawing he says he wants in.

The three of us now form a corporation, Capitol Auto Sales, and right away we go to work. I write the General Service Administration in Washington asking them to place our name on their bidders list. I know the government is more apt to respond to a company than an individual solicitation, so I have a big corporation letterhead printed up.

Sure enough, after a week or so an envelope arrives full of bid forms for government automobiles across the country—Chicago, Los Angeles, Butte, Sioux City, Burlington, Miami—any place large or small that has a government agency. None of the cars offered has more than 40,000 miles on them. All are standard models, all certified in top condition, and all can be purchased via mail for around $50 regardless of make or design.

Not bad.

So we send in a few bids and before long we're buying cars all across the United States at $50 apiece. After each of our bids is accepted Mel travels to Cincinnati or Boston or Milwaukee or wherever the car is and picks it up. Here he pays for it with a money order and immediately drives it to the used car section of that particular city where he makes a deal with the highest bidder, often at a 100 percent profit from what he just paid.

Now this is all great, of course. The trouble is, there are a lot of automobiles out there in America and only three of us to run the business. We decide to set policy.

We divide the business into three departments: the Marty Department, the Mel Department, the Dot Department.

Dot does the books, keeps the records, and sends in new bids from our office in Albany. Mel takes care of selling cars east of the Mississippi. I cover the cars west of the Mississippi. Presto, we're a "national" corporation.

It was the beginning of a true commercial enterprise, the first I had ever been involved with. Though we didn't realize it at the time, we had laid the foundations for a business that would endure from 1937 up to the war. It was an enterprise that would make us, well, if not rich, certainly a lot more comfortable than when we were conducting business from two-by-two telephone booth back at Silverman's Service Station in the capital city of Albany.

On the Road

For the next six years I took to the road, leaving my new wife behind, my family, my life in Albany, crisscrossing the West like Johnny Appleseed, visiting every known form of government agency, institution, reservation, preserve, national park. It was border to border, coast to coast, running, buying, selling, and most of all learning the used-car ropes and educating myself in the ways of the world, and in the ways of all its various people.

Capitol Auto Sales might, for instance, win a bid at auction for four Chevrolets on an Indian reservation in Oklahoma.

So I'd drive cross country to the reservation, pick up one car, hitch a second behind it and hire a local guy, usually an Indian, who'd do the same with the third and fourth cars. Then we'd tow our acquisitions in tandem to a dealer in Omaha. In these days automobiles were built with solid metal bumpers, none of today's fiberglass junk, which meant you could tow a vehicle around the world with a tow bar without worrying that the back of your car was going to fall off.

Once in Omaha I'd then visit my dealer friend who was always glad to see me coming and always ready to fork out

$100 for a car that he'd then turn around and sell for $200 or more, or God knows how much. Everybody scratched everybody else's back, and we were all happy.

Part of the fun, of course, was meeting local color along the way. One of the places I ended up visiting most frequently, for example, was Pierre, South Dakota, a poke hole in the snow not far from one of the larger Indian reservations. The good citizens of this habitation were very fussy about their town's name, insisting that it be pronounced *Peer* and not *Pierre*, as you might say in France. Many of the salesmen who passed through Pierre picked up on this sensitivity and taunted the poor locals with all kinds of evil mispronunciations such as "Pee-hair" or "Pee-i-er-ee" or even "Piss-off" or "Queer."

The townsfolk didn't take kindly to these jokes and there was always a good deal of tension between them and the city slicker salesmen who banded together in the lobby of Pierre's one hotel to trade road stories and inform the locals how things were *really* done back in Chicago, or Atlanta, or Detroit. The natives, in turn, dubbed the salesmen "drummers" (because they carried their samples around in fiberboard cases with straps on them that looked like drums), and went out of their way to make life miserable for them.

I, on the other hand, made it a point *not* to tell the citizens of Pierre how things were done back in New York or anywhere else, and I tried to keep as low a profile as possible, sitting quietly in the hotel lobby listening, laughing, taking it all in and not saying a whole lot.

My silence made the townspeople and salesmen alike a bit wary after a while, and their suspicions were compounded by the fact that I was rumored to be connected with the government in some mysterious way, that I had "contacts"in Washington. Before long the gossip mill was churning out fantastic tales: I was with the FBI, I was an agency man in disguise, I was a spy.

I did nothing to disabuse them of these notions, of

course, and as a result I always got the red carpet treatment whenever I arrived in Pierre, South Dakota. No one there ever did find out that my only connection with the government was selling their agencies' used cars and voting once a year.

The Thing Grows

The best part of the business was that it was all-cash. We'd buy a car Tuesday afternoon, turn it over Wednesday evening, and have enough to piggyback on the profits and buy another car on Thursday. Sometimes we'd make a bid on a batch of cars without having enough money in the bank to cover it. By selling the cars off piecemeal, just as I'd done with Quigley, we were able to cover our flanks. Everything seemed to fall into place on its own.

In 1938 we bought 200 cars. Next year we acquired 300 cars. In 1940 we were doing 400 cars a year, and by 1942, between Mel and me, sales exceeded 500 cars a year.

Now think about it: I'm covering half the United States of America all by myself, logging hundreds of miles every day like a traveling salesman, driving, say from Topeka to Salt Lake City, back to Sioux City, down to Houston, up to Omaha, and from here, say, to San Diego or Portland or St. Louis or Elk River, Idaho, all in a few days' time. Mel, meanwhile, is doing the same thing in the east. Each of us is responsible for selling approximately 250 cars annually.

Considering that there are 365 days in a year, this meant we were selling one new automobile every other day, on the average, which is better business than many used-car lots were doing at the time.

By the early 1940's we were thus earning around $10,000 a year, ironically, the same salary that I and my fellow students used to fantasize about back in Albany Law School.

Used Cars

But, again, it wasn't the profits that intrigued me so much as it was the chance to observe my fellow man. Soon I was meeting the darndest people from the most exotic places— Mexican border patrol guards, slick-talking FBI men, forest rangers who hadn't set foot out of the woods in a year, Indians who still dressed as if they were in a Tom Mix movie. Each of these characters had a different view of the world, a different set of values, a different story. Some even spoke a different language. It was like going to a museum every day of the year.

Take, for example, the used car dealers. They were a caste unto themselves, a friendly, outgoing, slightly seedy bunch of compulsive salesmen who knew their cars inside-out, but who were looked on as second-class citizens by their rivals, the new car dealers. You never—*never*—saw a used-car on a new-car dealer's lot. It meant the dealer trafficked in second-hand goods, and this was a social no-no, even though we were in a Depression.

Used car dealerships thus catered to less affluent, sometimes less-educated buyers, and in the process unscrupulous dealers would occasionally wire on a broken muffler or "forget" to tell a prospective buyer that a piston was shot. It was during these Depression days that used-car dealers got their poor reputation, not entirely undeserved but also, I think, a bit exaggerated.

At the same time, odd to tell, many of the dealers I met during these years were a strangely conservative bunch who were rarely willing to go out on a limb.

I recall once traveling to Omaha in the middle of the Dust Bowl days where everywhere you looked you saw sand circles blowing up in clouds, abandoned houses, ghost towns, barnyard animals dead along the roadside, entire families of ruined farmers hitchhiking to anywhere you'd take them.

None of these sights augured good business. And sure

enough, when I reached Omaha the first used-car dealer I spoke with told me how he's was dying on the vine because no one could afford to buy his used cars, especially his kind of used cars, the expensive models, Packards, Caddies, Graham Paiges. They cost too much, and they used too much gas.

Then he looks at me strangely for a minute and takes a step back, sort of sizing me up.

"How much you getting for your autos these days, Marty?" he asks. He knows I deal in the lower-priced models.

"Around $100 per," I tell him. "Usual price."

"Know what?" he says. "I'm going to make you a trade. You give me eight of your small, cheap cars, I'll give you eight of my big, expensive models. Even-steven."

"Why would you want to do that?" I ask. "Gives you the raw end of deal, doesn't it?"

"I can't sell these big fancy chariots anymore," he replies. "Folks around here need transportation all right, like all of us, but they're poor folks now, mostly, they want those little, cheap models you sell. How about it?"

"So what am I going to do with the big cars?" I shot back. "If you can't sell them, neither can I."

"You're a traveling man, right?" he answers.

I say I am.

"You drive out west sometimes, don't you?"

I do.

"Then here's my suggestion. You trade me your cars, take these big models all the way to California where folks have more money and can afford fancier get-arounds. That way you'll make yourself a big profit, and help me out too. What do you say?"

I thought about it for a moment, and the more I thought the better the idea seemed. I even began to wonder why I hadn't thought of this before?

"Why don't you do it yourself?" I asked.

"I'm a family man. Hard to pull up stakes and travel."

"But there might be a lot of money in it for you," I suggested.

"No matter. I'm a family man."

Like I said, they were a conservative lot. This fellow knew I'd make myself a big profit from the deal. But he didn't care. It was all the same to him. And so, as has often happened in my life, someone came along, dumped a golden opportunity in my lap, then walked away, not knowing what they were passing up—or, perhaps, not willing to take the risk.

So we traded: my eight little buggies for his eight luxury monsters including two Buicks, a Packard, a Cadillac.

I then found several car salesmen who wanted to leave Omaha and relocate out West, and who were willing to drive a car there for room and board.

The next day my motorcade set out and soon we were in Denver where a dealer I knew fell in love with one of my Buicks and bought it on the spot for five times what I'd traded it for. I picked up several more cars in Denver at a good price and continued on.

To make a long story short, after making several more stops along the way we finally reached Los Angeles where jobs were plentiful and auto prices inflated by the high cost of freight. Here I sold off my bevy of beauty boats for many times their market value, and many, many times the value of the cars I'd traded them for. It was the first really big killing I'd ever made in the business world. The profits were so high, in fact, that Dot, Mel, and I used our share of the earnings to help my parents buy their own retirement home in Florida.

Cars, as I said, have always been my friends.

Why Don't They Do the Same Thing Today?

Whenever I tell this story, by the way, the first thing people ask me is: why aren't people doing the same thing today? The government still sells its cars at bargain rates. Why aren't people getting rich from it?

The answer is, first, that the cars have to have title certificates today. Not so in 1937.

Second, they now need to be inspected. Not so in 1937.

Third, they need to be insured. Not so in 1937.

And fourth, you can't really tie a tow bar onto a bumper today.

At any rate, all I can say is: God bless good timing, good luck, and Henry Ford.

➤ ➤ ➤

Chapter 9

❧ ❧

CLOUDS OF WAR

All Good Things Come to an End

All good things come to an end, the philosopher tells me. And he's right, I suppose.

I think back, and I remember. It's 1936, 1937, 1938. The used car business is great and getting greater.

Now it's 1939. Still going strong. The shortage of used cars is very evident.

Then 1940. Leaps and bounds. Prices of used cars are going through the roof.

And no end in sight.

Everything is going great guns. Only problem is, watch out for those changes of decade.

I woke up one morning and suddenly war spears were flying back and forth across Europe. People were dying by the millions and guns were going off on several different continents. All this madness filtered back to the United States and caused the mood in the country to take a sharply conservative turn. Hostilities in Europe and the Orient were too violent, we all felt, too widespread and dangerous not to eventually draw us in. How, when, and where we would be drawn in, however, no

one knew. No one was even certain who the enemy would ultimately be (pro-German sentiment at this time in the United
States was surprisingly strong). Our government was starting
up intern camps for American-born Japanese and their parents,
and that was an ominous sign. Most Americans knew in their
bones that it was only a matter of time till something popped
and that somehow, some place, conflict was inevitable.

This explosion of global hostilities and the demands it
created caused American factories to work overtime manufacturing weapons of war. Some of these weapons were for our
own defense; most were marked for export to the Allies and
some even to Nazi Germany.

Ironically, this increase in manufacturing activity
caused the flow of goods and services at home to slow to a
crawl. You'd go shopping, say, and discover that household
items like paper, salt, cotton, tin goods, sugar, petroleum, and
rubber were removed from the shelves. Where had they gone?
To China, to England, to Australia, to God knows where. I
remember a magazine joke at the time depicting an old miser
sitting in his room, rubbing his hands together greedily, surrounded by treasure. His loot wasn't gold, however, but a stack
of rubber tires.

Among the industries that were most directly affected
by this surge in production was automobile manufacturing. The
raw materials needed to produce cars, the metals and welds and
hose required for assembly line production, were suddenly
channeled into planes and tanks, not Chevrolets. This meant
that cars were increasingly difficult to find as time passed, and
worse, a good deal more expensive.

Now understand that even during the deepest part of the
Depression, the average middle class American family had at
least one automobile on display in the driveway and sometimes
two. Come what may, we Americans were going to have our
cars.

This fools' paradise lasted until the 1940's when, almost

overnight, car prices shot up abruptly, car production slowed, gas prices went through the roof, rationing began, and automobile showrooms that had once been chock-a-block full of new Chryslers and Fords displayed one or two models at most and you'd better put your order in early, buddy, because there's not enough to go around.

What did all this mean for our little business in Troy, New York?

Doom, basically.

We watched helplessly as the competition doubled, then tripled, then quadrupled. Once upon a time car dealers held their noses when a used car drove by. Now they were strangling each other to get their hands on used cars. In some cases the government was selling cars for more money than we could get from the dealers.

Meanwhile, because of the sudden boom, business expenses multiplied dramatically—postage, gasoline, train fares, hotel rooms, meals. These increases raised our costs even more, and reduced our margin of profit. Everything seemed to go into overdrive all at once as the 1940's came roaring in, and many small businesses like ours were caught in the whirlwind.

The long and the short of it was staring us in the face: we were no longer competitive in the business.

What stepping stones now? Where to go from here?

Lose One, Gain One

By 1940 my mother and father had left Troy and were happily ensconced in the home bought for them in Florida. Consequently, there was nothing compelling to keep us here in Troy. I was very discouraged over the loss of the business and couldn't imagine what I'd do next. I had a wife to take care of now, along with my mother and father, and soon, we hoped, children.

Then one day Mel came up with an interesting proposal: why don't we all move back to New York City and try our luck in the used machinery business.

Mel, you will recall, was an expert at buying and selling industrial equipment, and Dot, who'd been his partner for several years, knew almost as much about the business as he did. Between the three of us we had thousands of hours' experience buying and selling one kind of machine or another, and we all worked together as a team.

We thus agreed—moving to New York was the smart thing to do. Within six months we had closed the used auto business, disposed of our house, moved our families to the Big Apple, and rented apartments in Long Island City where the living was pleasant and the rents cheap.

•+ •+

Once settled in, we then found a storefront on Jackson Avenue for $35 a month with plenty of storage facility and easy access to the 59th Street Bridge. Then we started buying and selling used equipment in earnest.

We had been in business only a short time when Morris Lester, my oldest sister's husband, joined our company.

This gave us a needed shot in the arm. Morris had spent years buying and selling used equipment, especially gaskets and garden hose. I would hazard a guess, in fact, that Morris knew more about garden hose than any man on the planet at this time. He had also established a network of relationships with a number of rubber manufacturers. After his company failed he brought these contacts to us as part of what he referred to as his "portfolio." Rubber was, of course, especially hard to come by at this time; but with Morris's contacts we were able to purchase huge lots of it and turn it around at double and triple the price.

Demand varied. One customer needed lead pipe, another rubber hose, a third assorted machine parts or rope wire or copper tubing. We advertised in the *New York Times*, targeting factories and industry.

On the whole, we did rather well. We didn't make the Fortune 500, mind you, but we earned enough to feed our families.

What's more, except for my mother and father, we were all together now, a solid unit of three loving families working in the same business toward a common end. The sense of togetherness was special and heightened the excitement we felt from our growing success. A few years earlier surplus machinery dealers couldn't get arrested. But now with war shortages all that had changed. The difficulty, in fact, was not finding a buyer for the goods, but locating the goods to sell.

Rambling and Gambling

Our business day was thus spent rambling through Brooklyn, the Bronx, the metropolitan area, and in far away, exotic places like Paterson, New Jersey, paying visits to factories and warehouses, and ferreting out what of their supplies, if any, was for sale.

Most of these places maintained a separate room for their surplus equipment, and we'd purchase everything we could find and ship it back to our shop in Long Island City. Here we'd store it in the basement in an area that Dot dubbed "the General Store."

We didn't always have to go far afield to find our materials, however. Sometimes the goodies came right to our front door.

Once, for instance, Mel and I went to the local Sears Roebuck warehouse on a tip from Morris, the hose expert.

Here, sure enough, about 300 lengths of 50-foot hose were on display, all of it Dunlop hose, Sears' special high quality brand. Garden hose was practically impossible to find, and when it did show up anywhere in the city the price was prohibitive. This time, however, for reasons known only to the prophets, Sears was selling it off at $5.95 a length, a bloody steal.

So I hunted down the warehouse manager and persuaded him to give us a 10 percent discount if we took the whole lot. He agreed and even suggested that we keep the hose stored in Sears' warehouse and pick it up as required.

Which we did. Right away the stuff starts to sell off the floor like wildfire at $9.95 a length.

Then one day while our sale is in full swing a guy comes in and asks how much the hose is per 50-foot length.

Mel tells him the price and he hits the ceiling.

"Sears was just selling the same hose," he hollers. "Certified Dunlop hose! Around the corner. For $5.95! What kind of stunt are you trying to pull!?"

"Well, sir," I replied. "Why don't you go to Sears and buy it there?"

"Because," he answers "They've all sold out."

I smiled at him smugly. "And that, sir, is why our price is $9.95."

Then there was the stirrup pump episode.

For the past several months the papers had been full of reports about the Japanese war machine, and about how the "Nip menace" was using a terrible new weapon on their enemies called an "incendiary bomb," a distant ancestor of napalm.

As a consequence of these reports and of the somewhat exaggerated rumors concerning the bomb's kill power, panic spread across the country, especially in the big cities like New York where the prospect of fires in tall buildings haunted everyone's dreams.

As a reaction, the city enacted an ordinance decreeing

that public buildings have pails of water on every floor, along with stirrup pumps to spray it with. This, presumably, to douse the 50-foot high walls of flame that would be caused by incendiary bomb attacks.

Most people don't remember stirrup pumps. Once upon a time, however, they were a staple in every household. A handy water spray contraption shaped like a bicycle pump, they were usually stashed somewhere in the pantry or basement and then forgotten till you needed them to bail out a wet basement or water a fern.

The absurd flaw in this so-called "pump law" quickly became apparent. Why waste time filling and squirting the stupid pump, everyone asked, when you can just toss the pailful of water directly on the fire. An obvious point, perhaps. But wartime government regulations were like this.

At any rate, stirrup pumps quickly become the law and delinquent landlords were fined right and left for not adhering to the code.

The result was that stirrup pump mania broke out across New York, and within two weeks they were as difficult to find as walruses in a teahouse. Our own shop immediately started receiving dozens of requests for the little critters, but like everyone else in town we had none in stock.

Then one day I was taking the train down to Philadelphia to check out some advertised equipment when about halfway through the trip a guy gets on, sits next to me, and starts reading the Philadelphia newspaper. A few stops later he gets off and leaves the paper on the seat. I pick it up and start reading. Immediately my eye falls on a bold half-page display advertisement:

GIMBEL'S DEPARTMENT STORE SALE:
TODAY AND TOMORROW ONLY:
STIRRUP PUMPS—ONLY $4.95
GO TO THE THIRD FLOOR

A sale! Of stirrup pumps! A bloodhound couldn't have found a stirrup pump anywhere in the five boroughs, and here in Philadelphia there are so many of them that they're going at half price!

I turned the page. To my astonishment another ad for stirrup pumps appeared, this time at Wanamaker's. Then another listing at another store.

And several more at assorted shops and department stores all across Philadelphia.

Stirrup pumps, it seemed, were as common in Philadelphia as Quakers once were.

When the train arrived in Philadelphia the first thing I did was gallivant over to Gimbel's, where, just as the ad promised, hundreds of pumps were on display, all ticketed at the ridiculously low price of $4.95 per. In New York, I'm thinking, landlords are paying as much as $20 per pump, desperate to avoid the stiff fines for noncompliance. And here I am in pump Valhalla and they're practically giving the things away. Ain't no justice.

I hunted down the manager.

"How much for all the pumps on the floor?" I asked.

He does some figuring and gives me a price.

"Take 10 percent off because I'm buying them in quantity?" I asked.

"Certainly, sir" he said.

"And, of course, you'll deliver them to my store in New York?"

"We always deliver, sir."

"On an as-needed basis?"

"That can be arranged."

I bit my lip and took a breath.

"You'll take care of all freight charges too, I assume?"

He had to think about this one. Was I pushing him too far?

"Of course," I said, making a slight movement towards

the door. "They're having a sale on stirrups at Wanamaker's too, I noticed in the papers."

"All right, sir," he replied. "The freight charges are not a problem as far as Gimbel's is concerned." Apparently he was working on commission.

Next I ran to Wanamaker's and offered them the same deal, which they quickly accepted. Finally I made an agreement with Winthrop & Hathrop on the same terms.

Then back to New York where we advertised the stirrup pumps in the classified section of the *New York Times* at $14.95 per. Within 30 days we sold them all.

Now the thing that interests me most today about this transaction, thinking back, is that Philadelphia and New York are only a few hours apart. Yet in the era before instant communication one city might be chock-full of a certain product, and the next one down the line might not have any of this product, and neither city would be aware of the difference. Opportunities like this were thus based on *lack* of technology rather than the presence of it. There were, after all, advantages to living in a simpler time.

Our Bear Mountain *"in"*

Then there was the time our three families decided to drive up to Bear Mountain State Park in upstate New York and spend a day *au naturel*.

The drive takes about an hour-and-a-half from Long Island, and by the time we arrived the woods and lakes were warbling our names. We hiked, rowed, smelled the flowers, and by the time dinner rolled around we were so hungry we decided to splurge and eat at the Bear Mountain Inn, a restaurant-lodge famous for its Lincoln Log architecture and great food.

At the restaurant the whole family was sitting round the table anticipating a lusty meal when I happened to glance out the window and could see a large pile of galvanized pipe in the distance.

Most of the metal pipe in the world was pumping steam under the decks of battleships or flying around the sky in DC6's. Shortages were rampant and demand high. That very moment, in fact, I knew of four or five dealers who would pay a king's ransom for this cache. And that was just for starters.

The waitress came by to take our order. I asked her who owned that ugly pile of pipe out there.

"Oh, that," she said. "That's the old skating rink, what's left of it. Thing burned down last year. They tore it up months ago and just left it in a heap. What an eyesore, huh?"

"I'll say," I said. "Got any idea what they're going to do with all of it?"

"Beats me, honey," she answered. "You want stuffing with that turkey or plain?"

The next morning I wrote a letter of inquiry to the Superintendent of Bear Mountain State Park, and a few days later a reply showed up in our mailbox.

To whom it may concern: yes, all equipment from the skating rink will be available by open bid. In addition to the galvanized pipe there will be industrial tools and machinery of all kinds—tractors and trucks (worth their weight in gold at that time), fire equipment, saws, drills, grounds-keeping supplies. The sealed bids will be open to everyone.

Amazing! At the time this kind of equipment was like rubies and pearls.

After carefully going over the variables and calculating what we could afford, we mailed in our bids. We'd had plenty of experience dealing with the government by now, and we knew how to pace our bidding. Still, we thought that every company from here to San Francisco would be bidding against us, and that our chances of success were small.

We waited for what seemed like years.

Then one day a letter brought remarkable news: not only were we the winning bidders, we were the *only* bidders. Or practically so.

For some reason few other companies had bothered to compete with us, perhaps because they thought it was a lost cause, perhaps because they hadn't been hungry enough to eat at the Bear Mountain Lodge that day and didn't know this pile of equipment existed. Who knows? All we did know was that we were now the owners of 22 tractors, 841 pieces of pipe, 15,007 couplings, 212 hand saws, 98 lengths of chain, 99 hammers, 394 boxes of nails—on and on.

We spent the next six months sorting the stuff out and selling it to an anxious and large-pocketed group of buyers. By the time we'd finished our families were not only able to have as many meals at the Bear Mountain Inn as they pleased but were more or less able to buy the right wing of the place as well.

Well, almost.

Up in the Air

It was 1941. December. The Day of Infamy.

Unlike most people, I can't remember the exact place I was standing when the news broke. Japanese over Diamond Head, fleet destroyed, sneak attack, rain of death.

War!

I do remember listening to Roosevelt's famous "Day of Infamy" speech, and realizing that once again everything in my life was going to change dramatically, and forever.

I also realized that my draft number was distressingly low—the draft was run on a lottery basis then, just as it would be later on during Vietnam—and that I'd better do something about it posthaste if I was going to maintain at least a modicum of control over fate.

Growing up in post-World War I and Jazz Age America, I'd read a great deal about Air Force aces and daredevil johnnies, about wing-walkers and traveling air shows and the loop-de-loop. All this aeronautics stuff had a feeling of romance and daring to it that I found extremely exciting. I especially wanted to fly my own plane.

I reasoned: with war breaking out all over the place and my country already a great air power, why not parlay my interest in flying into a means of taming the draft? I'd recently heard that NYU was offering a course in aeronautics for college grads, a combined study plan of airplane engines, instrumentation and navigation. This seemed like just the ticket. I'd study aviation, learn to fly, then join the Air Force as a flight instructor. This way, I figured, I could indulge my boyhood wing-walking fantasies and satisfy my military obligation at the same time.

For the next six months I thus spent my time in three different places doing three entirely different things:

✔ 1) Working at our store in Long Island City hawking used equipment during the day.
✔ 2) Studying aeronautical engineering at NYU at night.
✔ 3) Learning to fly an airplane in Pennsylvania during the weekends.

The most exciting of the lot was, of course, flying a plane.

The war was on in earnest now and the air raid siren was a fact of life in every urban area.

Flying a private aircraft over any major city was outlawed.

For aspirant New York aviators this meant that the closest airport was several hours west of the city, in Easton, Pennsylvania.

And so, that's where we spent the weekends.

Think Ahead

As time passed and as I logged more and more hours in the air, it seemed clear to me that my advance planning was paying off, and that I was on my way to a new career.

I'd always enjoyed planning ahead. I'd been a planner since the days when my mother taught us never to open the icebox door without knowing which articles you wanted to take out and which ones you wanted to put in, a decision one made ahead of time to avoid keeping the icebox door open too long. (My mother, I always liked to say, was decades ahead of everybody, including IBM, one of whose slogans was and still is: "Plan Ahead.")

At any rate, things were going according to plan, everything was on target, and I saw no reason to suppose that anything would stop me from becoming a certified Army Air Force flight instructor within the year.

Man Proposes, God Disposes

One bright, clear Saturday at the airport in Easton I was standing by a fence eating lunch with Dot and awaiting my 1 o'clock flying lesson when a fellow student hailed us across the field and walked briskly in our direction. He was a young guy about my age, tall, gangly, always smiling. Like me, he was learning to fly so he could join the Air Force.

"Morning," he said, holding out his hand. "Great flying weather, huh, Marty?"

"You bet" I answered. "Can't wait to get up there."

"Glad you brought that up" he continued. "I got a real big favor to ask you. I sure hope you won't mind."

"What's up?" I asked.

"Well, I just found out I have a wedding to attend today at 3 o'clock. A real important one—my boss's daughter. It wouldn't look very good if I didn't show up."

I nodded and smiled. "How can I help?"

"Well, they told me over at the office you have the 1 o'clock flying slot. I was hoping maybe you could switch with me. I'll take your 1 o'clock slot, you take my 2 o'clock. That way I can get to the wedding and make my boss happy. I sure would be obliged if you could help me out."

I told him that we were planning to hang around most of the day anyway and that it was no big deal changing time slots.

"Gee, thanks, Marty" he said, shaking my hand again. "I'll repay you the first chance I get."

He walked off a happy man. A few minutes later we saw him climb into the cockpit and take off with his instructor.

Dot and I found a grassy area nearby and absently watched our friend do several loop-de- loops and then head up into the clouds.

Realize, of course, that flying a small plane in these days was quite a different experience than it is today. The planes were mostly open-cockpit Piper Cubs that couldn't go higher than 2,500 or 3,000 feet, and even that was pushing it. They also had an air speed a few mph's faster than a bulldozer. And, of course, we didn't know from radios or instrument flying.

Still, 3,000 feet was high enough to make you pay attention.

And high enough to send a bolt of terror through us when we suddenly heard a loud metallic snapping noise overhead, looked up, and saw that the wing of our friend's plane— the same biplane I had been scheduled to fly—had sheared off and was plunging to the ground. Along with the plane itself.

We watched in disbelief as the engine sputtered, and the plane plunged earthward for two-thirds of a mile, fragments of metal and rubber flying off it in all direction. Then the plane went belly-up, twisting and gyrating in weird ways as it came down.

When it finally hit at the edge of the landing field they heard the noise, I was told, ten miles away. The moment it impacted the craft burst into flame, causing what was left of the fuselage and the two pilots inside to crinkle up and melt.

Dot and I quickly gathered our belongings and headed back to New York, driving all the way home in shattered silence.

The whole return trip I'm thinking to myself that I'm 29 years old, still young, still healthy, still alive (though only by the Grace of God), still planning to live a long life and raise a family. Once again the Good Lord has snatched me from disaster. But this time He's left his calling card. On it, printed clearly, it says: Marty: Don't overtax your guardian angel.

I had no right, the message said, to place my life in jeopardy now that I was married man. How unfair it was to my wife and perhaps to our children who might one day see the wing of their father's aircraft snap off, just as it had snapped off for this pleasant young man who was so very anxious to please his boss and who, like me, wanted to be a flier.

From that day on I never again flew an airplane.

Out of the Flying Pan

This decision did not, however, stop the draft board from breathing fire down my neck.

By now I'd passed the NYU exam and received an instructor's license to teach aircraft engine instrumentation and navigation. Why not continue with my aviation career, I thought to myself. Nothing's changed that much. I have the knowledge and the skill. I'll just avoid the flying part.

As if they'd divined my very thoughts, the Civil Air Patrol sent me a letter a few weeks later and making me an offer I couldn't refuse: a special training course in aeronautics was being given for college graduates in Lynchburg, Virginia. Would I like to join? The course offered advanced instruction in air navigation, plane engines, and instrumentation. Participants would graduate as qualified Army Air Force instructors. Their job would then be strictly land-based and would entail teaching, instruction, navigation, everything but actually flying a plane. The pay was unusually generous.

I applied and was accepted the next week.

For the next six months I then trained, drilled, exercised, studied, got haircuts, read the newspapers, marched in circles, visited home as often as possible, and generally had myself a pretty good time in Lynchburg. Could be worse, I thought, in this man's army.

Then the draft board reared its head again: If Silverman is going to remain in the program, they insisted, he must be given a commission as an officer.

This was fine with me, but while the notion posed no problem to my commanding officer in Lynchburg, he was too low on the pecking order to grant a commission. He'd write me a letter of recommendation, he explained, and I'd then have to deliver it personally to his C.O. in Washington, D.C.

A week later I arrived in Washington with the letter, headed for the Pentagon, and handed it directly to a general who read it over, contemplated the matter, and replied that before he could grant me a commission I'd have to receive 12 weeks of Air Force basic training.

This was not part of the plan, but still it seemed a small price to pay for a commission *and* a well-salaried job doing what I liked *and* a means of paying off my military obligation.

The general had a set of orders prepared directing me to Camp Upton, a reception station on Long Island.

I reported to Upton for duty and received a physical, shots, a uniform, and my dog tags.

After two grueling but endurable weeks in Long Island I was transferred to Charleston, West Virginia, where, I was told, I was to finish Air Force basic training and return to Lynchburg where my commission would be waiting for me at last.

Again, fine, though this moving around was taking its toll on both Dot and me. No matter, though—it would be over soon.

In Charleston training proceeded at approximately the same pace as in Long Island, and everything went smoothly until we got about halfway through the program.

Then the sky fell.

From the depths of the War Department word came down that our training program was being terminated. No second chance, no reconsideration, no alternative plans. Just finis.

Where would be go now? we all wondered. What did the Air Force have in mind for the next leg of this infinitely protracted journey? I brought the question to my C.O.

"You'll have to take it up with your new commanding officer," he replied in standard military monotone.

"New C.O.?" I asked. "What do you mean, sir? You're leaving?"

"No, *you're* leaving."

"Could I ask, sir, to where?"

"You didn't get the news?" He seemed genuinely surprised.

"No, sir, I didn't."

"You're all being shipped out tomorrow night."

Another transfer, I thought. Oh boy!

"Where are we going, sir, if you don't mind my inquiring?"

"Harrisburg, Pennsylvania."

I thought about this for a minute. "There's no Air Force base that I know of in Harrisburg, sir," I said.

"That's right, Silverman" he replied. "There isn't. Like I told you, you boys are all being reassigned—out of the Air Force."

Loss of Appeal

The army is famous for two things: the unreasonableness of its policies, and an infinite pliability that allows anyone to finagle anything as long as he does it in the right way.

Knowing both these facts from experience, and reeling from my sudden and ominous change in fortune, the first thing I did when I arrived at the Harrisburg camp was to find my personnel sergeant and lay my case before him. I found him at his desk in the camp administrative office.

"Sarge," I pleaded. "I'm a few courses away from becoming a full-fledged aeronautics instructor. I was trained to teach Air Force recruits how to fix engines and navigate planes, not to march or shoot guns. There's been a big mistake."

"No mistake," the sergeant answered, an expression of inestimable boredom on his face.

"Beg pardon, sir, but there's got to be an administrative error of some kind," I repeated. "I'm in the Air Force, not the infantry!"

The sergeant stared at me with steely blue eyes and made no reply.

"I'm also a lawyer," I continued. "If they're going to reassign me they should at least send me to the Judge Advocate General's office. I can earn my keep there. But infantry—Sir, I'm almost 30 years old. Everybody here is 18. I don't even know how to throw a hand grenade."

"You will," he replied. "Anything else, Private?"

"Sir, there must be *something* that can be done!"

The sergeant thumped his pencil on the desk. "Right now we need infantrymen. Later on we'll need lawyers."

"But I—"

"You're in the infantry. That's all, Private."

"But sir, I—"

"Listen, buddy," he said, leaning forward at his desk, his cold eyes motionless in his head. "There's a war on, you understand? Lots of people are doing lots things they don't want to do. Not get your ass out of here!"

My head was reeling, I called Dot and told her what had happened. So much for my powers of planning.

At least you're stationed close to home, she said. And anyway, you're a lawyer, for God's sake, Marty, and an aeronautics expert. Surely the army will realize the mistake and reassign you.

Surely.

But the fact of the matter was, as I soon came to realize, that we were in the middle of the biggest, bloodiest war ever fought on this planet. Not only did we need fighting men to defend hearth and home, but a big push of some mysterious kind was being planned behind the closed doors of the Pentagon. It would be known as D-day.

To carry off the most ambitious military operation of all time, the U.S. military needed grunts, not aeronautics engineers; and so thousands of training operations like ours were being tossed out and the participants sent off to become dog-faced, rat-chewing, hard-fighting American GI's.

That was the long and short of it. Of course, as Dot said, at least I was close to home and could visit now and then.

Trouble was, I couldn't get a pass.

Nor could Bernie Rosenberg, a friend of mine in my same company. Or Howie Slatterman in D Company. Or Nathan Endelman in A Company, and Larry Meyers. Or Bob

Figman and Steve Bauman in G. All of us were in the same boat here at the Harrisburg training camp, all Jews at a time when anti-Semitism was not only condoned in the United States armed forces but, in many circles, encouraged.

Thus began one of the most grueling experiences I have ever endured

The Training Camp from Hell

At first you get mad and take a swing at the guy.

Maybe you win the fight, maybe you lose.

Then an hour goes by and you hear the same thing. "Hey, Jew bastard" or "Hey, kike face." "Hey, you sheeny ass hole." "Hey, you Christ killing son-of-a-bitch."

So you swung. But at a different guy.

Maybe you win again and maybe you lose. A couple of hours later the same thing happens.

After a while what do you do? You stop swinging and ignore the bunch of them. You going to fight 180 men?

Nor is there any way you can keep your Jewishness a secret. How do you disguise a name like Silverman or Rosenberg or Schwartz? Your name tag says "H" for Hebrew. There are no secrets about it from the world.

The only guys who can carry it off were the blond, blue-eyed Jews with goyish last names like Colin or Richards. Even then they usually get discovered—assuming they want to disguise their Jewishness in the first place. A friend of mine, a nice goyish looking war correspondent named Carroll, liked to handle this moment in a special way. When it was discovered that he was Jewish and the guy who discovered it said something like "You're Jewish?! I didn't know that?" Carroll would reply, "Sure. You are too, right?"

The other guy would shake his head and look confused,

and Carroll would keep at him. "You're not!" he'd say. "That's really strange. I could have sworn you were Jewish. You *look* so Jewish."

At any rate, after you were at camp a while everybody knew you were an H, and they made you pay. All the 18 and 19-year-old punks with their front teeth missing and their big biceps and their beer breath and their long hit lists of who's okay and who's not okay in this world.

Fact is, you come to realize, the military has always been a Mecca for good old boys. Many of them came from the deep South and had never seen a Jew before. They'd just heard the stories — "everyone knew" they were true — about how Jews ate Christian babies and controlled all the money in the world in their secret cabals.

The worst offenders were the 20-year men, the brainless, skill-less, luckless guys who had joined the peacetime army or National Guard years ago because they had no skills and couldn't find a job. Once in the military they spent their lives hanging around the base, drinking, sleeping, womanizing, goofing off, and finally, by default and seniority, were promoted to the rank of sergeant.

They were a tight-knit little club, these fellows, and in a way an exclusive one too: if you were a Catholic, Jew, foreigner, weirdo, intellectual, black, brown, yellow, striped, no need to apply. Anyone a centimeter different from what they took to be the norm and they'd taunt you, taunt you good, taunt you till you dropped.

It started with detail assignments. Is this the chummiest job on the base? Good, give it to Silverman and Rosenberg.

Think KP is bad? Scrubbing pots and pans in the mess will make you puke with fatigue. Give it to Silverman and Rosenberg.

Latrines need cleaning? Silverman and Rosenberg.

Emptying the garbage? Silverman and Rosenberg.

Dead animal burial brigade? Call the Jew boys.

Filling in a trench? Where are the kikes?
And on it went.

●+ ●+

How did I stay sane through it all? Well, I waited till it
got dark. Then I'd stow my gear in the bunk, walk to the latrine,
and sit myself down in the farthest stall to the left.

That's right, the latrine. Here I was finally alone, away
from the catcalls of prejudice and hatred and doom. And even
better, I was in front of the most wonderful piece of graffiti in
the world that some soldier angel had scrawled on the side of
the stall. It said the following:

**The only man in this fucking army who really knows
what he's doing is sitting right here.**

Don't ask me why, but I drew enormous consolation
from these words. I'd read them aloud, read them again, and
pretty soon I'd start feeling that it was true, that all the officers
and enlisted men were nuts, and that I was the only one with my
head screwed on right. Maybe it was true, maybe it wasn't. But
watching the tomfoolery around me, seeing the bombast, self-
importance, the illogicality of the brass and worse, soon to wit-
ness hordes of young men fresh out of their mothers' arms sent
to miserable deaths by vainglorious officers and thoughtless
commands, well, it sure seemed that way at the time.

That silly little piece of graffiti helped keep me from
going crazy.

Excel, Excel

On the rifle range we were given the worst firing positions. The bunks were the worst. They woke us up earlier, yelled at us more, gave us more details, marched us more, blamed us more, withheld leave from us more often than anyone else on the base. The old favorite: the Jew as scapegoat.

It was terrible.

But here's what they didn't bargain for. The more they taunted us the more we strived to excel, both Rosenberg and I. And all the other Jews on all the other bases in the Army as well Our records of achievement, decoration, and valor under fire were consequently among the highest in the military.

This, despite the rumors you heard at every base, that the Jews were afraid to fight, that they ran when the firing started, that they held the cushy jobs behind the fire lines.

Don't you believe it. And don't take my word for it either. Go to the battalion records and the division yearbooks and look it up. See for yourself the disproportionate number of Jews who won medals. And Bronze Stars. And Purple Hearts. The disproportionate number who served in combat, who fought on the beaches and in the rubble, who threw themselves on live hand grenades and carried their wounded buddies a mile on their back to safety. It's all there in black and white—where you'll learn that given the ratio of Jews to gentiles in the armed forces, more than *five times more Jews* gave their lives for their country during World War II.

Look it up, you'll find it there. And you'll also find a saying: that's even more important: there's no race, religion or creed in a foxhole.

Which is also true. The moment we landed on the beachheads and the bullets started flying and the noises got so loud grown men peed in their pants, a strange thing happened. All the "Jew boy" talk stopped. All the prejudice evaporated. Suddenly there were no Jews on the beachhead, no Protestants or Catholics. Just Americans. The guys who had gone out of their way to taunt us were suddenly calling us "buddy" and sharing their last cigarette.

In all the time I spent during World War II fighting in the hedgerows, in the broken towns, among the ruins, I rarely heard a bad word about the Jews. Rarely. It was as if all the hatred and the prejudice and the mean-spiritedness had been refocused onto the enemy, allowing us countrymen at last to be allies. And friends. And sometimes buddies.

It seems to me that we all need someone in this life to love, and someone in this life to hate.

Wouldn't it just be better if we just stopped at the love part?

➡ ➡ ➡

Chapter 10

❧ ❧

INTO BATTLE

A Special Time

Time is forever when someone's trying to kill you.

When you're at war. When the war never stops.

Of course, a lot depends on who's doing the time-keeping. By calendar reckoning, from the hour America invaded Normandy till the day the Germans surrendered it was almost exactly 11 months. But there's another way to calculate time that isn't based on dates or clocks, or even on the past or future. It's measured by a sense of the conditional: by the number of days, hours, minutes and seconds that you *might* continue to live.

This type of time is most evident when you stare at your hands and feet, and wonder if they'll be there when the bombardment is over. Or when you wake up in the morning and ask yourself if you'll live to eat lunch that day. It's difficult to put it into words. We fought among the shattered forests, hanging upside down in ditches, inside abandoned wineries and around the piles of exploded German bodies, hour after hour. Day after day, it finally began to seem as if we'd come out of our mothers' wombs firing M-1's; it began to feel that we'd all just go on killing each other across the hell fields until God Himself shouted "Enough!"

Those of us who were there, who saw the face of battle in France and Germany and Belgium, who survived their way from D-day through the Bulge, knew all about this kind of conditional time. For us, the readings on our wristwatches and calendars were different from everybody else's.

For us the hands of the clock and the dates on the calendar simply said: "perhaps."

The Chosen People

But before I wax too philosophical, let's back up a bit and pick up where we left off in the last chapter.

This brings us again to Harrisburg, Pennsylvania, in the year 1943.

Here we meet our untrained, unprepared, not entirely willing entrepreneur and used automobile salesman from Troy, New York, a 32-year-old refugee from Air Force training shanghaied into the bloody 379th Infantry, 95th Division, tormented there by goose-nosed sergeants and Georgia grunts, then drafted by a power over which he had no control to participate in what was soon to become the goriest and most prolonged battle ever fought by an American military force on foreign soil.

Mercifully, none of us knew about the carnage that lay ahead. We simply waited, content to be diverted by rumors. Scuttlebutt had it that we were not headed for Europe at all but for the Far East. There were several variations on this theme.

> *Rumor one*: We were being shipped to the South Pacific to help MacArthur take back the Philippines.
> *Rumor two*: We were being parachuted into the mountains of Indochina on a top-secret mission.

Rumor three: We were being trained to take part in the full-scale invasion of the Japanese mainland.

Rumor four: We were going to Chicago.

All these rumors except, perhaps, the last one caused me concern. From the day I'd been yanked out of the Air Force and dropped here in Harrisburg I'd had no real training in infantry tactics or in ground warfare, and I was basically unprepared for combat.

When I mentioned this matter to my officers they assured me I needn't worry, that they'd teach me all I needed to know right here. They'd also give my friend, Bernie Rosenberg, the same attention. "That's a promise, soldier!" the sergeant bellowed.

They were as good as their word. Both Bernie and I were given in-depth courses in such essential fighting skills as pot- scouring, cleaning privies, picking up other men's garbage, and standing guard duty at 4 in the morning while the rest of the barracks went home on leave.

In fact, we learned just about everything there is to know about Army routine *except* how to protect ourselves from enemy bullets. They never got around to this part of the syllabus, at least not to any extent.

All of which gave Bernie, me, and all the other Jewish soldiers in our division a painful new perspective on why Jews are referred to as "The Chosen People."

Loose Talk

Then one day in May 1944 our unit was assembled on the parade grounds. We were told to put our personal affairs in order. Write a will, they ordered, file your life insurance papers, make out dependency forms, tie up the loose ends, say good-bye.

You're going to war.

A brief explanation was given of where we were head-ed and what we'd be doing, something about northern France, and a beachhead, and German bunkers.

This was followed by lectures on the importance of secrecy. The enemy has eyes everywhere, they told us; he hears everything Your best friend, your sweetheart, even your moth-er may be a spy. Be careful. Keep mum.

This wasn't just wartime paranoia either. There were plenty of German informers around in these days, and were lis-tening in the most unlikely places; in the next seat next to you on the bus, say, or in the neighborhood sweet shop. It was amazing how quickly a few innocent words from a soldier or sailor about a new weapon or a troop movement would find their way to the enemy. "Loose lips sink ships," the war poster on the fence said, showing a torpedoed American cruiser sink-ing in a ring of blood. And it was right.

Goodbye to All That

I telephoned Dot and broke the news of my leaving—the news that every wife of every young American serviceman knew was coming.

She took it with quiet courage, as did so many other wives. We made arrangements for her to come down to Harrisburg on the coming weekend to say goodbye.

That Saturday night the moon was full and Dot's hand was locked in mine as we strolled along the Harrisburg streets window shopping and flirting and trying to keep the mood untragic. Inside I couldn't stop from looking at her and think-ing: "This may be the last time. . . ."

Later that evening we went to a dance sponsored by the USO.

The dance floor was on a pier over a river. The irony of the fact that we had first embraced on a pier not so many years ago after our scrape with the canoe was not lost to either of us.

We danced.

I smelled the freshness of her hair, savored the light grip of her hand as we moved across the floor. We laughed and touched and stopped occasionally to gaze at one another. Many of the other soldiers were with their wives and girlfriends too that night, and a mood of poignant, even desperate romance filled the air. I tried my best to enjoy the moment and not dwell on my departure.

This was easier said than done, however, especially when the orchestra broke into several bars of "There's No Place Like Home," and then a chaplain, quite uninvited, stood up and delivered an interminable speech chock-full of such lines as "We bid you God's speed, all good luck at the front, and a fond last farewell," and "When you get to Germany and do fierce battle there give Hitler the holy hell he deserves."

When this last line was intoned I could feel Dot's body stiffen. She turned, looked at me, buried her head in my chest. What was there to say?

We walked slowly back to the hotel trying to prolong each moment, to grab time, stretch it out, pin it to the wall. We had been together seven blissful years and we wanted more. We deserved more. Now suddenly, like a thief in the night, here was life, fate, whatever you want to call it, conspiring to steal it away from us.

Most of all we wanted children. Were we going to be deprived of that privilege too?

Perhaps.

Would I ever see her again?

Perhaps not.

If I did return, would I still be in one piece? Would I

have my eyes? My hands? Would I be able to walk? To speak?

No one could make any promises. We'd all seen the soldiers recently returned in wheelchairs, in iron braces, in permanent hospital beds.

I began to rationalize, to philosophize. Perhaps the Good Lord knew that we'd be better off if we didn't have children right now, I said. Perhaps it was not the right time. Later on, no doubt, when I was home and the timing was better—probably then.

But Dot wasn't buying it. "Without you I would have nothing of us," she said quietly, and held her face in her hands, and sobbed.

Neither of us slept that night.

I blamed myself for dragging her down here, and exposing her to all this. We clung to each other as the hours passed, and as we lay there in the dark hotel room I thought about the countless men and women down through the ages who had clung to each other on the eve of battle. In some mystical way I felt connected to them.

We talked, embraced, made love, were silent together. Then we prayed. I don't remember the words. I only recall crying out, "Please, please, Lord, please—don't let it end here!"

The next day Dot was gone and I was back in camp. For the first time since I'd been in the military the war now seemed real.

Preparing to Go Overseas

Back at camp preparations were going on in earnest, and it was difficult not to get caught up in the excitement.

Though we knew that these activities might bring us to our deaths, there was something exhilarating about it all, something rousing. A proverb I'd heard once went through my head: an adventure, it said, is a hardship rightly considered.

I think it was during this period that I also learned how impossible it is to think of two things at the same time.

That is to say, part of me wanted to hang on to every memory of my weekend with Dot and stew over my fate. Another part was kept too busy to think about it. Thank God for the one-track human brain.

After several days of packing up, our division was transferred to Camp Miles Standish in Massachusetts close to Boston Harbor. From here we were to sail overseas.

Predictably, there were delays, and we ended up getting an extra week of leave. Glorious!

I phoned Dot and told her to meet me at Palmer House in Boston. I filled our hotel room with flowers, candy and fruit, and when she arrived we hunkered down, not leaving the room for two straight days. We even had our meals sent up. After our painful farewell in Harrisburg this tete-a-tete felt like a reprieve, and we both squeezed every drop from it that we could.

Then another goodbye.

Back at camp they told us we'd be crossing the ocean on two transports. Half the division would be on the *USS Mariposa*, the other on the *USS West Point*. The ships would sail two days apart with a naval escort, and would disembark at Liverpool.

We were leaving tomorrow.

The Crossing

Of all the people I met during my years at war none is more memorable to me than Paul Steinfeld.

Like myself, like Bernie Rosenberg, and like all the

other soldiers with "H" stamped on their dog tags, "Steiny" had been singled out in boot camp, and given every slop detail his K Company sergeants could dream up.

But this didn't deter Steiny. In fact, I think it inspired him.

A small, ordinary-looking guy, you wouldn't notice him at a cocktail party, and you certainly would never pick him out as someone special. He was just a nice little man who didn't mind trouble, and sometimes got himself into amusing scrapes. We found it especially funny when he volunteered for mess duty the first day on the transport ship.

Volunteered? He hadn't have enough KP in boot camp?

But as it turned out, there was method in Steiny's madness.

Any soldier signing up for kitchen patrol, it had been announced, would be assigned a deckside stateroom complete with private showers, soft bed, and ocean view. Luxury appealed to Steiny, so he volunteered.

Trouble was, he hadn't counted on one thing—soldiers on a transport ship, bored to madness, have nothing to do but eat.

And eat we did. From dawn till dusk. Any time you looked into the mess you'd see a long line of guys cued up, piling their plates with every morsel in sight, taking a second helping, a third, a fourth. Some guys literally ate all day.

Now this was well and good for the soldiers. But for Steiny and his grandiose plans it meant he had to labor below in the mess from morning till night, ladling out the soup and cleaning pots and pans. There were no breaks in the schedule, because the eaters on board kept eating round the clock. In the end Steiny didn't have much fun in his stateroom. As a matter of fact, he never saw it by the light of day.

"I thought I was pretty clever volunteering for KP," he told me at the end of the trip. "But would you believe it, Marty—every time I got back to my room it was dark outside and I was so bushed I didn't care. I'd just plop down and fall asleep, then wake up in time for the next shift. The whole trip over I never laid eyes on the ocean!"

Steiny wasn't the only one with stateroom dreams. A certain General and his staff had made the crossing with us, and because he was heavy brass he'd been given the most luxurious room on the ship.

The day we landed in England, Bernie Rosenberg and I happened to be standing on the top deck. We observed the General and his entourage vacating ship, and leaving the door to their quarters wide open.

We looked at each other. Neither of us had taken a shower in a week. It was fate.

Five minutes later Bernie and I were in the General's private bathroom lathering up in the shower and singing at the top of our lungs.

We were so immersed in the luxury of it all that we forget to lock the door of the stateroom.

Then, sure enough, a few minutes later several orderlies entered the cabin looking for the General. The bathroom door was wide open and the orderlies peered in, seeing the two of us standing there buck naked in the shower.

Fortunately, all officers and men had been stripped of insignias during the trip over, so the sight of our insignia-less clothes on the bed didn't tip them off. In fact, to the contrary, the intruders thought we were the brass itself, and they started falling all over themselves begging our pardon and beating a hasty retreat.

We graciously gave them amnesty and waved them out, only to have a second round of arrivals enter moments later and perform the same genuflection. Then a third group came. It got so we began to anticipate the next arrivals. By the time we finished our shower we'd been saluted more times than Eisenhower.

What would they have done if they'd caught us there in

the General's marble bathroom? Two naked Jewish privates
with soap on their scrotums?

Who knows? I hadn't read much on army protocol at
the time, so I didn't know the legal consequences. Ignorance is
bliss. I also had the attitude that if they weren't happy with my
performance they could send me home.

That wouldn't have been so bad either.

But they didn't.

Orgy Time

We disembarked at Liverpool and were immediately
transported to Camp Barton-Stacey a few miles outside of
London. Except for the weather nothing much changed during
the next few weeks—same old drilling, same old military delay
and double-speak. Mostly it was plain boredom.

By now we knew what our assignment was, which
meant we were frightened as well as bored. We knew that we
were going to attack a fortified beachhead in Normandy across
the English Channel; that we'd be transported there in special
landing boats; that if the weather was bad we might all tip over
into the ocean and drown with our heavy gear on; that we'd be
left all alone on the beach to fight it out with the Hun who'd had
several years to dig in, and who was probably expecting the
invasion; and that if the invasion failed we'd lose the war.

It was sobering news. Already you could see hundreds
of empty landing craft pitching and rolling ominously below on
the docks, waiting for us like empty coffins. The only thing we
could do to keep our minds off the coming conflict was to relax
and watch it all go by.

To raise our spirits and keep us from going stir-crazy,
the authorities showered us with passes to London.

Piccadilly was the main attraction. It had all the movies

and dance halls and, of course, the red light districts. If you were looking for love, the nights were the best time. The Square was pitch dark then from the blackouts, and a soldier could find an anonymous partner, professional or amateur alike, in a few minutes just by asking around. Some women supplied their own condoms.

Trouble was, anyone looking for easy romance had to be careful not to step on the coupled bodies that were lying all over the place, even in the middle of the sidewalks, doing just about anything your imagination might conjure up.

Amazing! You don't read much about this episode in the history books, but I saw it with my own eyes. Everyone in that crazy square seemed to be embracing everyone else all at once. It was, I guess, a last desperate fling before the flower of English and American youth went plunging ahead into a do-or-die confrontation with the largest and most ferocious military machine the world had ever seen.

A Word from Old Blood and Guts

My outfit landed on Omaha Beach, Normandy, at D+3.

By now everyone in our battalion had heard stories about the GI's who'd reached the shores in the first wave and stepped out of the boat so loaded with gear that they sank into the ocean and never came up. Most of us were thus traveling light, and some men even threw their knapsacks and extra ammunition overboard before we hit the beach.

All these worries turned out to be unnecessary. The Normandy beachhead was more or less secured, and all casualties had been evacuated. This was both a relief for us, but also a disappointment.

We climbed the cliffs overlooking the Channel, and in a short time joined up with General George Patton's Third Army which was just then being organized into what would become one of the most deadly American fighting units in the European theater. Orders quickly came down from Patton's command: now that the landing zone had been secured, and the bulk of the army brought ashore, our job was to move inland, hunt down the enemy wherever we found him, and show him no quarter.

I saw General Patton several times during my stay in Europe, and the impression he made lingered. He was a tall man with a raw, sunburned face, chiseled features, and narrow eyes that bored out at you with a look of cruelty, intelligence, challenge, and, well, perhaps compassion is too benevolent a word. But there was something in him that seemed to sincerely care about his men.

The first time I saw him was in a forest grove at the edge of the Normandy countryside. He stood on the hood of his jeep talking to us with, sure enough, his fabled ivory-handled pistols strapped to his side.

"I didn't bring you men here to die for your country," he boomed out. "I brought you here to make those other sons-of-bitches die for *theirs!*"

He looked around from face to face, pausing for effect. We were in the middle of a war zone with hundreds of GI's milling around. But you could have heard the proverbial pin drop. He was magnetic.

"And don't stay in those damn foxholes. The longer you lie there the sooner you'll get dead. The enemy will dump mortar shells on you. Keep moving ahead, keep going."

He seemed to grow taller as he spoke.

"We're here to kill these guys," he went on, "and to kill them as fast as we can. Don't mess around! The quicker you kill them, the sooner you go home!"

His voice got louder and more shrill.

"It's your job to keep going no matter what! Until you're captured or killed. If you're wounded, I'll expect you to keep fighting anyway. You don't just give up if you've taken a bullet or two. You keep shooting as long as you're alive and conscious! You keep fighting the enemy until someone comes along and puts you out of your misery!"

He paused for effect.

"That's what I'd do. I expect you all to do the same. Is that understood?"

The whole mesmerized group of us shook our heads in assent.

"Then good luck, men! I know you'll give me your best!"

When the talk was over and the general had zoomed away in his jeep we understood clearly why they'd nicknamed him "Old Blood and Guts."

Trouble was, as one of my buddies remarked, it may have been his guts, but it was our blood!

War and Remembrance

In the next few pages I hope you will pardon my lack of orderly sequence and syntax. Sometimes the best way to tell a story is to let the memories flow on their own, as if taking notes. Because as anyone who has been on a battleground can tell you, combat happens in fits and starts, in disjointed flashes, not in a nice little story with a beginning, middle and end.

Years after the war, I was once watching a television documentary with several young people. The documentary was a real "go-get-em Marines!" kind of thing, trumped up with thrilling military music. In the middle of the film one of the youngsters turned to me and said, "Wow, war must really be exciting!"

"It is to some extent," I replied. "But always remember this, son. The music isn't playing when the battle's going on."

So at any rate, here it is, a scrapbook of fragments and

notes remembered from the bloody war to free Europe, and rec-
ollected 50 years later in the relative safety of my New York
City office chair.

Hedgerows—The hedgerow, an encyclopedia tells me,
is "an ancient and picturesque farm wall largely indigenous to
the northern French countryside and especially to Normandy."

I don't know my geography all that well, but as far as
I'm concerned Normandy is nowhere, and they can keep their
picturesque farm walls. They caused us nothing but heartbreak.

Built of shrubbery and packed earth, French hedgerows
run for miles across open fields and countryside. Crisscrossing
in random patterns, these ancient walls form mounds five and
six feet high, and in some places they angle out into a maze of
bulwarks that resemble formally constructed military battle-
ments. If I hadn't been assured these walls were hundreds,
perhaps thousands of years old, I'd think the Germans had
built them themselves, so impregnable are they to any but the
heaviest gunfire, and so perfect for concealing a defending
army.

Facing these formidable fire lines, our job is to move
from one hedgerow to the next, find the enemy, flush him out,
obliterate him.

Straight ahead—The only direction you know when
you're attacking hedgerows is *forward*. No such thing as back
or turn around. You move ahead if they're shooting at you, and
you move ahead if you're shooting at them. Just ahead. Each
day we measure our success in hedgerows rather than miles.
"We took three hedgerows today," is a familiar phrase.

Even when we think we've cleaned out the enemy from
behind one of these accursed mounds, there's always some zealous straggler popping up, shooting at us, sometimes killing us.
When we work the hedgerows I make sure to carry a good stash
of hand grenades. Lob one in, and hope it will finish off the

wise guys. It becomes a standing joke in our outfit that Silverman is never without a pack full of grenades.

Death everywhere—A day never goes by in the hedgerows without seeing dead bodies.

Dead American soldiers. Dead German soldiers. Dead roosters and sheep. Dead farmers. Dead children. Dead school teachers, bicycle riders, mailmen, pretty young girls blown to bits by land mines or bombs. It gets so you can't imagine a day without seeing a corpse.

I start to count the hours in each day. That's a bad thing to do. I keep wondering when it will end, and where, and if I'll ever be able to resume a normal life when it's all over. Day after day you see your friends shot up, killed, dismembered. You know your chances of returning home are small. Minuscule, perhaps. But what choice do you have?

None. Just keep moving ahead.

Reserve units—Men are killed and the replacements arrive.

Most of them are 18- and 19-year-old high school kids anxious to prove how brave they are. They're here, they tell us, to "get at the enemy."

It takes a week or two of combat to make them understand that we're all afraid, all the time, everywhere. It's okay to be scared out of your mind, they learn. Everyone is.

Since I'm the oldest and most experienced man in the outfit, and since most of the guys I came over here with, including the redneck sergeants and Georgia crackers who tormented me in training, have been killed or wounded, it becomes my job to teach these greenhorns how to stay alive.

I do the best I can.

I show them how to move along a trench, how to recognize the right target before firing, how to walk across a field and not attract attention, how to tell the sound of different shells coming in and know which ones to worry about. Most of all, I show them how to attach themselves to an experienced vet and learn from him. After a while they start calling me "Pop Silverman." I'm the old man of the outfit at 32.

Where do all these kids keep coming from? I ask myself. Just coming and coming—an endless supply of bright, smart faces. I'm a young man, but I feel old now. The kids make me feel old.

I remember one replacement in particular. He arrives from New York in late December telling everyone how the day before shipping out he'd eaten a big Christmas dinner at Lindy's Restaurant in New York City. He died a few weeks later, and I never knew his name. That's all I remember about him—his big Christmas dinner at Lindy's.

Survival—So much of survival is pure ass luck. Sometimes you think that no matter what you do you're still going to get hit.

Sometimes you get superstitious, but that doesn't help. You see guys going through crazy compulsive routines each day for "luck," putting on one shoe, standing up, putting on another, standing up, that kind of thing, then later that afternoon getting blown to bits. Didn't work. If you want to keep breathing it's a better idea to just stay on your toes and think of ways to outwit the enemy.

While you're under fire never take *anything* for granted. Always look both ways, right and left. Avoid bravado. Learn how the enemy thinks. Don't take unnecessary chances. Stay calm. Take care of what's in front of you, and don't worry about the rest.

But all this helps only a little, because like I said, it's mostly luck.

Underestimating Jerry—I'm walking along a railroad track. Shells are falling at half- minute intervals directly in front of me. You can set your watch by their arrival.

So I deflect 50 yards to the left and think, "Stupid Jerry, always so orderly and predictable, even when he's firing artillery. His lack of imagination is going to lose him this war."

Then a big shell zigzags out of nowhere, and explodes with a mocking laugh a few feet away from me. I hit the ground just in time to save myself.

Moral of this story:

    1. In war, don't get cocky or think you're smart.
    2. Move quick.
    3. Never underestimate a German soldier.

R&R — We're in continuous contact with the enemy for 105 days.

That's almost four straight months without a break. (To this day when I hear the words of the song "Those were the days, my friend, we thought they'd never end," a shiver runs down my spine.)

During this time we never change our clothes. Once we live on cold K-rations for four straight days. No fires allowed; the enemy will see them.

Imagine then my happiness when they bring a laundry unit up to the front line one morning and we get to take a shower.

I've already told you in the first chapter how the army creates instant cleaning facilities by joining several large trucks together to form one extended shower installation. And how you walk from one trailer to the next soaping up, removing what we called the "top soil," checking to make sure all your body parts are still there, and being overjoyed that they are (we haven't been able to take a look for weeks), scrubbing down and working the lather into every nook and cranny in your body, a joyful moment, then continuing on to the drying room where they have two honest-to-goodness terrycloth towels waiting for you, and you wonder if heaven itself could be as fair.

Imagine also the distaste you feel when, dressed in your warm, clean clothes and a fresh pair of socks, you have to put your stinking army jacket and greasy ammo belt over them, say good bye to the laundry trucks, and trudge back to the war!

I guess if any of us ever thought of deserting it was then.

Regimental reserves—During battle, three units are kept fighting on the lines and a fourth is always held behind in reserve.

Usually this reserve unit is the one that's taken the most casualties.

They pull it back to give the men R&R, and slowly build it up with replacements. When they've repopulated the unit they move it to the front lines and bring another back.

They keep up this rotation until we're all killed, or the objective is secured.

Mail call—Whenever they bring the laundry unit up to the front lines they usually tote a sack of letters with it. One of these mail calls brings a welcome letter from Dot.

I open it, read the first few lines, and almost fall into a swoon.

I reread. Is it possible?

Yep. Same words, same golden words as before: *I'm going to have a baby.* My eyes fill with tears. Many years later when the war is a distant memory and our children are almost grown I tell Dot that of all the experiences I've had in my long, rich life the one that made me the most joyful was reading that letter.

Suddenly all that matters is to be alone.

I walk to the edge of a nearby woods clutching the letter to my chest and looking up at the sky. All I can say over and over again is, "Thank you, God!"

But somehow that doesn't seem enough.

Now praying on one's knees is not a Jewish custom.

Perhaps it's became we wear yarmulkas on our heads as a sign of respect and fear of God. I don't know. At any rate, I'd never prayed in this position in all my life; and yet today, why I don't know, the urge is overwhelming and I fall to the ground in prayer

A few minutes later I return to the unit, having decided not to share this news with anyone. Our unit begins to move out.

And suddenly I didn't want to move out. I wanted to stay right here where it's safe and quiet, and read the letter a thousand times. Then I wanted to turn around and sprint for all I'm worth back to New York City; back to our unborn son or daughter; back to my wife and my parents and to all the people I love. Suddenly, with every vein and fiber in my substance I want only to live.

What does this mean now? That I have to be careful from now on, have to be smart, have to stay out of the way of a bullet, have to stay alive. . . .

Wounded—On December 6, 1944, a piece of shrapnel from an artillery blast catches me.

The medics haul me off to the battalion aid station where the surgeon in charge assures me it's nothing serious, and that—what fantastic luck!—I'll be back in the lines with my unit in four or five days.

He seems so delighted when he gives me the news, so happy over my "good fortune," as if all this time I've been foaming at the mouth to return to the battle lines so I can be killed and never see my newborn child. I begin to wonder if I'm living in an insane asylum.

They give me a Purple Heart.

Shot in the head—A few weeks later I'm hit by a sniper's bullet square in the head.

The force of it knocks me to the ground. I lay there in

a pool of blood thinking I have a bullet upstairs somewhere in my cerebellum, and amazed to find myself still alive, not to mention awake.

After a few minutes I start thinking that since I'm still thinking I must still exist too—I think, therefore I am, right?— and that I'd better get myself up-and-at-em before the sniper takes another pop at me.

Question is, where is he?

I look around the area. Finally I spy a large haystack about 200 feet away.

Struggling to my feet with blood trickling down, I find shelter and hail an armored vehicle that just happens to drive by. I tell him what happened, and we decide to investigate. On the way over I pick up six incendiary grenades.

At the suspected danger site the driver wheels his vehicle around the haystack in wide circles and I start to toss my grenades into it one at a time. Then we pull back and watch the thing burn to the ground.

As I'm looking at this terrible sight a strange sensation starts to come over me, like there's something important I've forgotten and I should be thinking about it. Then I remember what it is: I've been shot in the head! I should be dead, or at least stretched out on the ground somewhere. Up till now I've been operating on pure adrenalin. Suddenly I don't feel so good.

Back at the aid station I learn what really happened. A bullet has passed between my steel helmet and the plastic liner, skated across the top of my scalp, run straight down my back and grazed my butt. After examining the wounds they assure me there's no real damage, and that barring infection, O lucky man, I'll be back with my unit very soon.

They also point out that the trajectory the sniper's bullet has taken is by scientific standards an impossibility, and that my being here at all, alive and more or less in one piece, is one of nature's stranger mistakes.

Once again, I figure, the Man Upstairs has been looking after me. Even in the middle of the flames.

The hospital ward—I'm in the hospital this time for a week.

As I lie there I watch the casualties being brought in. This sight, so indescribable, causes a constant swing to take place inside me between gratitude and despair. For a few moments, surrounded by screaming half-torsos and the remains of men, I ask myself: wouldn't I be better off dying right now and getting away from this horror.

Then I remember Dot and the child. The will to live is strong. I try to put these thoughts out of my mind and concentrate on staying alive.

They gave me my second Purple Heart.

Steiny again—Remember Steiny? The guy on the transport ship doing KP?

Well, after a few months of combat he had become transformed in everyone's mind from a harmless, likeable character to a mighty hero.

I could fill this book up with stories about him. One will have to do.

It was the beginning of 1945. Fighting like a gladiator one minute and a chess player the next, Steiny managed to outlive everyone in his unit and was promoted to sergeant (the last surviving man in any unit automatically becomes sergeant by default—which is one reason why it's so easy to get a promotion in time of war).

This meant, of course, that all the new recruits were his responsibility.

One day Steiny and his squad were holding up in an abandoned farmhouse waiting for orders when a huge German tank comes rolling by. Steiny's men know enough to stay down and let the damn thing pass.

All, that is, except one greenhorn who for reasons known only to himself, opens up on the tank with his M-1, which is, of course, like trying to kill a rhinoceroses with a spit ball.

The bullets ping harmlessly off the side of the vehicle and it grinds to a stop.

Everything goes strangely quiet. For a moment you can almost sense the drivers inside the tank looking around, trying to figure out where the shots came from.

Then the obvious dawns.

They turn their big rattling machine around, drive it up to the farmhouse as close as they can get, revolve the fearsome gun on its turret, and start blasting away.

A heated and largely one-sided fire fight ensues, and several of Steiny's men are quickly killed.

Knowing that it's only a matter of time before everyone in the farmhouse is roasted, Steiny orders his men to keep firing, then sneaks out the back of the house and begins to crawl towards the side of the tank. Having been close to German armor before, he knows that the drivers inside this thing can only see out a few narrow slits in front, and that visibility from the sides and the back is almost nil.

Steiny crawls along for several minutes until he gets so close to the tank that he can't miss. Then he stands up in full view, loads, and fires his bazooka point blank. The tank explodes in a blaze of incendiary light. The flash is so intense that Steiny instantly goes blind.

Maneuvering on instinct alone, he crawls into a nearby ditch and lays there until one of his men gets help. The medics take him back to the aid station and from here he is shipped to a hospital England. Eventually his sight returns, and he is awarded the Bronze Star. But for Steiny, this will be just one decoration of many.

You never know who the heroes are going to be. I'm still friends with the man today.

The bazooka—The type of bazooka we carried and that Steiny used so well to his advantage was an amazing weapon. It looked more like a stovepipe than a death machine and was amazingly light considering its length and firepower.

When you leveled one of these things against a tank—it was about the only piece of small armor that could destroy these huge crawlers—the shell would drill a hole in the vehicle's side and stay intact. Only after it was inside would it explode.

This is ho-hum pyrotechnics today, perhaps, in our era of computer-guided missiles. But in its time it was a fearfully effective technology, and one that the Germans came to loathe. As far as they were concerned, the little guy, the foot soldier, wasn't supposed to have so much fire power against their major weapons. The bazooka was one of the weapons that helped us win the war.

Metz—After several months of war in the hedgerows we moved deeper into France where the battle terrain shifts from country to town.

Now we're fighting from city street to city street, building to building, using flame throwers, grenades, close-in fire weapons. Snipers are posted against us everywhere. There's hand-to-hand combat, fierce one-on-one struggles that are settled with pistols and sometimes knives. The streets in the French towns are narrow, and this is a good thing because now the Germans can't get their tanks in.

The first city we invade is Metz, which has never fallen to an enemy in all recorded history. They call it the "Bastion City."

The Germans have surrounded this quaint place with a network of bunkers and pillboxes. Most of them are constructed in an ingenious cocoon shape that causes our artillery shells to bounce off them like rubber bullets. By the time the softening-up bombardment finishes and we arrive, the only things that have been knocked down are the stores and homes of the poor

French inhabitants who stand by watching as their beloved city is blown apart stone by stone.

Yet in the end the German bunkers are vulnerable. We pull our tanks up as close as we can get to them, fire a shell, knock off a few pieces of the cement, and pull back before the Germans return the insult. Then another tank pulls up and fires a few more rounds.

We do this over and over again, all day long, losing tank after tank but slowly chipping away at the cement fortification. Finally holes appear in the sides. Roofs collapse. The outside perimeter begins to fall. Some of the Germans surrender; most, however, move back to the inner city where the fighting now becomes intense.

All along the boulevard fire and smoke are pouring out of storefronts, men are running and shooting from house to house, grenades are going off, pieces of buildings are being ripped off by explosions and gunfire, sometimes crushing unwary soldiers below. Back alleyways are choked with bodies from firefights. Blood is spattered on the walls of cafes and tailor shops. Bullets zing and whiz and crisscross overhead till it seems to us that there's a German sniper at every window. The noise is deafening; then for a moment it stops and a strange silence falls over the street. But only for a minute. Another explosion breaks and the furor returns.

Distant music —It's the dead of night. A German shell has landed in the middle of a city square in Metz, blowing up our radio lines and turning the wires into spaghetti.

Radio communication is, of course, critical during any battle, and the only way to get it back is to resplice the wires. A group of us volunteer for the job. I'm in command.

A dozen men move cautiously and silently into the square, creeping towards the damaged wires. Though everything is dark and still, we're in a part of the city notorious for snipers and firefights. The moon is full and it's throwing a bright orange light over the street. Perfect light for sharpshooters.

The men form a circle around me and I go down spread-eagle on my belly and start to splice the wires.

It's late fall. The ground is already icy and feels like the surface of a frozen lake underneath me. The only light is moonlight; a flashlight would be too risky.

While I'm working away the men are aiming their weapons at the rooftops and the windows circling us. Every dark hole, every doorway, shadow, every side alley is a potential sniper zone.

Am I splicing the damn thing properly? I ask myself. Will it work when I'm finished? Is some German aiming his gun at my head right this minute through one of his goddamned little peep holes? What's that light over there? Who made that sound? I'm cold. I hate France. Are these guys watching or falling asleep? Why'd the bomb have to fall here? Hell, I want to go home!

In the middle of all this, with me spread-eagled in the middle of the street and this group of frightened, shivering GI's in a circle around me, a faint wisp of music starts to come floating towards us from a distant radio. I strain to listen while I crawl around on the ground. It distracts me in a pleasant way. There's something familiar about the tune.

I strain some more. All of a sudden it's as if I *have* to understand the words of this song—as if understanding them will keep me safe in the middle of this madness, and get me home, and make life okay again.

Then all of a sudden someone turns the volume up on the radio, and the words of the song pour out at us:

> Clang, clang, clang went the trolley,
> Ding, ding, ding went the bell. . . .

It's Judy Garland. With her Hollywood soundtrack orchestra. Serenading me here on my belly in the middle of World War II.

I laugh to myself and continue splicing now with a light heart, unafraid. Somehow at this moment I know everything is going to be okay, and that I'll make it home again safe and sound.

I don't know how I know. I just do.

After this I'm never quite as scared again.

Long barrel and short—Every time you turn the corner of a building on the streets of Metz a German seems to be waiting there for you on the other side.

To make matters worse, our M-1 rifles have long barrels. This means when you're sneaking round a corner you can't hold it in front of you where you need it most; if there's an enemy on the other side he'll see the end of the muzzle coming and be ready to pop you. I always hated the M-1.

One day a few miles outside of Metz I come upon an M.P. lying on the ground wounded in the leg and waiting to be evacuated.

I ask him if he needs anything, and soon we get to talking. While we're chatting I notice a Thompson submachine gun lying at his side. Now the Thompson has a very short barrel, shoots a lot of 45 rounds in a short time, and is the perfect weapon for negotiating city corners. On a lark I ask him if he's willing to swap his machine gun for my M-1.

"You can keep them both" he answers with a grin. "I'm not going to need either of them for a while."

It didn't take more prompting than that. Thanking this amiable M.P., I left him my cartridge belt and M-1, and strapped the machine gun over my shoulder.

I could turn corners now without telegraphing my arrival to the enemy. Several times I was sure it saved my life.

I sometimes think back on how this chance meeting

with a wounded M.P. in the middle of nowhere saved my life. In war, the smallest incident, the briefest conversation, the most casual hesitation or sudden impulse can be critical to survival.

As an officer, you tell your troops to stay put, then you advance 100 yards on your own and finally return to get them — and thus miss the shell that lands exactly where you'd be standing if you hadn't come back for your men. It happened to me once.

Or, say you're walking to a communication trench. You meet an officer on the way and stay behind an extra half-minute to pay your respects. Another man takes your place. He walks the route you would have walked, and — *Crash!* — a shell lands on him and he is no more. This happened also.

Or again, your commander orders you to move to the right of a tree, or to the left; and this seemingly random order decides whether you go home on a transport ship or in a box. At one time I was the officer who had to make these decision.

Napoleon once remarked that "As a general, I beat the Austrians in battle simply because they did not know the importance of five minutes."

In war, little things count.

The Iron Men of Metz — As I told you, Metz had never been taken.

Not until the 95th American Army Division got here. The fighting was murderous and it seemed to go on forever. But gradually, slowly, our planning, firepower and plain guts began to tell. After weeks of ferocious combat the "Bastion City" fell.

This victory was a crucial one for the European theater of operations; the military command appreciated it so much they gave our division two honorary titles.

The first was "The Iron Men of Metz."

The second was decided by Patton himself. He visited the battle area and noticed that our division patch was a 9V. He declared that the V stood for Victory, and that the ninth would herewith be known as the: "The Victory Division."

It was hard not to be proud.

Giving up the command—When you're an officer in the army and you're in combat, you get accustomed to being obeyed. After a while you simply assume that you're giving the orders and others are following them.

Thus, when the war was over and I returned home, I still have something of the officer in my blood. I'd given orders so long by now it had become a kind of conditioned reflex.

Trouble is, here at home holding my first-born in my arms, my beautiful three-year-old baby daughter—hearth, safety, bliss—I hasn't dawned on me yet that my beautiful daughter is also used to being obeyed.

One day after I'd been back in the States about a month Dot and I decided to take our daughter for a weekend trip to a resort in the Catskills. In these days the mountain highways were pretty rough going, and it might take ten or 12 hours just to travel a few hundred miles. Stopping along the way at a rest stop was always mandatory.

We'd been traveling some hours and my daughter, who'd been very good through most of the trip, piped up from the back that she wanted some milk.

I pulled into the first wayside restaurant we came to, a big place called The Apple. Dot and my daughter sat down on a bench outside while I went into the restaurant. A few minutes later I returned with a carton of milk.

"I don't want it anymore!" my daughter hollered, and pushed it away.

I handed it to her again. "Take it!"

Same response.

"Drink!" I insisted, expecting to be obeyed. After all, if I can order 180 men around in life-or-death situations it's not unreasonable to expect to be listened to by a three-year-old.

Is it?

"No!" she screamed back, and set her jaw in a scowl.

A battle of wills now began, with me pressing the container of milk on her and she shaking her head and trying to knock it out of my hands.

Back and forth, with Dot looking on helplessly: yes, no, yes, no. The child had made up her mind and nothing on earth was going to change it. I was getting more and more angry—not just the anger of a frustrated father, but the pent-up frustration of years; frustration at being plucked out of the prime of my life and made to spend several seasons in hell; at seeing my friends and colleagues die all around me every day for no reason I could understand; frustration at the uncanny cruelty of the human species.

All this was inside as I sat there on the bench in the peaceful Catskills glowering at my baby daughter. This, plus the feeling that though I'm in command, the whole thing is *insubordination!*

I stood up, uncertain what to do with this little monster.

Suddenly I felt a tap on my shoulder.

I turned around and a little old Jewish man was standing there. Apparently he'd been watching the whole scene.

"I have to leave now, sonny" he said. "But before I go I want to say one thing to you: so what will it be if she *doesn't* drink the milk?"

He shrugged, turned, and walked away.

Somehow it was the right thing at the right time.

My wife cracked up and I did too. Suddenly I realized how ridiculous I was being. The anger and fear and frustration suddenly departed, like a lot of bad air expelled.

I picked up the milk container and tucked it into Dot's purse. "You can drink it later, Sweetie," I told Carol, and we laughed again.

After this incident I had no more problems readjusting to civilian life—or family life—again.

And the phrase "What will it be if she doesn't drink the milk?" has become a family joke. When something goes wrong, when we don't get what we want, we say, "So what will be if we can't make this deal?"

And then we do something else. Thanks to the little old man.

In life, as in war, you never know where your help and your protection is coming from next.

➤ ➤ ➤

These 17 serious young men had survived the rigorous testing by Albany
Law School's professors and had qualified for their Bachelor of Laws
degree (LL.B.) in the Spring of 1936. They had entered in the Fall of 1933,
the worst year of the Great Depression as part of a much larger class.
Academic attrition is traditional in law schools, but dire economic circumstances created additional problems for the Class of 1936. Among those
who struggled successfully was Marty Silverman
(center in the seated row).

For optimistic ("No problem!") Marty, the gratification of receiving the all-
important professional certification obviously overrode the discouraging
picture nationwide. He had just marked his 25th birthday.

Very significant in the borderline acceptance of Marty's credentials for Law School admission was a decision by the Dean, Harold D. Alexander. Greatly impressed by the young man's earnest appeal, he settled the issue affirmatively. Marty never forgot the Dean's confidence and the challenge offered. Many years later, he made possible the creation of this important addition to the academic program—the moot courtroom which he stipulated be named in the Dean's honor.

Part of the Dean's challenge to Marty was to find the means to pay the Law School's fees. Inspirationally, Marty determined that this site—just off the western side of the busy Menands bridge over the Hudson—would be ideal for a profitable service station. He persuaded the Socony-Vacuum Corporation to help him establish the station. Throughout his Law School career, he worked long hours developing a successful business while carrying out the demanding hours of studies.
He prevailed on both counts.

Marty's mother and father, Charles and Fanny Silverman.

Marty and Dot in
"The Canoe."

Marty and Dot
on their wedding day.

Dot and brother-in-law Mel Rosen
in the office of Marty's first leasing company.

Marty and his family (from left to right)
Dot, daughters Carol and Joan, son Lorin, and Marty.

May 30, 1980

To our children:

Remember, if you ever need a helping hand, you'll find one at the end of your arm. As you grow older you will discover that you have two hands. One for helping yourself, the other for helping others. While I was growing up I took as many hands as I gave. I still do. Your "good old days" are still ahead of you, may you have many of them.

We leave you a tradition with a future. The tender loving care of human beings will never become obsolete. People even more than things, have to be restored, renewed, revived, reclaimed and redeemed and redeemed and redeemed. . . . Never throw out any body.

At our age we don't know how many of your mazeltovs we'll be physically present at - Bar Mitzvah, Weddings, Graduations etc. etc. But we shall sincerely be there. Because our love for you all will be constant and forever.

A loving note from Marty and Dot to their children.
It captures the essence of their outlook on life.

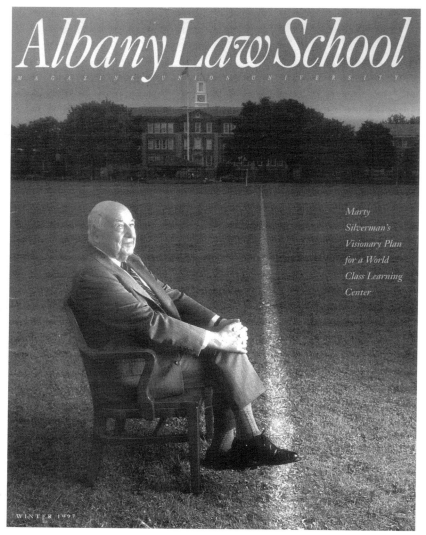

Two generations have passed since Marty Silverman's years as a student of the law, but his alma mater—a prominent beneficiary of his philanthropies—will never forget the gratitude he has earned in return for his dedication to the Law School and in enhancing its ability better to serve its oncoming generations of students. Pictured here is the cover of the school's magazine as the 21st Century opened.

In 1993, the Federal Government awarded Marty
the Livingston Medal for services rendered on behalf
of one of their intelligence agencies.
It is inscribed "To Marty Silverman,
In recognition of your outstanding service and support."

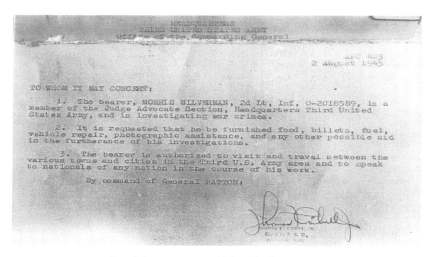

An old army pass of Marty's from 1945,
by command of General Patton!

Successful entrepreneur and visionary philanthropist though he is, Marty's approachable and personable style in pursing his farflung interests meshes well with his easy informality. Here in his midtown Manhattan office, the camera also catches his view of East Side office buildings (foreground) before they give way to a backdrop of the Hudson River and the world beyond.

As the saying goes, you can tell much about a person by the company he keeps. Here, Marty joins Governor George E. Pataki and President George W. Bush on what clearly was a happy occasion.

In October of 2002, Marty was a featured speaker at the commemoration and rededication of the New York State Military Museum and Veterans Research Center. Those hearing his message included (at his right) Governor Pataki and United States Representative John Sweeney.

150 East 58th Street, 29th Fl., New York, New York 10155
212-832-9170

May 21, 2003

Dr. Shirley Ann Jackson, President
Rensselaer Polytechnic Institute (R.P.I.)
110 8th Street
Troy, New York 12180-3590

My Dear Dr. Jackson:

It was a day to remember and one which I shall never forget!

It all started by finding a beautiful basket of goodies in my room at the hotel. I could not wait to tear the cellophane wrapper off the book and, although I could not read the type, I enjoyed the illustrations. Then, I unfolded the blanket which will comfort me on my trips back and forth to Albany. I usually take a pillow with me and stretch out on the back seat and I now have a blanket, too – thank you so much.

The dinner was exciting and delicious; unfortunately, I was too excited because I wound up with a "funny" tummy. I was determined not to let this spoil my evening nor for those around me. You were most considerate and kindly ignored my discomfort. In addition, when it came to the Colloquy, you let the academic honorees carry the ball and each of them did beautiful job. I indicated that I was not in their league and in no way did it distract me from listening to what they were saying. When you view the videotape you see that I was intently interested in what they said. Of course, I was most impressed by Dr. Robert Solo, especially when he said ... "if they need more nurses, let them pay more money!" - no wonder he won the Nobel Prize in economics! As your honorees were speaking, I couldn't help but recall a postcard of Albany Law School's building after my graduation which had an inscription on it. On that postcard there is a series of steppingstones leading into the building. As you continued to address the audience, I had the feeling that you were successfully converting obstacles into steppingstones.

As the day progressed and continued into the next, I was amazed at how you handled each and every situation and considered your guests, your students, and their guests. You were in complete control and I marveled at you.

Just when I thought things could not get better, they kept getting better and better. Let me tell you about Saturday. We were blessed with a beautiful day and, as a the Mullah recited the benediction, I didn't understand his words but had no problem converting them to mine – we

Marty's letter to
Dr. Shirley Jackson, President of Rensselaer Polytechnic Institute
after being honored at RPI's 2003 Commencement.

Dr. Shirley Ann Jackson
May 21, 2003
Page Two

were speaking a universal language. When he finished I turned to Professor Eddie Knowles, who was sitting next to me, and jokingly suggested that all we needed now was a flyover. Would you believe three minutes later you announced there would be a flyover? Unbelievable! It had a strange effect on me. The first time the airplane flew over the noise and vibrations excited me, but when the pilot turned and flew back, I looked down at my red robes and hoped he would not change his angle of flight! My body became taut and the sounds recreated past memories. I looked up, the sun was shining in my face and I saw the sea of black caps that the students were wearing and realized I was sitting home in Troy surrounded by family and friends.

Being honored by you had a special meaning for me. When I was advised that I could keep the hood, believe me, I will treasure it. Michelle was very kind and considerate so after I received my honorarium and the gift, I was ushered off the platform down the steps into the golf cart. At that point Michelle indicated that they had a special surprise for me but it would not arrive for another hour. You know that I am a firm believer in the man upstairs. I suddenly realized I was less than fifteen minutes away from the site in which my parents were buried. You know the rest. We took your car and drove to the cemetery. What a joy it was for me to say my prayers, thank them and share with them this wonderful moment we dreamed of. Only you and Morris would understand my feelings as I shared my blessings with my parents and returned to the school.

When we returned the surprise was the 1926 Convertible and someone holding a raccoon coat. Could you imagine the joy and smile on my face and the excitement I felt as a group of your associates held the coat for me to slip on. Your photographer was outstanding! I wish I had a picture of his face because he was genuinely enjoying every minute of this and was as excited as I was. Together with the others, we really had a ball.

There is no way I can express my gratitude. The amount of preparation, planning and execution of this event boggles my mind and I will not forget that finally, when I went to R.P.I., I had my Convertible and a raccoon coat! Bless you all!

Sincerely,

Marty

MS:ms

Marty finally gets his raccoon coat
and 1926 convertible at RPI's 2003 Commencement.

Chapter 11

◆→ ◆→

BATTLE OF THE BULGE

The Big One

The largest, bloodiest battle of World War II was the Battle of the Bulge. More Americans died in this siege, more destruction was wrought, and greater danger to the Allied cause was threatened than during any ground offensive of the war.

The battle came about as a kind of desperation move by the enemy high command. In late fall of 1944 the Nazi army was defeated in France, defeated in Italy, defeated in Russia. This left only their military forces in Germany to fight invaders and hold the line. But Hitler, blinded by megalomania plus a belief in the invincibility of his cause, did not simply want the battle for Germany to be an heroic repulse of the enemy. He would accept nothing less than total victory, nothing less than the total annihilation of the attacking British and American forces.

Based on this dicey strategy, the Fuhrer made one of the truly critical decisions of World War II. Instead of fighting a defensive battle to protect the German homeland his troops would attack.

German strategy was to use three of the most formidable German armies (including the elite Sixth Panzer Division) to launch a surprise counter-offensive across the Ardennes Forest to the Meuse River. From there the German armies would swing northwest and capture the city of Antwerp, a maneuver designed to cut off Montgomery's British troops. This move, in theory, would then split the Allies, and allow the Germans to make short work of both British and American troops.

Approximately 600,000 German soldiers were manned for the assault, among them the best and most seasoned Nazi divisions.

The attack began on December 16. When it came it hit with tumultuous force, penetrating 50 miles into Allied territory, and generating horrendous casualties on both sides. (The name of the battle was taken from the large, balloon-like "bulge" the German armies made in the Allied lines of defense.)

My unit was about 10 miles from the city of Bastogne when the Germans launched their counterattack, and Patton, with his usual slave-driver intensity, marched us through ice and snow for eight days to face a massive German attack on December 24, the day before Christmas.

It was the coldest winter ever recorded in Germany and France.

But I'm getting ahead of my story. Let's go back a month or two before the battle began, to Metz. The battle for this beleaguered city has just wound to a close.

Uncle Sam's Reward

Metz fell to the Allies in early December 1944, after a heartbreaking struggle and enormous loss of life. In deep acknowledgment of our superhuman efforts Uncle Sam gave us a special reward the day of our victory: dinner. A Thanksgiving dinner, to be exact.

During the November holiday we'd been fighting street to street, sometimes hand-to-hand, and it was only now, with Metz secured and the action on hold, that General Patton ordered his troops given a belated holiday meal: turkey, turkey and more turkey, all we could eat.

And eat we did. For months we had lived on whatever we could scrounge up. Now it was payback time, honest-to-God meat on our plate along with something that passed for cranberry sauce and an ooze they called gravy. But though the meat was a few days (weeks?) old, and though the meal was delivered in thermos containers rather than on a Thanksgiving tray, it was hot, it was turkey, and we ate it.

Wall to Wall Fighting

Finishing up in Metz, our unit headed east to the Saar River bordering France and Germany. As we crossed the dark waters and moved through the towns of Saarlautern and Fraulautern in Germany, resistance stiffened. We had a foot in the "Fatherland" now, and this was a new and stunning experience for the Deutsche soldier and householder alike. The German government vowed to make us pay for every inch of German earth we took.

Despite heavy resistance, we pushed ahead, and were soon forced into more street to street city fighting. This time, however, we discovered a novel method for eliminating the problems that had tormented us in the French cities, namely snipers, and turning corners on city blocks.

This method was based on an ingenious military concept. Who dreamed it up I don't know, but it was deadly efficient: make the walls of the German houses into doors.

I'll explain.

You see, even to this day most buildings in German towns are built with common-wall construction. The right wall of one building forms the left wall of the building next to it, and so on from house to house, down to the end of the block.

This architectural convention presented an intriguing alternative to fighting in the open: simply blow one long, tunnel-like corridor all at once through all the walls of all the building from one end of the city to the other.

We accomplished this feat with the help of a little plastic gizmo that looked more like a box of Chiclets than a deadly explosive cap. To use it you walk into the first house on the block, tie the Chiclet box onto a stick, dangle it near a wall, and detonate it.

Boom! The charge blows a hole in the wall, and you walk through into the living room or dining room of the adjoining building—where you then blow a hole in the next common wall, and the wall after that, until you're made one continuous series of holes straight through every common wall on the block. Now you have a nice protected passageway to walk down or in some cases drive through—wide, safe, quiet, and furnished along the way with tables, chairs and overstuffed sofas in sensible burgher fashion.

Sounds pretty destructive in retrospect, and I'm sure the monuments department would have a thing or two to say on the subject. But when you're getting shot to pieces out on the streets, and every building is a sniper's lair, well, as far as I'm concerned those little Chiclets boxes saved us a lot of bloody fighting, and a lot of American lives.

Sideshow in Holland

We were moving swiftly from German city to German city in early December when word came down that the British troops were under heavy attack in Maastrick, Holland, and that our regiment, the 379th Infantry, was being sent there to help out.

In what seemed like no time at all our transportation units commandeered a number of so-called "40 and 8 boxcars" from the local freight yards. These were the same cars that French cavalry troops had been transported in during World War I and were, to say the least, antiquated (the name was taken from the fact that each car held 40 men and eight horses). Our unit was crowded into the makeshift troop trains and whisked to Holland.

I'd never been in contact with British fighting units before. The thing that sticks out in my mind most about them is the fact that compared to our troops these men were drastically under supplied, and had learned to make maniacally efficient use of every scrap of food, weaponry, and ammunition.

Once, for example, during the fighting at Maastricht I began to feel that my extra ammunition belt was weighting me down and interfering with my mobility. I slipped it off and tossed it to the ground. Then I heard a voice behind me.

"Hey, mate, you dropped your belt."

I turned and saw a smiling Limey walking towards me holding the jettisoned equipment.

"Oh, thanks," I said. "But the stuff's too heavy. I just wanted to get rid of it."

He stopped in his tracks and his smile thinned to a look of utter wonderment.

"You *meant* to drop it?"

"I threw it away, yeah," I answered casually, not knowing what his problem was. "Got too heavy."

"Perfectly good ammo? You threw it *away*! How about giving it to me?"

"Be my guest," I said, suddenly getting his point, and feeling a little sheepish for my wastefulness.

The Britisher picked up the belt and fondled it as if it was a newborn babe. "You Americans certainly have it ready to be plucked," he said absently, and carried away his treasure in an ecstatic daze.

After this incident I was careful to be less profligate around my English brothers-in-arms. We soon learned that the British were, in fact, compulsive about conserving their resources, and would literally pick their shots before they fired while we Americans whaled away all day with our M-1's and machine guns, going through clip after clip without thinking twice. It even became a joke among the Americans that the British soldiers thought they had to pay money out of their own pockets for every bullet they fired.

The reality was, of course, that the British had been fighting longer than we had, and were desperately short on food and equipment. Theirs was a carefulness born of privation, long-term suffering and loss.

Once on a mission outside of Metz, I remember, I captured a German officer who was packing a brand new Luger pistol. Especially made for German officers (the grunts used the far louder and less accurate Schmeizer), the Luger was the Cadillac of pistols and may well have been the finest piece of pocket weaponry ever invented—sleek, accurate, aesthetically beautiful. Everyone wanted one. Now I had one.

I strapped on my new toy and returned to my unit. Soon, however, I discovered that the thing shot only 9 mm rounds, and as it turned out these were extremely difficult to find on the American side. The British, on the other hand, used 9 mm bullets in several of their weapons. I approached one of my British counterparts who I knew was going returning to

England soon and asked if he could leave me some of his ammunition.

"Delighted," he said. "When I go next week I'll give you what I've got."

Next week came and I reminded him of his promise.

"Oh yes, yes, " he said, "reaching into his pocket and taking out nine 9 mm bullets. "Here you are" he said, fingering the bullets lovingly "And please, Marty—use them carefully. . . ."

Nine bullets weren't enough to fill a single clip.

The Battle of the Bulge

On December 16 the Battle of the Bulge began.

We had just completed our assignment with the British in Holland, and were just then stationed in an area near the place where the attack was launched when, as I mentioned, Patton sent us on a forced march to the town of Bastogne situated at the very center of the fighting.

Hitler's counterattack, though it ultimately proved a foolhardy tactic, took the Allies by surprise, and for some days the issue was in doubt. For weeks friendly locals had warned the American command that the Germans were massing numbers of troops along the lines. But the brass refused to believe it. No one, they reasoned, would be fool enough to attack under such circumstances. Then the Germans attacked.

From the moment the offensive began every soldier in our unit, and, I would guess, every American soldier in every unit of the 3rd Army became a rifleman. This included men who had never picked up a gun before—cooks, barbers, bakers, clerks, sometimes even members of the marching band. All were suddenly riflemen.

No matter how many coats and blankets and canvas

caisson coverings you piled on top of yourself, you couldn't escape the cold. It went beyond anything I've experienced before or since. If a soldier received even a superficial wound he might freeze to death in minutes before a medic reached him.

The cold turned the ground iron-hard, and this made it impossible to dig trenches, or even foxholes. When the German 88 shells came whistling in there was nowhere to hide. We crouched, shivered, tried to squeeze in between rocks and trees, and prayed to become invisible. Even going to the bathroom was a nightmare. The ground was so hard we couldn't dig latrines, which meant we had to squat wherever we could. After a while the stench became pervasive, mingling with the smell of gunpowder and burned flesh. Even the cold didn't cancel out this smell. I sometimes recall it today.

No one, of course, knew that weather conditions would be so dreadful that year, and so we went into battle woefully underdressed. Combat boots are made of thin leather, and once the cold gets to a soldier's feet it doesn't go away; frostbite was the inevitable result. Literally thousands of troops were disabled during the Battle of the Bulge simply from the cold. Many lost an arm, a leg, even their lives, to gangrene.

Snow was everywhere.

At first we tried to use it as camouflage. Men covered the front of their uniforms with it to blend into the snowy landscape. What they didn't realize was that body heat melts ice, which then refreezes, forming a frosty coating over the entire body. Many of our GI's froze to death before they could get out of these uniforms into dry clothes.

After the first several days of fighting our unit received a large influx of reserves, most of them kids who had been hastily and poorly trained. They'd had basic training under garrison conditions, it was true. They knew how to fire a rifle and throw a hand grenade. But battle conditions are different than life on the rifle range, and most of these kids were dead in a few days, victims of inexperience and foolhardiness. Within a month we went through two, maybe three complete turnovers of replacements

In the beginning of the attack things went Hitler's way. The cold helped his cause immensely. The German troops came into battle dressed far more warmly than the Americans, and a thick fog covered the Bastogne area for one straight week, making American air support an impossibility.

Our 95th was lucky, however. The day after we began engaging the enemy the clouds lifted, and hour after hour sleek squadrons of American planes filled the sky above us. We could see them strafing German troops, buzzing German artillery, hammering at the dreaded Panzers along the roads. It didn't stop the German advance entirely, but it slowed them down long enough for our troops to retrench, settle in, and begin to launch a counteroffensive.

Meanwhile, the indefatigable General Patton had a plan to neutralize the German thrust. Our troops were to drive up the middle of the German forces, he advised the top command, while other segments of the army would attack the German flanks.

This tactic was immediately overruled by Eisenhower, who realized this was no ordinary enemy we were fighting, but an army of home-defenders whipped into an ideological frenzy by Hitler who was broadcasting the same message over and over to his troops: "This is your finest hour. You will succeed in overpowering the enemy. The only land we will give them is burial space."

These broadcasts had a mesmeric effect on the German fighting man who entered battle now with glazed eyes and a strange transfixed look on his face. I saw it up close many times. All these human killing machines wanted to do now was die for the Führer and the Fatherland. I sometimes had the uncanny feeling that we were fighting automatons.

Living with Dying

Do you know how difficult it is to get a teenager to shoot a man?

The recruits were coming in droves, and it became a do-or-die situation: either learn to kill the enemy or we all go down.

When the fighting came to a lull I'd gather two or three of the new recruits around me and with my best "voice in command" explain the rules of war:

"You have only one job here: kill, kill, kill!"

"Never hesitate!"

"Shoot first, ask questions later."

"Shoot or be shot—these people you're fighting are *not nice*!"

Sometimes I'd paraphrase Old Blood and Guts:" This is not the Salvation Army! We're not here to save souls! We're here to *kill* souls, and the faster we do it the sooner we get home!"

The kids I was talking to were wholesome American stock. They didn't want to hurt anybody, and they certainly didn't want to kill anybody. Behind their macho masks it was clear they were not only frightened of the enemy but of themselves, of the barbaric task they were being asked to perform in this utterly inhuman war.

But all wars are inhuman. And the miserable fact is once you're in the thick of it you have to do what's necessary to survive. We were fighting a cruel, implacable, well-trained enemy who was battling to defend his homeland. Show him no quarter—because he'll show none to you.

"Don't stop to take prisoners," I'd holler at them. "We can't afford the time. We can't afford the extra rations. Either shoot the bastard, or stay behind the lines while we advance and take care of him."

Every day at dawn we moved ahead, always remembering Patton's command: forward, never back, even if it means certain death (rumor was that Patton had once threatened to take up the rear and shoot anyone who didn't advance).

We scattered the new recruits among the old-timers, and told them to listen up and watch and learn. Some of them did. Most of them—well, a few lived long enough to become "old-timers." How many weeks did it take at the Bulge to become an old-timer? Two or three. Anyone who stayed alive that long was an old-timer. No exaggeration.

Most of the time I didn't remember the recruits' names cause they died so quickly. But some made it through, usually on dog-assed luck. Once, I remember, a group of us were advancing across a field with a new recruit named Joe. We reached a shell hole and started to go around it when a German soldier popped up like a jack-in-the-box and pointed his weapon at Joe's head.

Instead of reacting, Joe froze. He would have been sauerbraten in a second if one of the other guys hadn't fired first, blowing the German away.

When the smoke cleared I looked around. There was Joe stretched out on the ground with his rifle in front of him. I knew what he was thinking: he wanted to run.

"Stay down!" I shouted. "We're under fire. Don't get up, stay there!"

I gave him the thumbs-up signal.

"There are troops behind you—be careful of the cross-fire."

He nodded and seemed to understand. But the next minute there was a lull in the shooting, and he was up on his feet running towards us.

As if this wasn't bad enough, when he reached the still twitching body of the German who'd ambushed us he stopped in his tracks and stood there, gaping down at what must have been a bloody mess. Two or three bullets whizzed over his head, but he continued to stare, hypnotized. Several more pinged around him in the mud.

"Move it!" I screamed, "Move it, Joe!" This seemed to jar him awake.

He dashed towards us and somehow managed to stay alive till he reached shelter. He'd been incredibly lucky. The Germans were good shots.

I made a note to talk to him that night, but I don't recall if I ever got around to it. If I had I would certainly have told him rule number one—"In combat never stop to look at a dead body, ours or theirs. The sight of it will stay with you for a long time. Maybe for the rest of your life."

I was speaking from experience.

Death by Incompetence

After the initial fury of the counteroffensive was spent, the Nazi war machine slowed down, stalled, and finally came to a clanging halt, their last card played out, their gamble gaining them nothing but obliteration and the utter loss of morale.

The Battle of the Bulge lasted a little more than a month, from December 16 to January 20, and then took another two or three weeks to tie up loose ends. For both sides the encounter was the costliest of the war. Our army suffered 4,000 dead plus 30,000 wounded, captured, or executed by the SS (along with uncounted thousands of French and Belgian civilians). The numbers of German soldiers killed and wounded was far greater

From now on the outcome of the war was never in doubt.

Penetrating all the way to the Meuse River, the enemy had been stopped at the tip of the "bulge" by American and British forces who fought with a persistence and ferocity that gave the death blow to the German's already waning sense of invincibility. American air power helped the process along by chopping up the German supply lines for a distance of 50 miles, keeping them from equipment and reserves when they were most needed.

Gradually the German army pulled back or was destroyed, and the shooting died down. At the end of this incredible ordeal most of us in the 95th were totally spent in body and soul. Perhaps, we now thought, the High Command will give us some rest time and let another division do the dying for a while.

But no, not at all. The 95th was immediately dispatched on a mission down the Rhine where we were commanded to take and hold every bridge we found there.

Still, this assignment was tame compared with what we'd been through. Replacements were coming in on a regular basis, and pressures were reduced. We had time to work with these new men, to prepare them for the coming push. Things got easier.

One day along the Rhine my unit was ordered to protect a bridgehead over the river, and to make sure that the Germans didn't blow it up it (as far as the Germans were concerned, every bridge left standing on the Rhine was one more doorway into Germany). As evening fell word came down that the Nazis were planning to drop a paratroop unit on us that night, and blow the bridge.

Fine. We were ready.

Night came and with it a full moon. Our men were old-timers. We were strategically well positioned and felt confident. We had enough light from the full moon to keep a watch on things. No one was worried.

But there was one problem. A new lieutenant was put in charge of our unit, a seven-week wonder who, besides lacking sound military judgment and everyday battle experience, insisted on waving his hands ridiculously whenever he issued orders, a habit that made him look like something between a whirling dervish and a windmill. Halfway through the night he suddenly announced that the German paratroops had landed, and that we were under attack.

The moon had set by now, and the Rhenish countryside was cloaked in a deep, solemn darkness. I was the sergeant in charge, and had been watching all evening with extra caution. Neither I nor any of the others saw any signs of infiltration, and our judgment in these matters was finely tuned. Yet orders had been given. We opened up with everything we had.

For the next several hours a steady stream of rounds were emptied into various sectors around the bridge where the lieutenant insisted the paratroopers had landed. Now and then his silhouette could be made out in the darkness, spinning his arms convulsively and shouting orders.

As soon as light came the next morning we crawled out of our holes. Making a search of the area, we did in fact find several dead bodies—all of them our own men! These, it appeared, had been meticulously picked off by our riflemen in areas where the lieutenant had directed the fire.

Truly the horrors of war. But there was a gruesome justice to it all as well. Among the dead bodies brought in that morning was that of the hand-waving lieutenant, killed, apparently, by stepping in front of his own line of fire. How he managed this feat I've never understood.

My Almost Court-Martial

The strange death of the young lieutenant caused a stir in Division HQ, and the next day the Inspector General's department sent a major over to our sector to investigate.

Since I'd been the sergeant in charge when the incident occurred, I was ordered to give a full explanation.

This I did, with such animation and pique that the major quickly saw I was bitterly critical of the young lieutenant's fitness to command. He stopped me in the middle of my report.

"Sergeant, do you really think you could have done any better?"

"Sir," I replied instantly with a good deal too much challenge and attitude in my voice. "I sure as hell couldn't have done any worse!"

Interview concluded. The major left without further comment.

Two or three days later I was summoned to Division HQ.

The major was waiting there in one of the main offices along with several other military bigwigs, all of them looking as hard and cross as seasoned soldiers can get.

I'd really done it this time, I told myself, making a wise-ass remark, being insubordinate to a ranking officer. I wondered if they were going to court-martial me.

Salutes were exchanged, then one of the officers motioned for me to sit down. The others remained standing. This didn't bode well. I felt like I was already in the electric chair. One of my questioners asked me if I'd really said what I'd said to the major.

I told him yes, I had.

Expecting the worst, I sat silently as four battle-hardened faces stared down at me from military valhalla.

Then a strange thing happened: they all started smiling. One even laughed.

"Well, if you think you can do better, then go ahead," one of the officers said, taking something out of his pocket and handing it to me. "Let's see how good you are."

I had no idea what he meant by this, and had no time to think about it either. The seat of the chair I'd been sitting on was missing some of its cane and had a wooden plank covering the hole. As I stood up to take whatever it was the officer was handing me I knocked the plank off the chair. *Clunk*! It fell loudly to the cement floor.

I bent over awkwardly to get it, embarrassed out of my mind to be bungling around like this in front of these seasoned officers.

One of them sensed my confusion and embarrassment. "You don't have to do that, *lieutenant*," he said. You're an officer now!"

I stopped and glanced up.

It took a minute. Then I got it.

I looked down at what the man had given me. They weren't going to shoot me. They weren't going to court-martial me or ship me to Leavenworth. They had just given me my officer's bars.

I was being *promoted!*

❧ ❧

Somehow I managed to smile and thank my way out of the room, then stumbled into the hallway outside gripping my new officer's bars. Not only had I been made an officer, I'd been given a seven-day pass to Paris, recently liberated, to pick up my new uniform. I was to leave at 0:800 the next day.

Private transportation would be provided, courtesy of HQ.

An Officer and a Salesman

There was more. As a rule, when a soldier is promoted he's instantly transferred to another unit. They figure, I suppose, that familiarity breeds contempt, especially if you've been fighting side by side on an equal basis with a guy and suddenly you become his senior officer.

In my case—why, I'm not sure—they made an exception, and let me stay with my company. I wired Dot the good news.

"Just received a battlefield commission," I said in the telegram. "And they have also given me back my own company to command. Love."

Two or three days later I got a reply. It was signed in bold letters by both Dot and Mel.

"Mazeltov," it read. "We knew you would never be happy until you had your own company—and already you're making commissions!"

How Sweet It Is

The next day I traveled to Paris, heading straight for the supply depot where I picked up my new togs: uniform, ribbons, hat, infantryman's badge, shoes, socks, the works.

I raced back to my hotel room, locked the door, peeled off my old clothes, lay them on the bed (crisp hotel bed, clean sheets, fragrant linens) and jumped into the shower. I'd already had four showers that morning. But just in case the bathroom vaporized I wanted a fifth.

I lathered up for a few minutes, then rinsed off and strode out of the bathroom squeaky clean.

Alone. Myself. For the first time in months. Or was it years? A room of my own—what could that be? Privacy. Noiselessness. No bomb shells blowing off pieces of chimney on top of me. No groaning or grousing men. No blood and flies and hedgerows and smelly feet. No waking up in the morning and taking a head count to see how many men had been killed last night. As Jackie Gleason would have said, "How sweet it is!"

I lay there mentally rolling in the extravagance of it all,

then I slowly I sat up, picked up my old combat boots, and carried them to the wastebasket. The poor things were worn down to a grizzle and were no good to anyone anymore. But we'd been together a long time, these boots and me, and now that the time had come to trash them I felt a wave of sadness and even remorse sweep over me. They'd protected me all these months. How could I be such a faithless friend? (In times of war, understand, you think of anything as your dear friend that helps you to a) stay dry; b) get warm; c) eat; d) sleep; e) remain alive.)

With a deep sense of nostalgia I finally dropped them in. Then I took my new officer's boots out of the bag, and suddenly there were no more regrets.

Next came the officer pinks. Lovely; perfect fit. A pair of dry socks and the new boots over these, and the shirt and the officer's tie and jacket, and, and—it was like eating a meal.

There. Done. I walked over to a full-length mirror on the bathroom door. *Benissimo! Wunderbar!* I threw myself a kiss in the glass. I couldn't believe what I was seeing. Class. Rank. Master tailoring. I hardly recognized the face smiling back at me. The big smile I tried to look stern and in command like an officer, but I couldn't stop grinning. I snapped to attention and saluted my reflection. I winked at him and smiled. What a guy. I was proud of him, proud of all the brass covering his chest. Now he—me—was one of "them."

But as I continued to stare into the mirror, slowly, gradually, a new face and figure began to emerge. A tired, skinny face and figure worn out by fatigue, fear, bad food, imminent death.

I studied this tired face for some time. It looked back at me almost accusingly, as if asking what I was doing here all dressed up in this officer's costume. I was just another GI. Remember? Just another dogface sent out into the fields to die for God, nation and—who knew what? Just another unknown soldier.

Then yet another face appeared and took this one's

place. This time it was Sad Sack Silverman of L Company, Harrisburg training camp, Pa.

Sad Sack looked out of place here in his new officer's khakis — 32 years old, couldn't keep up with the kids on the forced marches, could barely wiggle his middle-aged backside through the obstacle course, was fit (his sergeant and officers all agreed) for kitchen duty mainly and scrubbing the crud off the sinks — an out-of-place would-be pilot, used car salesman from Troy, New York, who'd certainly never make a soldier.

And so it went, one incarnation after another in the glass. All those weeks of training and fighting and killing had added up in calendar time to less than 365 days. Barely a year from then till now. How was it possible, I wondered, for so many experiences to be packed into such a short time? But it was mostly over now; all that remained was to mop up.

And I was mopping up my life too, trying to clean off the spatter, to look around at the wide world and remember how normal people led their normal lives. Lives without K-rations or rigor mortis or the bedevilments of weaponry.

Three days remained on my Paris leave. I vowed to make the best of them. Little did I know that these next three days would change my life forever.

Paris

When you walked down the Champs Elysee or in the Trocadero or past the Cathedral of Notre Dame in April of 1945 it seemed that most of the people you saw were American soldiers. A majority of them looked like men who'd been suddenly lifted out of hell and dropped into the world's biggest candy store. Even the most sophisticated of them were dazzled by this city and its delights.

Determined to have fun, I hopped from hot spot to hot

spot across Paris, drinking, laughing it up, seeing the sights. Along the way I noticed a curious thing. Everywhere I went enlisted men and officers kept buying me drinks. "On the house, pal," they'd say. "Must have been rough."

I couldn't figure out why everyone was being so accommodating, until one night an officer paid my bill and then nodded towards the combat infantryman's badge displayed on my chest. This badge told other soldiers that I'd been in the thick of the fighting, and that I'd lived to tell the tale.

Back in my own unit everyone I knew was wearing this badge. No big deal. This made me assume that every man in the army had seen as much fighting as I had. We were all soldiers, weren't we? It wasn't till the combat was over that I learned there were only 3,200 riflemen in an infantry division of 15,000 men, and that the rest of the division did things like cooking, communication, administration. I also discovered that 20 percent of our division suffered 70 percent of the casualties.

When I learned these facts it became clear to me why so many soldiers were buying me drinks. Partly awe, partly envy—and mostly survivor's guilt.

The Officers Club

After I'd been in Paris a few days I was told the best place to eat was the French Officers Club.

I found my way there one evening towards the end of my leave and upon entering was told that I'd have to purchase a chit for the meal. Not a very classy beginning. But this first impression was wiped away the moment I entered the main dining room and beheld a sight that took my breath away.

Gilt mirrors. Mahogany tables. Silver place settings. Bowls of fruit. Waiters in white. Tablecloths. Bottles of wine. Smiling officers at every table. A beautiful French dining room pleasantly abuzz with good food and sensible conversation.

I hesitated. Should I go in? Me, a lowly GI? Then I remembered my promotion. My new place in space. I belong here, by God. I'm an *officer*.

Perhaps. But as I entered that room I never remember feeling more sorry for myself and angry at the world. Looking around at all the well-fed faces I thought back on the months of half-frozen K-rations for dinner with snow and ditch water to wash it down. And here were these non-combatants gorging themselves on grouse and custard and *chateau la fite* every night. That was the kind of war *they* were fighting. Tain't no justice.

And yet, they say that the first sign of intelligence is an ability to adapt—and you would have been amazed to see how quickly I adapted. After the first meal, I adapted. After the second even more. By the third I was a native. For the rest of my stay in Paris I took all my meals in this heavenly place and never thought about K-rations or the fat-faced non-combatants once the whole time.

Table for Three and Destiny

When you entered the French Officers Club and walked around looking for a place to sit, it was customary and polite to ask the officers at the table if you could join them. Strangers were usually welcome unless a private conversation was taking place.

One evening I happened to sit down at a table where three officers from the Judge Advocate General's department were having dinner. A fascinating discussion was in progress concerning the prospect of setting up a war crimes office. I listened in rapt silence.

Given the nature and extent of the atrocities performed

by the Nazis, the three men all agreed, it would be necessary to bring many of the German high command to trial. Mass murder of Jews and political prisoners had taken place in the concentration camps. Allied prisoners of war had been shot while surrendering. The Gestapo had tortured untold thousands of innocent people. The SS had perpetrated extreme cruelties on civilians and soldiers alike. The list went on and on.

This conversation was particularly riveting to me since I had recently been present at the liberation of the Dachau concentration camp and had witnessed firsthand the devastation visited on my people by the Nazis. Though this subject is one I find almost impossible to speak of today other than in passing I was, as you might imagine, more than a little anxious to see justice served.

The discussion continued in this vein for some time until one of the men, seemingly out of the blue, announced that his office would be needing lawyers who understood these issues to work at the coming trials.

I couldn't believe what I was hearing. I wondered if the Man Upstairs was trying to tell me something again.

"I'm a lawyer," I piped up.

They all turned and looked in my direction. Until this moment I hadn't contributed a word to the conversation and had gone entirely unnoticed. "I'm also Jewish," I continued. "I was at Dachau when they liberated it. And I have all the legal expertise you're looking for."

I could see them all staring at the brass on my chest and at my combat infantryman's badge. The ranking officer looked at me in a particularly interested way. He opened a bottle of wine and filled all the glasses.

"Interesting," he said, "interesting," never taking his eyes off me.

He raised his glass and made a toast. "To the bastards who made it all happen."

We drank and then set his glass down hard on the table.

"Let's get them!" he hissed, looking directly at me.

"Let's get them!" I answered back.

We drank, vowing to make these bastards dance in their own blood.

In Living 3-D

The four of us agreed to meet again the following evening for dinner. This time, as requested, I brought my orders with me.

The officers read them over, conferred among themselves for several minutes, then assured me I was the man they were looking for and that they would arrange all transfer details. I was to report back to my division at the end of my leave, they said, and my transfer papers would be waiting there for me.

It was difficult to believe. A chance meeting, a seemingly accidental event, and once again fate added a surprise squiggle to my graph of life.

This good fortune delighted me, of course, yet experience said that in the army things are not always the way they seem, and that it's better to see it in writing before you celebrate.

Still, I wanted to share the news with Dot and Mel. I decided to compromise. Instead of wiring them directly I'd send them a photograph of me smiling and let them draw their own conclusions.

Several times while I was in Paris I'd passed a photography shop that advertised "three-dimensional pictures." I decided to take a chance.

"Bonjour, Monsieur American" the proprietor said as I entered. He was standing behind a huge camera mounted on a long metal track. He looked as if he'd been waiting there for me all day.

"Have the seat, Monsieur" he said without asking why I was here. "You want with the big smile, yes?"

"Yes" I answered.

"As you wish, Monsieur American." He lit a cigarette and handed it to me. I was told to extend my hand with the cigarette directly towards the camera to get the full 3-D effect, then hold the pose.

I obeyed for what seemed like an eternity while the proprietor fiddled with the camera controls and moved his contraption back and forth on its track. Then finally: snap, wheeze, *swwwwwttt*, click!

A few minutes in the dark room and he emerged triumphantly with the latest in photographic technology, a true 3-D picture, a cross between a stereopticon and a hologram; and this, remember, was only 1945.

I paid the proprietor, left the shop, and sent the picture to Mel and Dot on the next post.

How I would have loved to be a fly on the wall when they opened it. They hadn't seen me for a year. Would I look too thin to them, too burned out? I didn't think so. They were seeing me at my best here, with a smile on my face and something to hope for. (This old 3-D picture, a bit frayed at the borders now, still hangs on our wall today. It's achieved the ultimate status in the Silverman household: a family treasure.)

The Map Readers

The last few days in Paris passed rapidly and before I knew it the time came to ship out. My orders this time—why, I never knew—routed me through an REPL depot where replacements were waiting to be sent into combat. I was to remain here for several days, then return to my unit.

Arriving at the REPL depot, I reported to the C.O., who

immediately placed me in charge of some black troops who were waiting to go into battle. My assignment for the next several days was to teach them to read a map.

This seemed like a strange thing to do at this late date in the war, but orders were orders. After lunch I told the sergeant to assemble his men and we marched straight off into the woods to begin our lessons.

As we stepped along I could hear disgruntled murmuring behind me: "Waste of time!" "Who uses maps in combat anyway?" "What does this guy know?" They were right, too; I was a lousy map-reader.

We marched till we were well out of sight of camp, then I ordered a halt.

"At ease, men," I shouted. A company of black recruits came to rest and stared at me with surly glances.

"Now look," I said. "We're going to stay here in these woods for the next three hours. You guys can do whatever the hell you like: shoot craps, go to sleep, take a piss, I don't care."

They looked at me disbelievingly. Then smiles started to break out.

"That's not all!" I bellowed. "When we start back to camp we'll march there straight and proud like we've just won the war singlehandedly. We'll sing a cadence march as we go. I'm going to make you guys look good."

This met with no objection, and for the next few hours we all goofed off. In late afternoon I assembled the ranks and like Caesar's conquering legions we marched back to camp, shouting out cadence counts and keeping perfect step for the impressed groups of onlookers.

I stayed in the depot two more days, and both days my troops assured me in front of everyone there that they couldn't *wait* to learn more about maps.

When the time came for me to leave the depot the C.O. called me over.

"It was a pleasure to see how a combat officer handles

his men!" he said, and he whipped off a snappy salute.

"Few things more important in combat than reading a map, Sir," I answered, and gave him my best salute in return.

Never Look Back

Next day I took the train to the camp where my division was stationed. I had no sooner arrived when one of the old-timers in L Company spotted me and shouted "Hey, Pop Silverman's back!"

Friends gathered round. It was a wonderful moment; everyone started talking all at once, and as they did I was relieved to see that my new rank made no difference to anyone. One of my buddies even reminded me that since I was an officer I was entitled to a liquor ration. We marched en masse to the supply building where I ordered several bottles.

Changing into a pair of fatigues so I could keep my new officer's togs pressed and clean, I sat down on the floor with the guys and passed the bottle around as the new replacements stood to the side listening in awe to the war stories that criss-crossed between us. The more we drank the better the stories became. But we were entitled. It was the reward of survival. Of the 180 men in the unit when I arrived probably no more than 20 of them were here and alive.

That night I slept in the barracks with my buddies and the next morning I reported to HQ.

Here they informed me, just as I hoped, that I'd been assigned to a war crimes unit at Dachau, and that I was to report immediately. Since my orders had arrived several days earlier, I'd already been replaced at L Company by another lieutenant. Whenever I was a ready to leave, they told me, a driver would pick me up.

I walked out of HQ with deeply mixed feelings. The

fighting had died down to a trickle now, so I didn't feel like I was leaving my buddies in the lurch. But I would miss the old-timers. I would miss the camaraderie.

At the same time, I didn't want the dubious distinction of being the last man shot before the armistice was signed like something out of *All Quiet on the Western Front*. I remember standing there on HQ steps, gazing at the sky, saying a prayer of gratitude. I can honestly say that I had thought I'd never make it out of the infantry alive.

I returned to L Company barracks. When the hugging and backslapping was over and I'd shaken hands with the last of the old guard, the sergeant in charge shouted "Attention!" and every man snapped to.

I returned their salutes. It was the proudest moment of my life. I can't think of a prouder one. I was so proud to be a part of Patton's Third Army.

Then I called for the driver. He arrived in minutes and loaded my gear as I strapped on my faithful 45.

Without turning to the crowd of men standing there, the men I had fought with and bled with over the past several years and who I would probably never see again, I climbed into the jeep, gave the orders to drive on, and never looked back. On the side of the jeep, as per my instructions, were written the words "My Dot"—Dorothy, my wife.

In several hours I was in another world, and another life.

❧ ❧

Napoleon once said that the first quality of a good soldier is the ability to endure hardship.

I suppose he was right. I never set out to win those decorations. I had no wish to be a hero. I only wanted to survive and get home to my wife with soul and body intact.

But if putting up with hardship day after day after day is, as the Little Corporal claimed, part of being a good soldier then I'm here to tell you that I—and the rest of those magnificent men I fought with in the American army—qualify for the roll call in spades.

◆▶ ◆▶ ◆▶

Chapter 12

❖❖ ❖❖

HOME

The War Is Over

Or so they told me.

I was sitting in the back of a jeep on my way to work for the War Crimes Commission. This was the organization that eventually would bring us the Nuremberg trials, concentration camp infamy, and a legal concept that was, as far as anyone knew, novel to the world: the concept of "crimes against humanity."

I wish I could tell you that I was about to become a central player in this historical drama, that I would soon help in prosecuting the Nazis, and contribute to the sentencing of Goring and Hess, and all of Hitler's dark children. But no. Most of my work at the War Crimes Commission consisted of relatively minor legal cases plus a lot of daydreaming about going home. The thing I most enjoyed about my new assignment, besides not being shot at, was that I now had *only myself* to watch out for.

This sounds selfish. But it's difficult to describe what a burden it is to be an officer in a combat unit, and to have personal responsibility for hundreds of men's lives every day.

There's the constant worry over whether the new replacements will fit in. There's the guilt and pain you feel when one of your men is hit. No matter how many times this happens, you find yourself asking: Could his death have been avoided? Could I have done things differently? Each time one of your men dies, you die a little too. Each time one of them is wounded, you feel the wound. I was glad to be out of there.

And so, as I sat in the jeep bumping and shaking and dreaming, I did something I hadn't allowed myself to do for a very long time: I thought about the future.

Over the many months I'd been in combat, I'd learned to discipline my mind, to think of only one thing at a time. In the midst of a combat zone you learn to concentrate fully on the job at hand. When there's death all around you keep a low profile, and don't try to make like a hero. You think carefully about every move. You look before you leap. Do I turn to the right? Do I squat? Do I stand? Do I run? Do I shoot? Do I sneeze? Think, think, think—and stay alive. We were cold and we were hungry and we were tired—always. And we could handle all of this *if only* those Nazi bastards would stop shooting at us. That's about all we thought of then.

But the future? That was a luxury for non-combatants.

Now here I was safe in a jeep, well fed, feet dry, no command to think about, no metal parts flying over my head, no blood, no tears. I could go where I wanted, eat when I liked, sleep when the spirit moved me, get up when I wished. And most of all, I could dream of a future again.

As the miles of German farmland rolled by I thought of my parents and my wife, about my baby, my brother-in-law, Mel, who kept our family on an even keel while I was away. I thought of how my wife and Mel were running things, trying to keep our little business going. They were working every day so that I would have something to come home to. To me Mel was the unsung hero of the whole deal. While I was over here shooting at the Nazis he was back home wiping noses, paying bills, working 18-hour days, and providing the spiritual and financial help our family needed to survive. I hadn't appreciated all he'd done. Now I had time to reflect. He was as much a hero, I decided, as any soldier here. I understood how much people like Mel and all the other hard-working, self-sacrificing people back home had contributed to our winning the war.

"This is it!" my driver boomed out, pulling to a sudden stop, waking me from my reverie. "We're here!"

I looked around.

The place had changed considerably since my unit had liberated it a month earlier. I won't—can't— go into the details of the horrors I'd seen at the time. They are still too painful. But now, thanks to Yankee efficiency, what I saw was just another makeshift military post like many others across occupied Germany.

The name of this place was Dachau.

Yes, Dachau. Of concentration camp fame. Using German prisoners to clean things up, the site was now under Third Army command, and was being used as a holding place and trial court for minor war criminals.

After looking around for a while and getting my bearings, I reported to my C.O., Captain Corwin V. Edwards. After we exchanged salutes and a warm handshake, he introduced me to the other members of the war crimes team, and began to brief us on what we'd be doing in the months to come.

Right before the end of the war, he explained, a number of American pilots had bailed out over Germany. According to intelligence reports, the parachuters had been shot out of the sky by German soldiers. Our job was to visit the areas where these killings were reported, discover who was responsible, interrogate them, and haul them back to Dachau for trial.

I listened to the briefing carefully and made all the appropriate notes and noises. But inside I was sorely disappointed. This is not what I expected to be doing here in the War Crimes Commission. I had visions of participating in the big trials. Of avenging myself, and a good part of the human race, against the Nazi extermination machine. Instead, I'd be scavenging the countryside looking for potshooters.

Captain Edwards picked up on my disappointment.

"We're all in the same boat here, Silverman," he said. "It's not thrilling work. But it's necessary. And it'll keep us all plenty busy."

The Answer to a Prayer

Which it did. The other three men in my unit were combat veterans, tough, no-nonsense guys. One of them, Lieutenant Leonard, was a German-American who spoke fluent German, and understood the Germans inside-out. In the next few weeks we canvassed a number of small towns, picking up suspects here and there and watching as Lieutenant Leonard interrogated them. It wasn't a glamor job, but we felt we were making a difference.

In September new officers were added to our team. We now had eight men doing the work of four, and our efficiency level dropped by 50 percent.

Two months later four more offices joined us. Our efficiency dropped 80 percent.

The house we lived in, a former Gestapo headquarters, was small and overcrowded. We spent most of the time lying around waiting for assignments and listening to the new men bitch about being sent overseas. Suddenly none of it made sense any more. There was no moral to things now, no purpose or direction here. The burning need to win the war was over. We'd won; and the rest was a bunch of grimy details that I was just as happy to let somebody else worry about. As the Christmas and Chanukah season approached, the only thing I could concentrate on was my wife and child. I thought about my family at home lighting the candles and enjoying the spirit of the season with presents and music. The more I tried to focus on the job, the more I longed to be home for the holidays with my loved ones. I asked myself and the Man Upstairs the same question a dozen times a day: What am I doing here?

Then the Chanukah season passed, and New Year's Eve arrived. I woke up the morning of the new year and decided I'd had enough: *I want to go home!*

The next day I put in a request for leave and a discharge. In my case it was not a question of rotation. I had enough points and enough awards to go home any time I liked. However, having had so many disappointments in the army, I decided that I wouldn't count my chickens quite yet. I prepared a series of letters to be mailed at weekly intervals, and gave them to a buddy to send. I didn't want to raise anyone's hopes back home of my return until I knew I had that paper in hand. I kept praying.

On January 10, 1946, the answer came back clear and loud.

Discharge granted.

I was going home.

The Long Way Home

Nothing in the army is ever easy.

Instead of sending me directly from Germany to New York, the way they were doing it for most other guys on my post, my orders had me report to the French port of Le Havre hundreds of miles in the wrong direction. I was told I had to make this trip via a series of army bases and replacement depots located here and there across Germany and France. Hopping from one place to the next, and sometimes literally going away from France rather than toward it, it took me two weeks to get to Le Havre. A motorcar could have done it in a day. A plane in an hour.

Once in Le Havre I still wasn't out from under the army's thumb. As I boarded the liberty ship a functionary on deck shouted out my name and handed me a clipboard with a sheaf of papers.

"Sir," he said. "Here's the list of the 180 men you'll be in charge of during the trip back."

More responsibility! I almost screamed, "Why me?" but bit my tongue. After all, the only threat to life and limb now was to make sure the guys I was in charge of didn't kill each other over a craps game, or shoot each other arguing how my unit was tougher and saw more action in the war than yours!

There was a positive side too. Being an officer, I had privileges in the ship officers mess. I also had my own room and plenty of time to think about how to announce my presence once I reached New York. During these last months I had been writing letters to family members on the average of once a week, and had sent supplementary messages with returning buddies. Knowing the army as well as I did, I never gave anyone at home a specific return date. As far as Mel and Dot were concerned, I could show up at any time, or no time. Like me, they just waited. The war had taught us all to be patient.

Six uneventful days at sea later, our ship sailed into the generous, loving arms of New York Harbor.

This was it. The great hero's return. Statue of Liberty (I saluted her as we passed). Flags flying. Confetti. Brass bands. Couples kissing. Fathers holding their children in their arms for the first time. Mobs of people standing at the dock to welcome back the conquering warriors. I could see it all from a distance as our ship sailed through the Harbor, made a wide turn, proudly headed for the landing place and then—stopped dead in the water!

We were having engine difficulties, of course. No problem. But the hours passed and still no forward movement. So near and yet so far. What was going on?

An announcement over the P.A. made it all too clear: New York Harbor, the voice told us, was overcrowded with returning soldiers. As a result our ship was being diverted up to Boston Harbor where we would be kept until there was room here in the processing stations.

How long would that be? we all wanted to know.

No one was sure. *We'll keep you posted.*

◆→ ◆→

My reaction to this nasty trick of fate would probably have been more grim if it were not for the amazing coincidence that next unfolded.

As it turned out, everyone on board our ship was sent to Camp Miles Standish a few miles outside of Boston. This bleak compound was just then being used as a holding place until space could be made for us in Fort Dix where official discharge papers were being issued. The fascinating thing about my ending up here was that centuries earlier (so it seemed) my division had shipped out to Europe from this same location.

The chances of this happening, several of my friends agreed, were almost non-existent. I was returning to the same place I had been sent from, *but in reverse,* as if someone were running the film of my life backwards. On the way to the war I had ridden a bus from Camp Miles Standish to the train that took me to the ship that sailed me across the sea to Europe and the war. Now I was leaving the war, taking the ship from Europe back to the train, back to the bus, back to Camp Miles Standish. This sensation of living life in reverse and of fate's circle completing itself in an uncannily perfect way, still astonishes me to this day.

At any rate, as it turned out we sat around in Boston for a week or so until the powers-that-be shipped us to Fort Dix where we—guess what?—sat around some more. By now

thoughts of mutiny were on my mind, and I was literally ready
to do anything to get officially discharged. One day, with my
major campaign ribbons pinned to my chest, I walked into the
dispatch office and demanded to see the officer in charge. I was
ready for a fight, ready to do *anything* to get out of there.

The officer was a reasonable fellow. He pulled my
records, studied them for a minute, then announced that there
was no way he could process me right away. Thousands of
troops were returning, and all of them clamoring to get home.
Confusion was the name of the game. It might take a week to
get me processed, he said; it might take a month. Who knows?

He thought for a minute.

"Where do you live?" he finally asked.

"New York City."

"Be smart," he said. "Just go home, take some leave
time, enjoy the weekend. Come back Wednesday night, and
we'll try to have you out of here by Thursday evening."

I'd promised myself I would not leave Fort Dix until I
was a completely free man, and didn't owe Uncle Sam another
minute of my life. Still, I was getting to the point of desperation, and I figured I'd better seize the opportunity. I went back
to the barracks, picked up my gear, and boarded a Jeep bound
to the railroad station, where I boarded a train for Penn Station.

Imagine that ride into the city! For over a year I had
spent most of my mornings thinking I was not going to live
through the day; and most of my days thinking I would never
live through the war. Now here I was on a train, alive, healthy,
with my arms and legs intact, on my way home. How do you
choreograph such a reunion? How should I announce my
arrival?

As the train pulled into the station I figured, what the
heck, why not have some fun?

Dot and Mel were running the family business from an
office on 44th Street between Madison and Fifth in the center
of the city. As soon as the train arrived I walked up to 44th,

found a drugstore with a telephone booth in the back, and called the office.

Dot picked up. I disguised my voice.

"Hello, this is Lieutenant Wofnisky. I'm a friend of your husband's from overseas calling from the X Hotel in New York."

Immediately I heard a flurry of discombobulation and excitement at the other end of the phone. My wife wanted to know how, why, when, where. I cut her short.

"Look, I don't know any of the details. Your husband just wanted me to call you and play you this record he made for you overseas of his voice. You want to hear it?"

Yes, yes, yes!

So I told her she'd have to wait a couple of minutes because I have to set up the record player, plug it in, find the record. Would she mind waiting?

No, no, no!

I put the phone down, walked over to our nearby office building, took the elevator up to the office, and walked in the door.

When the telephone receptionist saw me she started to scream. I held up my hand, and she stifled her excitement. I walked quietly to my wife's office.

Sure enough, there's Dot still standing with the phone to her ear, waiting patiently for Lieutenant Wofnisky to crank up the record player in his hotel room and play the damn record so she can hear my voice for the first time in a year. I crept up gently behind her and tapped her on the shoulder. She jumped and turned. For a moment she didn't recognize me. Then she did. . . .

How to describe such a moment? There's no way. In all my life—all my long, event-filled life—there was never such a moment as this one. Every GI returning from the war had his own version of this special encounter. For each of us it was different. But somehow it was always the same.

Dot and I didn't hang around the office very long that day. Her biggest complaint was that she hadn't had a chance to get her hair done for my return. Within 30 minutes we were opening the door of our apartment in Sunnyside, Queens, and I was being introduced to my three-year old daughter Carol—for the first time in our lives.

Who Are You, Daddy?

The whole family had written me about Carol over the past year, telling me how good she was, how adorable. Dot couldn't wait to show her off.

We arrived at the apartment and were greeted by our beloved housekeeper, Mrs. Becker, who had been with us for years. Little Carol was sitting on the living room floor playing with her toys.

Dot cried out several times, "Carol! Carol! This is your daddy! He's come home to see all of us!"

Carol glanced up at me for a moment, seemed very unimpressed, and went back to her toys.

Mrs. Becker, always a cheerful soul, tried to keep the mood light and prepared dinner for us. We all sat around our little kitchen table chatting, laughing, talking—except for Carol. Carol sat glumly in her chair. Something new had come into the house and had upset the balance of things. A threat to her mother's attentions had appeared on the doorstep. Never mind that the threat was her father. As far as she was concerned my arrival meant she was no longer the center of the universe.

To make Carol's pill even more bitter, when bedtime arrived Dot explained to her that now that Daddy was home she and Carol would no longer be sleeping in the same bed. Good old daddy would be taking her place. She would be sleeping in the living room every night from now on, on the couch. Wasn't that nice!

Dark silence.

Then Carol made a suggestion. Why didn't we all sleep in the bed *together*?

Through the years I'd heard stories about frustrated parents ready to hang the children out the window. I could never understand such cruel thoughts—until this night.

Now I understood. For the next seven hours Dot and I lay in bed staring helplessly at one another, listening to our daughter sobbing in the next room, telling her mother she didn't love her anymore, telling her father she hated him. She even tried several times to crawl into bed and elbow me out of the way.

I tried to be understanding, I really did. I lay there staring at the ceiling, hoping that this monster would hyperventilate and pass out for an hour or two so that we could just talk for a few minutes. I had so much to tell her, so many things to say. She had so many things to say to me. Just an hour. But no— this was to be an all-nighter from beginning to end.

⊷ ⊷

Next morning bright and early Mrs. Becker arrived. Carol ran to her in tears and threw herself into her arms,

Quickly sizing up the situation, Mrs. Becker sat down and put Carol on her knee.

"Carol, sweetie," she said. "I want to make you a deal."

"*What!*" said Carol with the petulant voice of a child who has not slept a wink all night.

"Let's send your father and mother away for the weekend," she said. "Then you and I can stay here together. And you can sleep in the bed with me!"

To our infinite delight and gratitude, Carol not only accepted the plan but was ecstatic about it. She returned to her security blanket, the deal made, and seemed to think no more about it for the rest of the day.

Meanwhile Dot and I decided to splurge. We'd heard about a fabulous weekend offering at the Waldorf Astoria—go to the theater, have dinner, live the life. Next day we said good-bye to Carol, who was so delighted to be spending the weekend with Mrs. Becker that she hardly noticed our leaving, and we checked into the Waldorf. The bellboy showed us to a dingy room—bare lightbulb, cracked paint (you get what you pay for). But we didn't care. Not at all. All we were interested in that night was the bed. . . .

Next morning the two of us went downstairs for breakfast. I was still in my uniform, and Dot was glowing and looking her best. As we walked through the dining room it was as if everybody knew the score—here was a returned GI with his wife, we could almost hear them thinking, first night back, first night together in years. Everybody smiled, nodded. Dot was so proud of my ribbons and decorations.

We walked along Fifth Avenue, looked in the store windows, went by Radio City.

It was like a dream. We held hands like kids. On almost every block we stopped, looked into each other's eyes, had a little kiss and hug. It was so good. It was beyond anything I could have dreamed of. It was perfect.

We walked over to the Plaza, stopped in at the bar to have a drink.

The room was rather small and full, not too many tables. A gentleman and his date seated at one of these tables spotted us in the doorway. Both stood up and offered us their table, then went to sit at the bar. They each shook my hand and said, "Welcome home, soldier."

This was how it went everywhere during those final 30 days I was home and in uniform (the Army wanted the civilian population to be exposed to men in uniform to make the reentry process smoother). During this time it was practically impossible for me to pay for a drink at a bar or a lunch at a fancy restaurant. I kind of wished I could stay in uniform forever. What a deal. Somehow in that glorious time so much of the pain and hardship and death that I had witnessed over the year began to leave me. All forgotten. It was so good to be with my people again.

We walked through Central Park for a while, passed through the zoo, sat down on a park bench, chatted, hugged, and decided to return to the hotel and nap. When we awoke it was 8 pm. We selected a fine restaurant. When we reached the desk the maitre d' looked down at us and asked if we had a reservation. I smiled and said no. He said he would find us a table, which he did. Then I noticed a banquette in the back of the room which looked especially comfortable and, reaching for a bill in my pocket, asked if he could accommodate us. Recognizing this familiar gesture, he smiled and quickly made the arrangements.

"Nothing has really changed" I said to Dot as we snuggled into our seats. "The Maitre d' is still the Maitre d'."

The next day we returned to our apartment and discovered that Carol was utterly delighted with her weekend, and wanted a repeat performance soon.

Seizing the opportunity, we asked Mrs. Becker if she could stay with Carol for a week while we drove to Florida to visit my parents.

Mrs. Becker was delighted, and Carol couldn't wait to get rid of us. We decided to drive rather than take the train, and to do so in one of the cars left over from our automobile-selling days, an old Chevrolet with an impressive shield on both front doors saying "U.S. Government, Official Use Only."

Since Dot had never enjoyed the privilege of being an officer's wife, we decided to take our time driving down, and to stop to along the way at as many army camps as we could.

Now I'm still in uniform, understand, and I have a number of impressive medals pinned across my chest. This means that Dot and I have visiting privileges at army bases, and because I'm a decorated officer we're eligible for the red carpet. What's more, we're driving this important-looking "government" vehicle that makes us look like big shots.

Every time we pulled into a base, the officers think we're VIP's, and they give us the blue ribbon treatment. The "U.S. Government" legend on our car piques their interest even more, and imaginations go wild. (The fact that the car is a 1942 Chevy doesn't seem to dampen their enthusiasm.) Some of the officers' wives even think we're being transferred to their base, and they leap on Dot, inviting her to join the country club, the bridge club, the mah-jong club. By the time we reach Florida we feel as if we'd been wined and dined by half the United States Army.

In Florida my parents were delirious to see us and they introduced us to all their friends. I watched the face of my mother and father as they introduced us. They were so proud.

A day or two later a little old lady came over and cornered me.

"Can I ask you a question, sonny?"

"Sure!"

She looked pensively at me for a moment, then at our "government" vehicle sitting in my parents' driveway.

"My son was in the army too," she said. "How come they didn't give him a big government car to come home with like you?"

◆→ ◆→

After a wonderful visit in Florida, Dot and I drove directly home, bypassing the military privileges. Both of us were anxious to see Carol but as might have been predicted, when we walked into the apartment she made a face and asked if we really had to stay home that night, that it had been so much fun sleeping with Mrs. Becker that she wanted to keep doing it.

We tried to explain that the reason we came home was to be with her. Whereupon she responded that she was perfectly happy to stay with Mrs. Becker.

For a moment I thought how good it would be to be back in Germany!

Cheaper By the Carload

During the first few years after the Second World War, it must be admitted, the American government took very good care of its veterans. One of the kindest things they did—at least in my opinion—was to form the War Assets Administration.

Overseeing an armada of warehouses from New York to California and everywhere in between, the War Assets Administration's sole job was to divest itself of thousands upon thousands of tons of surplus goods that had been earmarked for the war effort but that never even reached the docks. When I say surplus I'm not just talking about guns and ammo. I'm talking about every commodity that a human being could need to live and prosper: canned foods, soap, dredging machinery, reading glasses, undershirts, carpets, toothpaste, rubber hose, light bulbs, tires, grass seed, typewriters, easy chairs, kitchen sinks—you name it, the War Assets Administration had it in one of their warehouses.

Their way of getting rid of these goods was simple: sell them off cheap and fast to merchants across the country at approximately the same price they had paid for them, cash on the line. And due to a nifty clause in the charter, veterans got first priority. All we had to do was write to the War Assets Administration and tell them we were vets. The Administration, in turn, assigned us an I.D. number and we would then be permitted to go to any government warehouse in the entire United States, and select any of the materials there at cost. Lists were published periodically and updates came in all the time.

To appreciate what a momentous opportunity this was for thousands of newly returned guys like myself, you have to picture what it was like to walk into a supermarket or a department store in the first few months after the war. Today we take it for granted that store shelves will be fully stocked. If they weren't you'd walk out. But in 1946 you took it for granted that they *wouldn't* be stocked. There was simply nothing to stock them with. All the goods were "over there," being used for the war effort.

Now suddenly it's 1946, and there is no more war effort. Supply lines in the European theater are all filled to the brim, but back home, back in the U.S.A. they're empty. It takes a long time to gear down from a war.

Then we learned that the War Assets Administration was selling their stuff to veterans at cost, first come, first served, and any able-bodied vet could participate. With Mel's knowledge of the machinery business and my status as a vet we were a natural.

But as always there was a hitch. A vet couldn't just go to one of their warehouses and buy, say, ten boxes of twine and six cartons of flashlight bulbs. Not on your life. You had to buy these goods *by the carload*—carload, as in a boxcar on a freight train. Otherwise the Administration didn't want to be bothered.

This was a challenge. First of all, you had to have the cash on hand to pay for these enormous quantities of goods.

Second, you had to have a place to store the goods after you bought them; a place to keep them out of the rain till you could turn them over.

Third, you had to have an immediate buyer or you would be left holding the bag. Purchases from the War Assets Administration, you see, were always made on spec, with a strictly no-return policy. This meant that unless you unloaded your goods right away you'd find yourself with a freight car's worth of post holed diggers or pencil sharpeners or God knows what and nobody to take them off your hands.

At the same time there were compensations. The pipelines were so empty just then that merchants were buying anything—*anything*—to get stock back onto their stores. This solved the problem of demand. But you had to act fast. Also the government would ship the equipment once it was sold.

I remember, for instance, visiting a hardware store on Chambers Street in downtown Manhattan and telling the owner that I was a vet, and that I had a carload of 2 1/2-inch fire hose for sale.

"Only one carload!" he roared. "What can I do with only one carload? Haven't you got more than that? I'd like to help you out, pal, you're a vet and all. But it doesn't pay unless I can buy in quantity."

The guy humored me, and eventually bought my meager one carload of fire hose. The point is, though, that the demand was so great at this time, you had to offer enormous quantities of goods or no one was interested.

This magnificent sellers' market lasted only a short time. Six months later I went back to this same store on Chambers Street and told the guy I had four carloads of hose for him this time.

"Carloads!" he roared in the same voice as before. "Who needs carloads? You want to sell me maybe 20, 30 lengths, I'm interested. Who needs a whole carload!"

That's how fast the civilian pipelines were filling up.

On another occasion the government wanted to sell off its enormous surplus of barbed wire. During the war millions of tons of this wire had been stretched across Europe, and this left the people back home who needed it most for their businesses, the farmers and ranchers and herders, pulling their hair in frustration. Now that the war was over and the barbed wire was back on the market, the competition for it went crazy. I actually believe that in 1945 and 1946 certain people out there might have *killed* to get their hands on a roll or two.

The demand for barbed wire finally became so enormous that the government started selling it off in special sales.

One day, for instance, Mel and I received an invitation from the government. On such and such a date, they announced, they would take a special room and sell off five carloads of barbed wire. As regular buyers of war asset materials, we were invited to come and try our luck.

The big day came, and Mel and I walked into a room crammed full of hysterical barbed wire dealers. The person in charge immediately explained to the crowd that only one carload of barbed wire would be sold to each buyer. What's more, since the competition was so fierce, the government had decided not to auction off the goods at all. Instead everyone in the room was invited to submit their names or business card. These names would be placed in a hat, and five of them would be picked at random—quite a sophisticated system, I thought.

As soon as we heard these rules of the game Mel and I started writing. As luck would have it, we always operated under several company names, so we wrote each of these names on a separate card, down along with the names of our friends' companies and a few extras to boot. When the drawing took place and the names were pulled out of the hat, sure enough, one of our numerous titles hit the jackpot and we got our carload.

The interesting thing about all of this was that the carload of barbed wire we won would cost us $4.80 per hundred weight. As soon as the winners were announced several people approached us and offered $10 per hundred weight for this load of wire. All we had to do assign our contract to them. We left the auction room never having seen the barbed wire, never having paid a cent for it—but bringing home a hefty profit nonetheless. Those were the kinds of business opportunities that existed in this country after the war.

Another way in which the War Assets Administration helped veterans get a leg up was to allow them 30 days to pay for their goods. This took care of the problem of supply—you could acquire as much of a certain product as you wanted without having to pay for it right away. This meant that if you had a buyer lined up for this product you never had to put anything out of pocket, a dream situation. It also meant, however, that you had to buy and sell materials on a one-time, job lot basis— stuff you knew nothing about, which you sometimes never saw, and which you probably would never sell again for the rest of your life.

I remember once finding a massive quantity of hospital sheeting in one of the Administration's warehouses. I didn't know a thing about hospital sheeting then, and don't know a thing about it now. But in this Wild West atmosphere it didn't matter. I went to the local hospital-sheeting vendor, told him I had X carloads of sheeting at such-and-such a price, that I could deliver in a week, and was he interested? Yes or no. If yes I picked up the goods from the warehouse, delivered them on schedule, and had the check in my hands well in time to make the 30-day deadline.

Then there was also the comic relief. One day I remember visiting my War Assets contact in Philadelphia who took me down on one of the local piers and showed me a warehouse piled high with, of all things, OCD gas masks. OCD was the Office of Civilian Defense where these masks, presumably, had been kept on hand in case of home attack. The masks were molded out of a rubber casement and had a projecting canister on the bottom that looked a Coca Cola can.

I stood there staring at this mountain of rubber and metal, absolutely bewildered not only at the quantity but by the packaging itself. Each individual gas mask was enclosed in a carton, and there were literally dozens of cartons to each corrugated case. I asked my friend what he was selling them for. Three cents per mask, he said, I asked for several samples and he gave them to me.

I had no idea who would buy such an enormous quantity of gas masks, but the frenzy for goods was so great at this time, I decided, what the heck, I'd take a chance. On the train back to New York I happened to be reading the *New York Times* when, as luck would have it, I came across an article in the business section about a merchant named Henry Modell who owned a very successful army and navy store on Chambers Street. The article claimed that Mr. Modell was a public-spirited citizen, and that just now he was eager to help returning veterans.

This sounded promising, so next morning I showed up at Mr. Modell's store. Introducing myself, I told him I'd read the very complimentary article about him in the *Time*s. I was a vet, I said, and I had a supply of gas masks to sell. I showed him a sample.

Mr. Modell was a large man and very flamboyant. "How many these things you got?" he boomed out.

"I don't know," I answered. "Maybe four or five carloads."

He nodded sagely. "What you want for them, son?"

"Eight cents apiece," I said, thinking this was a pretty fair price.

Mr. Modell turned to his secretary with a grand gesture.

"If my young friend here, Mr. Silverman, will accept six cents apiece for his gas masks, give him an order for five carloads."

Needless to say, I accepted, relieved to get these things off my hands so quickly and to make a small but very definite profit. I wouldn't have to ship the masks either, or handle them, or see them, or even pay for them until I first got paid by Mr. Modell. We shook hands and declared it a deal.

Two weeks passed. One morning I arrived at my office

early and immediately the phone rang. I heard an hysterical voice on the other end.

"What're you trying to do to me! What are you trying to do to me?"

"Who is this?"

"Who the hell do you think it is!?" the answer came back in the unmistakable boom of Mr. Modell.

"What's the problem, sir?"

"What are you trying to do to me!" Modell screamed again, entirely out of control. "What the hell are you trying to do!"

It took several moments to calm him and get to the heart of the problem. "I got gas masks lying here from Fourth Street to Fifth Street," he hollered, "From Broadway to Lafayette Street. There are still two trailers waiting to be unloaded. And that's not bad enough? It's also raining!"

I told him I'd be down as soon as possible.

I drove to Modell's warehouse, and sure enough, cartons of OCD gas masks were stacked up completely around the block as high as a man could reach. On the street in front of his store were two huge trailer trucks loaded down with thousands more masks. The trucks were blocking the streets, and cars were honking, people were shouting!

Switching into my army training, I shouted out "Send those two trailers back for a couple of days right away! Until you get these boxes into your warehouse!"

Modell agreed this was the only thing to do, and for the rest of the day we worked getting the boxes unloaded and out of the way.

We parted on good terms, though in the weeks to come I got a kick out of reading Modell's weekly ads in the *New York World Telegram*. For the first few weeks they announced a sale on gas masks—only 18 cents apiece, get them while they last. A few weeks after that there was an even bigger gas mask sale—for 15 cents apiece this time. The last time I saw the ad the sale price was down to a nickel apiece, a penny less than Mr. Modell had paid me for them.

As time passed, the competition for goods in the New York area became increasingly cutthroat, and the amount of materials I could pick up locally decreased rapidly. But we were working with an unusual advantage: I knew the territory.

That is, when I was in the secondhand automobile business I'd spent years buying and selling merchandise in places like Denver, Kansas City, Phoenix—you name it, I was there. I knew the streets in these cities, I knew where to find things. I knew which hotels to stay at. I knew the people.

If we thus had a customer who was looking for, say, 50 carloads of business envelopes, and I knew that the War Assets Administration in Salt Lake City had a warehouse full of business envelopes, I had no hesitation about driving to Salt Lake City, making a deal, and shipping the goods back to New York in time to make a deal. That helped too.

Our policy, what's more, was *sell it quick*. Unlike many other buyers at the time, we didn't have much working capital and had turn over whatever we purchased right away or get stuck with it. The day we bought a load of goods was also the day we started to sell it. Those who had more money, I noticed, were often so busy buying and putting their piles of merchandise into warehouses, that they never stopped to sell. I know for a fact that even today there are warehouses in Brooklyn filled with rusted, broken goods obtained by zealous buyers at this time who believed in their enthusiasm that the boom markets would last forever.

All things considered, though, there was enough stuff around to make a lot of people rich. In fact, traveling the far corners of the country from coast to coast, and visiting one warehouse after the other piled to the ceiling with goods, I couldn't help feeling after a while that we had fought the war in a completely wrong way. All we needed to do for a speedy victory, I decided, was to dump this mountain of goods on the

Germans and Japanese all at once. That would have smothered them all instantly, and ended the war on the spot!

◆→ ◆→

It was a money-maker's dream; and like all dreams, it soon ended. We'd been given a year's grace, maybe two if you stretch it. But by late 1947 the stores were filled to the brim with merchandise, the warehouses were empty, and the party was over.

Mel, Dot and I worried, as one worries when a chapter in life comes to a close, and wondered what we'd do next. But somehow the Man Upstairs always had a new chapter waiting for us in the wings.

Brief Interlude

In this case the chapter—and a brief one it was—arrived by way of a fellow down in Tuscaloosa who called us one day. He'd heard we handled military surplus. Did we happen to have any Quonset huts for sale?

Perhaps you remember Quonset huts, those prefabricated portable storage sheds with the curved, corrugated metal roofs. You saw them everywhere in the first decade after the war looking like a cross between a huge vacuum cleaner and a small airplane hangar; ugly as all hell, but boy, so cheap to buy and so easy to maintain. There was a surplus of the things immediately after the war, and nobody knew what to do with them. Then the army got a bright idea. Millions of GI's were returning home just then and there simply wasn't enough housing to accommodate them. Why not settle the vets and their families in Quonset huts, said the government, until they can find more substantial living quarters?

In the next few years Quonset hut villages began springing up in every state and especially in the areas surrounding military bases. Measuring a standard 24 feet long and 48 feet wide, they could be divided into two apartments of 24 feet by 24, and furnished plain vanilla with a minimal kitchen, a dining area, a tin shower, and two small bedrooms, one for mom and dad, the other for the kids. Rent: $48 a month.

It was a pretty good deal if you had nowhere else to go. Good enough so that lots of veterans wanted to keep renting them indefinitely. The army, however, wasn't in the landlord business, and by the end of 1948 most of the occupants had been sent packing; which meant that the army had a surplus of Quonset huts on its hands again. It was around this time that the call came in to us from the guy in Tuscaloosa.

Now in my rambles round various War Assets warehouses I'd noticed piles of these pre-fab huts stacked up all over the place. Having been raised in upstate New York farm country, it occurred to me that these huts would make perfect outbuildings on a farm for tractors and equipment.

Mel and Dot agreed, so right away we bought a number of huts (they came in pieces, early ancestors of today's modular housing), and advertised them in farm journals across the East Coast.

Farmers have always had an eye for a good deal, and soon the orders came pouring in. Purchasing the huts from the government for $65 and selling them for $350, our role in the transaction was strictly middleman: no pickup, no delivery, just cash and carry. Buyers came to us, loaded the huts onto their vehicles, trucked them home, and set the buildings up themselves. They were simple to put together, at least in theory. The corrugated metal sheets snapped into place and were held together by double-sided nails. All you needed, we told our buyers, was a claw hammer, a screw driver and a free weekend.

As it turned out, assembly was a little more demanding. I remember one night a guy came to see me. He and his two sons had been working like dogs all day setting up their newly purchased Quonset hut and now it was getting dark. The guy comes into my office, a nice guy, quiet, mild-mannered guy, and says, "I got to ask you a question, Mr. Silverman."

"What's that?" I asked.

"Did you ever put one of these huts together yourself?"

"No."

"I didn't think so," he said. "If you ever had, you wouldn't be making it sound so easy!"

A New Business, a New Life

Then one day the Quonset hut reserve dried up, and there we were again, without a job. By 1950 all we had left from the War Assets days were odds and ends in our storefront in Long Island plus a few sturdy machine tools—a press, a sheer, various and sundry. Machines like these were still hard to find, so we decided to sell them off at a good price and capitalize another business. We advertised in the classifieds, and one day a local guy offered to take the machines off our hands. How much do we want for them?

I didn't know exactly what these things were worth, and I didn't want to let them go too cheaply. We argued back and forth for a while, and finally the guy starts to get impatient.

"Tell you what I'll do," he said. "I'll *rent* the damned things from you!"

Rent the damned things—the words had a certain ring.

I told him I'd talk about it to my partners, and let him know.

At first Mel didn't like the idea. He didn't believe in leasing, at least not machinery. Cars, maybe, or property. But machines?

Things just weren't done that way at this time, you see.

If you look in the Yellow Pages today under "Machinery Leasing" you'll probably find 600 names. But if you looked in 1950 you wouldn't find a thing. Like Mel said, it just wasn't done.

But at the same time things were changing, especially as far as taxes went. For the first time in history, depreciation was becoming a major factor in financial transactions, and businessmen were suddenly discovering that it made more sense to rent a business item and take the depreciation on it than to buy it outright.

Take a boiler, for example. According to tax law at the time, if you purchased a boiler it had to be depreciated over a seven-year period. If you *rented* this same boiler you could depreciate it in three years. Big difference.

I explained all this to Mel, and we kicked the idea of around for a while, and finally we decided to give it a shot. We would not only rent the machines to this guy from Long Island; we would try our hand at renting machinery to anyone who was interested.

And thereby begins a tale.

◦▸ ◦▸ ◦▸

Chapter 13

◆→ ◆→

AN ENTIRELY NEW IDEA

The Beginning of the Beginning

At first I didn't think very much about it.

We'd been a little creative, that's all, rented out a few old machines instead of selling them outright. That was that.

Now that the War Assets reserve had dried up, things were shaky for us financially, and Dot, Mel, and I were busy night and day sniffing around trying to find a business that would keep us afloat. We didn't have much time to dwell on the past.

Then one day about three months after we'd made this crazy rental bargain I received a phone call from the lessee, a Mr. Goldberg. He said he wanted to talk.

About what? I wondered. Maybe he wasn't happy with the way things were working out. Maybe he wanted to return the three clunkers and wiggle out of his contract. Maybe he was a crook or a crank. I was concerned.

We met the next day.

To my delight, not only was Mr. Goldberg innocent of any wrong intentions. He was wildly enthusiastic about the deal he'd made with us, and wanted to do another.

I asked him what he had in mind.

Well, he said, during the past year he'd been seriously considering buying a certain bookkeeping machine manufactured by Burroughs, the giant office machine conglomerate. At first he was going to buy the machine outright. Then it occurred to him: Why not let that Silverman guy buy the machine and lease it to me under the same rental terms as before? It worked once. Why not again?

Mr. Goldberg's proposal caught me unaware.

Without giving the matter much thought, I explained that I knew absolutely nothing about Burroughs bookkeeping machines; that I couldn't offer a warranty of any kind; that I had no idea how to repair a bookkeeping machine or how to install one, and certainly didn't know how to maintain one; and that anyway, I wasn't in the office-machine leasing business in the first place.

None of this perturbed my visitor. He assured me that he would pick out the machine himself, and that the Burroughs salesman would get it up and running. Burroughs would also provide the warranties, he promised, and the necessary servicing. All we had to do was purchase the machine and lease it to him. He—and Burroughs—would take care of the rest.

Mr. Goldberg handed me a brochure published by the Burroughs company describing the machine. It looked big and complicated.

"Go ahead," he said."Call the people from Burroughs. Talk to them about it. They have a sales office right here in Long Island City. What do you have to lose?"

I went home that night in a puzzled state of mind. At first I kept thinking that something must be wrong with this deal. Somehow it was too good to be true. I buy a machine, turn around and lease it for three years. This idea was weird enough—things like that weren't done in 1950's.

During these three years of the lease the lessee makes monthly payments with interest included. When the lease is up the lessee can either buy the machine outright for 10 percent of its original cost, or he can return it, and we get to rent it again to others.

Meanwhile the lessee doesn't have to lay out a big chunk of cash as an initial investment. He can pay it out monthly, a system with obvious advantages. At the end the lease he can then get rid of the machine if he thinks it's obsolete. Or he can buy it at a discount price. He also gets some terrific tax breaks along the way.

Meanwhile on our side, we've made a profit at the end of the three years, and we get to either sell the machine or re-lease it.

It's a win-win situation.

What's wrong with this picture? There has to be a catch, we thought.

I kept reviewing the concept with Mel and Dot, and try as we might we couldn't find anything wrong with the idea.

The more we talked the better I liked it. Despite our initial doubts, there *was* nothing wrong with the concept. In fact, it was fantastic. *Revolutionary* even. That's right, "Revolutionary" would not be too ambitious a word. As far as we knew, nobody else was doing anything like this with business machines, or with any other kind of equipment either. So why not us?

I called Burroughs and set up an appointment. I introduced myself to the Burroughs sales manager and to Mr. Goldberg's sales rep. The sales manager showed me the machine, explained its capabilities, and announced that its selling price was $6,500.

What kind of deal might I be interested in making? he wanted to know. Was I interested in buying the machine outright?

I explained that the only way I would consider purchasing this machine, or any machine like it, was to lease it to Mr. Goldberg's firm.

The Burroughs man seemed puzzled and asked why Mr. Goldberg wasn't planning on buying the machine outright. Or why he wasn't arranging for a bank loan or instalment loan if he didn't want to lay out the cash. He had no concept of how a leasing deal worked.

So I sat down, and for the first time—but decidedly *not* the last time—began to explain to the Burroughs representatives the way our leasing plan worked. I explained how the lessee could depreciate the machine more rapidly if he leased it than if he purchased it outright, and how this transaction would not appear on his balance sheet as a debt.

And so forth.

When I finished my sales pitch, it was clear that the Burroughs sales manager didn't get it, at least not entirely, but that something about it intrigued him. And anyway, as far as he was concerned he didn't really care who bought this machine, just as long as he could make a cash sale.

Once again I assured the manager that I knew nothing about business machines, that I had no intention of using this bookkeeping machine myself, and that my company would serve purely in a financial capacity. Burroughs would have to maintain the equipment, service it, guarantee it. We insisted that the lessee agree he had selected the machine, that the machine performed the functions he required, and that he would not look to our company for *anything* other than financing.

After a bit more discussion and further puzzled looks, the sales manager agreed to all the terms, and I issued a purchase order subject to Mr. Goldberg's signing my lease.

We shook hands all around, congratulated each other, smiled, made pleasant talk—and to this day I'm not sure if the sales manager entirely understood what the deal was all about.

Making It Up as We Go Along

That night I went home feeling extremely exuberant, and sat down with Mel and Dot at the kitchen table. So far so good, we all agreed. But it was now our job to figure out exactly what form our lease document would take. Mel, of course, was an old hand at leasing automobiles. But this was a different kind of deal. Basically we would have to make it up as we went along.

After putting our heads together for several nights, we came up with the following blueprint that we would stick to, give a little, take a little, for years to come.

The machine Mr. Goldberg wanted cost $6,500. We would buy it and rent it to him for three years at $227 a month. At the end of the three-year term, Mr. Goldberg could buy his machine for $650—that is, for 10 percent of its original cost, not a bad deal. Besides these advantages, Mr. Goldberg could also charge the rental expenses off as a balance sheet item under the category of "expense."

I packed off the new lease and sent it to Mr. Goldberg. He read it, had no questions or quibbles, signed, and promptly returned it.

After I received the signed lease, I visited the Burroughs office again, and made arrangements for delivery.

While I was sitting there chatting with the sales manager, one of his reps joined us and boomed out:

"You know, there are probably a lot of other customers that would like to use this plan! Why not get some of the guys together and tell them about it at the next sales meeting?"

The sales manager's ears perked up. You could see his wheels turning. Introducing a groundbreaking sales idea like leasing could make him look v-e-r-y good to his superiors. What did he have to lose?

"Sounds like a good idea," he said, turning to me. "Marty, do you think you could come over one of these days and explain how this leasing plan works to some of my sales-men?"

It appeared that the sales manager was getting a better understanding of how the lease worked, and was beginning to see the possibilities.

I agreed to visit the next week. Then the sales manager told me something that sweetened the pot even more. If one purchased more than $25,000 worth of Burroughs equipment in any one year, he said, Burroughs gave a five percent discount. This was a sizeable amount of savings when you added it up, and made the deal even more attractive from our standpoint.

A week later I returned to the Burroughs office. Five of his best men were there waiting to hear my spiel.

Introductions were made, handshakes; it was all very light, lots of smiles, jokes, coffee and buns—your typical sales meeting. The minute we sat down to talk, however, things became all business, and I discovered that beneath the sales-men's banter I was talking to an extremely eager, intelligent audience. Every man in that room was anxious to improve his sales, that was the bottom line. And I was about to explain to them how to do it.

The first thing I explained was that the leasing deal we offered was a *brand new way of thinking*, a new kid on the block, a fresh tool of the trade, unlike anything anyone else was currently offering. If a salesmen added this method to his repertoire, I said, he would automatically add to his sales as well. With very little effort.

I then described the ins and outs of how the deal worked, and showed the salesmen a model contract, which we now had printed and arranged. We give you our lease forms and you carry them with you when you make a sales call. Once your customer is interested in a particular machine, you tell them about this new leasing option. You explain that they don't have to go to the bank or find all the money at once. They can make monthly payments over a three-year period at a reasonable rate, then buy the machine for 10 percent of its original cost.

If the customer is interested, I said—and many will be—all you have to do is call us, put us in touch with that customer, and we'll take care of the rest.

Because leasing makes payment so easy, I added, and because of the inherent tax breaks it offers a lessee, this option automatically enhances your chances of closing the deal. Everyone comes out a winner. What's more, I added, if a customer wants to go the leasing route, this solves another perennial sales problem—the problem of what happens when a customer agrees to buy your machine, then gets turned down at the bank. With this new lease option, I explained, once the customer agrees to the deal there's no waiting around for a bank to say yea or nay. Assuming the customer has decent credit, you just go ahead and draw up the papers

The salesmen sat there taking it all in, whispering among themselves, trying to think up questions to ask. As I answered their queries one after the other, I could see their interest growing.

By the end of the meeting we agreed this was an everything-to-gain-nothing-to-lose deal, and within 30 days Burroughs' city office was offering our lease plan to all their customers.

Fortunately for us, the deal caught on right from the start.

Every time one of these salesmen came back to the office with a signed lease this generated new interest among the other salesmen. Soon they began pushing our lease plan too.

Not *every* customer wanted to go this route, of course. Some still opted to buy the machine in cash, or to borrow from the bank. This was fine because if only one out of five customers ended up leasing, this *still* increased sales considerably, and made the salesman's job a whole lot easier.

Word Gets Out

Burroughs' salesmen started offering leases as a regular part of the finance package, and the idea became increasingly popular. Five or six months after my initial meeting with Burroughs, sure enough, I received a call from a sales manager at NCR—National Cash Register. Their sales manager wanted me to come to their local offices for a chat.

The meeting at NCR was a kind of *déjà vu*—the same small talk as at the Burroughs meeting, the same handshakes and coffee—and raised eyebrows when I explained how our lease plan worked, then the slow realization, the shrewd smiles, the understanding.

Since we already had Burroughs as a client and the results were evident, NCR was an easier sell. We were helped even more by the fact that their salesmen were complaining that Burroughs salesmen were suddenly bringing in all the office machine business. A little investigation showed that our leasing plan was making a difference.

Now NCR wanted in. Did we have an exclusive deal with Burroughs?

I explained that we considered ourselves a kind of bank, and that we leased equipment to any solid company that was interested in doing business. I also mentioned that Burroughs offered us a 5 percent discount on all equipment we purchased over $25,000. Could NCR do the same?

The NCR sales manager thought they could. We had a deal.

I returned to our offices extremely excited, realizing that we had something really major on the fire here. It's one thing to have a single large company pushing our lease plan, quite another to have *two* such companies, both of them major Fortune 500's. The speed at which NCR agreed, moreover, was also a tip-off that the leasing concept was a viable one, and a sign of things to come. We had something big here, I sensed, something important and colossal. We just had to steer our course carefully to capitalize on the concept.

To celebrate our success with NCR, we decided to change our name.

We had been operating under the name National Equipment Sales. Now that the leasing option had been added, we wanted our name to reflect this fact. So we formed a new corporation, and called it National Equipment Rental Ltd.

The "Ltd.," by the way, was an afterthought. When we first sent our legal papers up to Albany to be registered, the State informed us the name National Equipment Rental was unacceptable. Don't ask me why.

So one of us thought of adding an Ltd to the title.

We sent the name in again with the added letters, and this time Albany accepted. Again, God knows why.

Ironically, in the years that followed those silly little initials would prove an enormous asset to our company, mainly because people thought we were a British outfit, and thus very rich and prestigious. We used to joke among ourselves about putting "Sir" and "Lady" to our names on the company letterhead.

All of this was of course tremendously exciting for three kids who had been stumbling around for years trying to find a business that would make it big. Now we'd found it. It was definitely catching on. But there was one problem that continued to haunt us, one major black hole: where were we going to get the money to buy all the equipment? If we didn't own the equipment we couldn't very well lease it. And if we couldn't lease it, we had nothing at all.

Our job was cut out for us.

But finding backing, as I'm sure you can imagine, was easier said than done.

At first we borrowed every penny we could from our friends and relatives. This source dried up quickly, and we were soon thrown back on the fickle generosity of the banks.

At this these venerable institutions still could not grasp the idea that an organization would pay rent on a piece of equipment they did not wish to own. Today, of course, you can go to a bank to finance the most outlandish deals—films, inventions, chancy real estate ventures. But in the 1950's, banks were a good deal more conservative than now, a good deal less willing to go out on a limb, even a short limb. Since we were a start-up company, and since we were peddling an idea more than a product, I knew it would be a tough sell to any financial institution.

But I had no idea how tough.

In the months that followed I went from bank to bank. At each meeting I patiently explained how we worked. I showed the bank rep all the facts and figures. I pointed out that we worked with several huge companies like Burroughs and NCR, and that all we needed was the cash to buy more equipment. With a little more money, I explained, we could become a major new player in town.

"Look here," I'd say, putting it as simply as I could to the man behind the desk. "We buy a piece of equipment for $6,500. We lease it out for 36 months at $227 a month. This gives us a profit of $1,672 over the period of the lease, which is almost a third of the value of the machinery itself. At the end of this time we either sell the equiment or rent it again for a similar profit."

I would then look the bank manager in the eye and challenge him to find a loophole or flaw in the deal.

He never could.

At the same time, the bankers never went for the deal. The more I explained, the blanker the stare in their eyes became. Then the same predictable questions:

✔ Why don't your customers go to the bank?
✔ Why don't your customers just pay on the installment plan?

✔ Why doesn't the manufacturer supply the funds?

✔ Why would anyone want to tie themselves up for three whole years with continuous payments?

And so forth.

I answered these and a hundred other questions as patiently and succinctly as I could. But to no avail. Bank after bank said no. They just refused to believe that any reasonable company would buy into such a deal. No matter how hard I explained the concept, there was a wall in their thinking that couldn't be broken through.

I'll never forget one banker in particular, a staid little man with white hair meticulously parted down the center and a three-piece suit with a huge carnation in the lapel, something out of central casting. I told him my story. He thought about it for a long moment, looked pensively out the window for several more moments, then turned to me.

"Son," he said. "You want to go into business on a shoestring. And you want this bank to supply you with the shoestring."

That was that.

Failure after failure followed. Bank after bank said no. Several months of sheer frustration and it became apparent that no bank was ever going to give us the money, at least as things now stood.

This meant we had to turn to the last possibility, the financial court of last resort, that one-way street to the brink— the factor.

The Factor Factor

Factors, as you perhaps know, are glorified pawn brokers.

Which means they are companies that accept accounts receivable as security for short-term loans. Which is a fancy way of saying they charge interest rates three times higher than anybody else to poor little start-up companies like ours that are too risky to qualify for bank financing.

I shouldn't talk too negatively about factors, however, because if it weren't for these clever gentlemen we might still be selling Quonset huts.

At the time there were only two factors in New York City. One was the firm of James E. Talcott, the other the firm of Walter E. Heller. We understood fully that doing business with a factor meant giving up almost all our profits in interest. But our debts were accumulating, our business was growing, and we had no alternative.

So one fine morning I took myself to Mr. Talcott's office where I was immediately taken in to see the president, Herb Silverman. Though his last name was the same as mine, there was unfortunately no blood relation here that either of us could trace, and I knew from the start that it would be all business with this old gentleman.

I went through my spiel on leasing, which by now I knew by rote, and after a bit of haggling and explanation, Mr. Silverman said he thought he could help. Here was the deal. After signing a lease with a customer, we were to bring the lease to Talcott's office. Talcott would advance us 80 percent of the face value of each lease, and in addition would receive a mortgage on the equipment. We would then make payments to Talcott monthly at a hair-raising 16 percent (the prime rate at the time was 6 percent).

Now at the time, the percentage rate was charged our customers on their monthly payments was 18 percent. Which meant that if we paid Talcott 16 percent, we were, in essence, working for Talcott. And this, even though our company had such a fancy English name.

It was a terrible deal, really, and yet an inescapable one. Sometimes, we knew, you have to take a step backward to advance two steps forward, and this was one of those times. I agreed to the terms of the deal, and signed on the dotted line.

Time passed

Before too long we owed Talcott almost a million dollars. Though they were getting concerned at our hefty bill, the good news was that the paper we gave them was always perfect, and our company was growing in leaps and bounds. Every day we were writing new leases, and though we weren't making much profit—almost none, really—we weren't losing, either. The business, meanwhile, just kept getting bigger and bigger. We simply had to hang on until we could find reasonable financing.

During all this time, moreover, I was still going to bank after bank hoping to get a break, hoping that I would find just *one* bright banker out there who understood the fantastic implications of what we were doing, and who was willing to trust and take a chance.

But alas, the more I hunted the more elusive that banker became. It seemed that for the present time, at any rate, we belonged to Talcott.

The Heavenly Mr. Heller

One day I received a phone call from a Minneapolis-based company called American Tractor asking if we could rent them $350,000 worth of machine tools. Without thinking I stammered out a yes. This was the biggest deal we had ever been involved with by far. While I negotiated with the sales manager on the phone, I motioned for Dot to check the company with Dun and Bradstreet.

American Tractor, it turned out, was an AAA company, the best there is. We were duly impressed, and I agreed to be in their office the next day with all leases signed.

Now at this time the shadow of World War II was still hanging over American industry, and machine tools were not easy to locate. In the office of American Tractor the next day I told their sales manager that it would take us seven or eight months to find, purchase, and prepare all the equipment they needed. Knowing the situation, the sales manager agreed. We completed the deal, went to lunch, and I returned home a happy man.

When I told Dot and Mel that I'd closed on the deal they were ecstatic, and the three of us started counting our money. It looked as if we had finally made the breakthrough. Not only did we have a $350,000 lease with a major company; this company was rated AAA. Which meant that raising the money at a bank to purchase the machinery would be a snap. It was a lot of cash, certainly. But we had more than half a year to do it in. And there wasn't a bank in New York that wouldn't jump at the deal.

But to my amazement, even with a Triple-A company in our pocket, the banks *still* didn't want to know us. All I had to say was the word "lease" and the door clanged shut. The harder I tried, the more I pleaded and cajoled and explained, the less luck I had.

Three months passed, then four, then five. I pounded the pavement, bank after bank. After a while I became increasingly alarmed. Time was running out. The equipment was being prepared. American Tractor was waiting. The contract was binding, and we had no money to float the deal. What to do? We were already in up to our necks in debt with Talcott. The thought of asking them for another $350,000 was out of the question.

There was only chance left.

Because we were up to our limits with Talcott, that left Walter Heller.

The day of my appointment at the Heller offices a fateful thing happened.

I arrived early for the meeting, and was shown into the waiting room.

Sitting across from me was a distinguished-looking old gentleman reading a magazine, and before long we were engaged in conversation. To pass the time, I supposed, he asked me in a fatherly way what my business was. I explained to him our situation with American Tractor, how we wrote leases, how we needed the money to finance our deal. The old man listened sympathetically and grasped the fundamentals of what I told him instantly. We talked for half an hour. Then a secretary came in.

"Your office is ready now, Mr. Heller," she announced.

The old gentleman stood up—it was indeed Walter E. Heller himself—stretched, smiled, and informed me that the custodial staff had been tidying things up a bit. Would I care to follow him to his office, and continue our interesting conversation?

What a stroke of good fortune! The famous Mr. Heller, well known in financial circles for his tight-fisted deals and merciless foreclosures, was a pussycat after all. We had gotten along splendidly, and I felt that at last I'd found a friend.

Once inside his office, however, the fatherly charm vanished instantly, and Mr. Heller bared his teeth.

"Look here," he said, leaning over the desk, staring at me in a predatory way. "I'll make it simple for you, Silverman. Here's how it works. We'll take over the lease with American Tractor. We'll advance all the funds. We'll collect all the money from them directly. And we'll give you 10 percent residuals at the end of the three-year lease. That's the best I can do. Take it or leave it."

If ever a man punctured my balloon it was Walter E. Heller. I'd been foolish enough to let him know how vulnerable we were. Now he was taking full advantage, knowing that we had no alternatives, dashing all our hopes for a profit in the process.

I told him I'd think about it.

A few weeks later, having failed to find money elsewhere, I returned to Mr. Heller hat-in-hand and agreed to all his terms. This way we could at least establish our credit and continue to build—and perhaps write smaller leases in the future.

One thing this deal would do, moreover, was insure our credibility in the marketplace. Even if we made only a few dollars, even if we didn't make any money at all, we would show the business world that our credit was solid and our word good.

And that counted.

Back to the Drawing Board

With our vision of riches dashed once again, we returned to the work-a-day routine of finding businesses that needed leased equipment. Half our working day was now spent preparing and writing these leases, the other half trying to find money to pay for the machinery.

More time passed, and gradually we began to build up a sizeable portfolio. Nothing as dramatic as the American Tractor deal, mind you, but a good lease here, a good lease there, and things progressed. We hardly noticed the way time flew by, and could hardly believe it one day when we produced a balance sheet with a $250,000 net worth.

Our patience was paying off, our business was growing on a daily basis, our credit and our reputation were impeccable. In three years time, Talcott had not lost a dime on any of our accounts. We continued to expand, and constantly found new manufacturers in the office equipment line with whom to do business.

Meanwhile, after the disastrous American Tractor deal, Mr. Heller came back and offered us the same terms that Talcott had given us. This opened up another avenue of financing, and we jumped at it. Heller's bite was exorbitant, however, and we still weren't making any profit. If only we could find a bank, Mel, Dot and I kept saying every evening at the dinner table. If only we could find a bank.

The problem was Dun and Bradstreet. By now our reputation was good and our business solid. But every time we applied for financing the same question came up: how are you rated by Dun and Bradstreet?

We explained that we were a new company just getting started, and that although we had some capital, we were still listed as a C3 company—which meant we had no more than a quarter-of-a-million dollars net worth. Given that we were in a so-called "risky" business, this rating was too low for the banks to bother with. Their doors remained closed.

●+ ●+

The good news, though, was that so far no competitors had appeared on the horizon. We were still the only name under "Leasing" in the Yellow Pages. Why no one had come along to give us a run for our money, we couldn't figure out. Word had certainly spread by now, and you would think that others would want a piece of the pie. Yet so far we owned the field.

We knew it wouldn't last forever, though, and that we'd better get ourselves well established in the field before someone else caught on. Which brought us back to our original dilemma again—financing.

What about going public? Mel suggested one day.

At first the idea seemed fantastic. But the more we

talked about it the more sense it made. Assuming we could get the capitalization to do so, the problem with going public meant we would no longer own our own business, no longer be independent, our own bosses—all the reasons you go into business for yourself in the first place.

On the other hand, how else were we going to grow?

I remember Mel asking me one night whether I would rather have 100 percent of nothing, or 10 percent of something really big.

His point was well made. I couldn't argue. We all knew it was true: we had to go public.

But how?

The only place I knew to begin was Wall Street.

It Only Takes One

So once more, dear friends, into the breach. This time I found myself making the rounds of the biggest firms on Wall Street, trying to convince them to do what their brothers in the banking industry had refused.

This was not entirely pie-in-the-sky, however. Wall Street financiers are a somewhat more speculative breed than bankers, and right off the bat several of them seemed, if not exactly interested, at least intrigued.

I did my regular routine at each meeting. I explained how our business was growing rapidly, that it was critical for us to get a AAA rating from Dun and Bradstreet in order to qualify for bank credit, that we already had $250,000 on our balance sheet, and that we were currently looking for an investor to give us the remaining $750,000 required to earn that rating.

No firm actually turned us down flat as had occurred at the banks. Each person I visited promised to review our balance sheet, discuss the proposal at board meetings, and so forth.

When nothing came of any of these promises after several weeks passed, I decided not to sit around and wait, and upped my number of appointments. After doing the rounds of the larger Wall Street businesses, I turned to the smaller firms.

It only takes one, they say, and they're right: only one. I don't know why it worked out this way. I don't know what made this one company say yes when all the others — so many, many others — said no. But that's how it happened the day I walked into the firm of Sutro Brothers.

The head of the company was Walter Florzeimer, a smart, efficient man who listened to my story once and once only, nodded his head a few times, made a few notes, and promptly announced that he liked what he heard, and that he would give us the money we needed right away.

Simple as that.

There was one condition.

I held my breath. Did he want my children? Would I have to work as a galley slave?

In fact, his condition was a fairly simple one. He did not wish to be involved with a family company, he explained. He would therefore allow us to conduct business in our accustomed way for two more years. At the end of that time we would then go public. Otherwise he would want out of the deal.

That was all.

It seemed a reasonable request, and an understandable one. Mom-and-pop businesses are fine in their place. But this was the big leagues now, and in the big leagues you do things in a big-league way. We shook hands on the deal.

Mr. Florzeimer then called in one of his managing partners, Harold Friedman. He told Harold to draw up the necessary papers, shook hands with me again, and left the room. Harold and I set to work putting the deal together. From that day on, from the moment we met, we have been best friends for almost 50 years.

A new era was dawning.

Back Home with the News

I left Sutro Brothers' office, walked downstairs, and found myself faced with an odd dilemma. Should I spend a nickel to call Dot and Mel with the news? Or just get on the subway and use the nickel to ride home?

Don't ask me why, but after having just spent months trying to raise vast sums of money, talking my head off, making tough choice after tough choice, this silly decision seemed enormous. Battle fatigue, I suppose.

Finally, I decided to grab the subway and go straight home. Standing there on the platform waiting for the train the truth of the situation hit me. We'd done it! Our next financial statement would have a AAA rating. Was I dreaming? Was all this real? Did it all really happen? I wasn't entirely sure. It all seemed so easy. You wait for something half your life. Then when it comes, instead of feeling real, it's vague—dreamlike. You have to pinch yourself. Why it's like that, I don't know. I needed to share the news with others.

Once I arrived and announced that we has a deal at Sutro it was like the dam broke for all of us. Three years of struggling to get our little company on its feet. Three years of turn-downs at the bank, closed doors, blank stares across the desk. Now this. The realization hit us all at once. We hugged, cheered, sang, fought back the tears. We understood that everything would be different from now on—easier, more manageable, better. Within a month of two we would be receiving a check from Sutro Brothers for $750,000. Unbelievable! More money than we had ever seen. Remember, this was the late 1950's when money still meant something, and when three-quarters of a million dollars was the equivalent of, say, 5 million today. Now, at last, we would have a balance sheet to take to the banks. Now, at last, we could get the lines of credit we so desperately needed—credit at 6 percent, not 16. What a difference! What a change.

At the same time, we also understood that our family-business days would be coming to an end, with all that implied. Two more years to run things our way, with all the fun and comradeship it brought us. Then: big business. It was a tit-for-tat deal, an offer we couldn't refuse. But that didn't make it any easier.

Looking Back

As we planned for our new future, as we put the details of the new deal into place, we also thought about the past, and of all the stepping stones that had brought us to this moment.

We thought about our early days in New York City, about growing up in Troy; about the gas station, the used car business, the War Assets Administration; about our parents, our school, the many friends and business associates we had met and worked with through the years.

All these people and places and events had somehow served as stepping stones to bring us where we were today. Tiny little pieces in a puzzle, drops of rain in the sea, all adding up, forming the stuff of which our lives and our fates were made.

Should we keep our offices here in Long Island City? we wondered. The rent was $35 a month, cheap even by 1950 standards. To date, our little storefront office had served us well. We saw no reason to move. At least not in the near future.

We also decided that from now on Dot would work directly out of the office, do the books, answer the phone, take care of business arrangements while Mel and I would go into the field and search for new customers.

The next question was, did we need to expand our staff? Not really, we decided. Mel and I could do most of the work. Perhaps in the future we would add a salesman or two. But right now this seemed unnecessary.

We did hire a bookkeeper to help Dot, though, and some time before the Sutro deal fell into place an old army buddy of mine, Bernard Rosenberg, had joined us as CPA. Bernie quickly became a driving force behind the business. He kept needling us, reminding us that we had to find financial help, had to locate that outside bankroll if we were going to make a real go of things. Without major funding, he kept hammering away at us, we couldn't grow, couldn't get that pot of gold. He suggested that we slow down on writing leases and spend more time developing sources for funds.

If we hadn't followed Bernie's advice, I should add here, we might still be working for the Talcott Company.

As for legal help, our company turned to Wilbur Silverman, another old army buddy who coincidentally lived in our neighborhood. Around 10 o'clock every evening Wilbur arrived at our house. The kids were put to bed, the coffee pot heated up, and Wilbur, Dot and I sat down at the kitchen table and prepared the next day's leases far into the night. With Wilbur and Bernie's help we probably conducted more business at that little table and wrote more contracts between the hours of 10 PM to midnight, than most companies do in a full day.

It was a small, tight operation. There were two salesmen, Mel and myself, a CPA, a lawyer, all of us not only business associates but personal friends as well. We were as much a family as a business. Over the years we had proved our credibility. With the Sutro deal we gained real net worth and a real balance sheet. Starting out as a tiny company in 1937, it took 20 years to reach success, to find the stepping stone that brought us to this plateau. Yet at no time during these two decades did we ever feel sorry for ourselves, or wonder why we had to work so hard just to keep our heads above the water. All we knew was that every day we came to our little office and did as much as we could. The Man Upstairs would take care of the rest.

Naturally some days were better than others. And some

years were better than others. Now and then there were supreme disappointments and seemingly disastrous setbacks. But we kept going, hoping that the next day, the next year, would be better.

During this 20-year period we picked up a great deal of experience, and became extremely savvy not only in the art and science of leasing but in the practice of business in general. By the time the Sutro opportunity came along we were ready to play in the big time. We had paid our dues. We were prepared to walk the next stepping stone.

Getting Down to Business

It has been said that, "people don't plan to fail, they fail to plan." We didn't want to make that mistake. So right from the beginning we reevaluated our position in light of our $750,000, and carefully thought out our next several moves.

We came to five basic conclusions.

First, we must get our balance sheet to reflect our new million-dollar status. We asked our accountant to give us a new certified statement.

Second, we must take this revised statement to Dun and Bradstreet, and receive our all-important AAA rating.

Third, we must immediately take this statement to the banks and land a line of credit for ourselves, thus reducing our interest costs to manageable proportions.

Fourth, we must notify the factors, both Talcott and Heller, that we no longer needed their services.

This last task, by the way, was a tougher job than I had anticipated.

While it's true that both these companies had charged us grossly usurious interest rates, this was their game and we had gone into the deals with our eyes open. Both companies played fair with us in all dealings, and occasionally shepherded us through difficult moments.

When the time came to move on, I thus thanked them both sincerely for their cooperation, explained our change of circumstances, and told them that without their help we would never have done it. Then I arranged to buy back our portfolio from them piece by piece. This would take some time, I knew, but with a little patience we would get it all done.

Finally, we had to change our way of thinking.

Up to this moment we had viewed ourselves as a kind of local street-corner operation. Now we would be becoming a public company traded on the stock exchange. We had to up-level accordingly—the only limitation we now faced was the Ltd. in our company's name. We even played with the idea of changing these little initials—not at all seriously, I should add—calling ourselves National Equipment Rental *Unlimited*. That's how bright the future now seemed to us.

Growing and building, I'm here to tell you, is a great deal of fun, perhaps more fun than anything a human being can do in this life. And no one enjoyed it more than I did, and Dot did, and Mel did. From this time on we would dream, we would plan, and we would hope—but we would also get down to brass tacks in a new kind of way, taking our little business a good deal further than any of us ever suspected it would go.

❯ ❯ ❯

Chapter 14

❥ ❥

ON OUR WAY

It Was a Miracle

Overnight our attitude changed, our reputation changed, our modus operandi changed, our bank balance changed, our company took off, our profits swelled, our name became synonymous with the leasing business, and our future seemed assured. It was a new ball game, a new show.

We had crossed the commercial Rubicon.

The only things that remained the same were that Dot continued to answer the phone and write letters, Mel continued chasing around after new leases, and I continued trying to arrange bank financing.

Everything changed, in other words, and nothing changed.

This, at any rate, was how it was in the beginning of our association with Sutro Brothers. Soon, however, the winds of serious change would be heading our way, and would blow our little mom and pop business away forever. After this nothing would ever be the same.

Finding a New Office

So the Sutro deal was clinched.

A few days after the meeting that clinched things for us I went by their offices and picked up the check—the $750,000 check—and deposited it with loving care in the bank. Then I waited for Lydesdorf, one of the city's largest accounting firms, to begin examining our books so we could produce a bona fide financial statement for Dun and Bradstreet.

It was all a formality, yet like anything that has to do with money, it took lots and lots of time; or in this case, along with a lot of other administrative chores, several months.

In the meantime it was evident that much as we regretted it, we could no longer stay in our little $35 a month storefront office on Jackson Avenue in Long Island City. Although at first we thought we'd remain there and work out of this *almost* rent-free location, things were changing. Our little office had met all our needs up till now: Dot did the secretarial work, took phone messages, handled the accounting, wrote the letters. Mel and I were out on the road. You don't need a lot of space to write letters and be out on the road. So it more than sufficed.

But now suddenly there was this check—this very big check—and with it a handful of new considerations.

Simple business prestige, for one. A Long Island City address didn't look very classy on our letterhead.

Second, we knew we'd have to expand our staff sometime in the future. When, exactly, we didn't know, but certainly the day would come. This would mean more desks, more files, more room.

Third, what if one of our customers came to visit us? It didn't happen very often. But when it did come, having a place of business in the bowels of an industrial district a subway ride outside of Manhattan Island wouldn't win us any points. Can you imagine a Triple-A corporation maintaining its facilities in a broken-down, single-room storefront with boiler pipes hanging from the ceiling, peeling paint, and front windows that always needed washing?

It was time to move.

So we considered the possibilities. And after several conversations, we agreed that we should move our location outside of city limits entirely. This way we wouldn't have to pay New York City taxes, and at the same time we could find the roomy accommodations we needed at a bargain price.

Searching various parts of Long Island, we soon discovered a good-sized office space in Floral Park situated one floor above a Chevrolet sales agency. The space was light and airy, and there was plenty of room to expand. The rent was $100 a month. This was more than double what we were paying in Long Island City, true, but it was a bargain nonetheless.

We took it.

Of course, with our new infusion of capital, you might ask, why didn't we find ourselves a fancy work space somewhere on Madison Avenue?

The reason is sound and simple. Other newcomers to the leasing business made this classic mistake and paid for it in spades. As soon as they began to earn a few dollars, they moved up town, shelling out thousands a month for a place with thick carpets and a pretty receptionist. Usually they were out of business in a year. How fancy does a leasing office have to be, anyway? Who cares? Certainly not the customers who lease tractors and office equipment and drill presses. All they want is their product. And every nickel we made in those days we reinvested back into our business so that we could write more leases.

What's more, most of our business was conducted by mail, or over the phone, or even in the customer's plant. Our offices were for administrative purposes only, and now with our new location we were fancy enough, just in case a customer happened to pay us a visit. We'd leave the leather chairs and the mahogany conference rooms to others.

Traveling Light

So we started to grow. And grow. And grow.

We had a million dollars to work with. Fresh money, We didn't have to hock every lease now. We could build a portfolio. And most importantly, we could talk to the banks.

Of course, the banks weren't about to give us all the financing we requested for every lease. Not the banks.

But at the same time, they now let us in their doors, and occasionally even showed us to their executive offices.

We soon found, in fact, that certain banks were willing—now and then, here and there—to take over some of our existing leases. We were, after all, an AAA business, and that's melody to a banker's ears. It all went slowly, mind you, and always with the understanding that we'd use both the equipment and the leases as collateral.

Best of all, it was clear that we were an equipment *leasing* business, not an equipment purchasing business.

This meant we never really owned any equipment unless we had a lease to use it. We never saw the actual machinery itself either; we simply made the arrangements by phone, then sent it by mail from the manufacturer to the lessee.

This also meant we didn't have to store anything, didn't have to maintain warehouses or equipment depots, didn't have to keep a fleet of flatbed trucks and cranes on hand in our backyard. The manufacturers we dealt with did all this. We were a paper operation, lean and simple.

And this was just the way we liked it. I don't think we could have planned the whole deal any better. It all just evolved as if by magic, as if on its own.

A Changing Financial Structure

With the changing of our financial structure, our mental attitudes changed too.

We felt more secure, more aggressive. We proudly proclaimed to anyone who would listen that at last—yes, at last—that we had become a triple-A company.

We realized that we now had two years to build our company to the point where it could be taken public. Our deal with Sutro Brothers stipulated that we should run our leasing business our usual way for two more years. At the end of this time we would either sell stock, or we would buy Sutro out.

Suddenly every day became important to us; and every day we felt we were making progress toward this commercial end.

We also began to focus on the operational side of our leasing plan, and to organize our systems in a more finely tuned way.

Our leasing program was now specifically aimed at small manufacturers who had a viable product to sell, and who wanted to compete with what was then the state-of-the-art in-house leasing program, the ninety-day cancellable lease of IBM. There were many such manufacturers in various types of businesses. Every one wanted to do what IBM did, to make it easy for their customers to acquire their equipment.

Understand that the concept of leasing equipment was still very much a bold departure from standard business practice of the time. While we found that we had to make the rules up as we went along—we were *creating* the leasing business as much as specializing in it—after a while certain fundamental operating procedures began to emerge. The basics of the deal we made with our customers in various fields of business and industry worked something like this:

First, we agreed to lease equipment to the customer, then arranged to purchase it from the manufacturers. The rental we charged the lessee was based on the cost of this equipment.

For example, say a piece of equipment had a list price of $10,000 but the rental price was $300 a month on a 90-day cancellable lease. We would pay the manufacturer $7,500. The manufacturer did not make full profit on the transaction, but he was selling and building up his volume, and growing in the process. In the long run the deal was as good for him as it was for us, since leasing was increasing his market share by enabling him to better compete.

Next, we give the manufacturer a set of our lease forms for his salesmen to carry with them on the job.

The salesman goes out into the field to rent these selected items. After the purchaser determines what equipment he wishes to acquire, the salesman offers him three methods of payment: cash, an installment plan, and of course, the third and newest option, a lease plan.

If the customer chooses the lease, the salesman whips out our simple printed lease form and the customer signs it. The form is forwarded to us in New York. We issue our purchase order. When the equipment is delivered, which takes about 30 days, and is accepted by the lessee, we then process the manufacturer's invoice for payment.

The end.

Why would a customer choose to lease a piece of equipment rather than buy it outright or pay for it on the installment plan?

We were constantly coming up with reasons why a lease was the best way to fly. The more time we spent in the business the more reasons we discovered. There were tax advantages in leasing. There were financial advantages, there were accounting advantages—the reasons just seemed to keep presenting themselves over time. It was as if we'd opened a treasure box, and the treasures just kept falling out.

Look at it from the lessee's perspective. He leases a piece of equipment with a depreciated life of five, seven, even ten years. When he signs a three-year lease he is in fact writing off the cost of the equipment in three years. It's obvious. In addition, the lessee's balance sheet does not show any debt for the equipment leased. Technically speaking, all he ever owes is a month's rent.

There were hidden advantages too.

After we were in the leasing business for a while we discovered that the real reasons people lease equipment are not always the ones they tell you about.

Many of our lessees, for example, tried to convince us they were leasing equipment simply to save taxes. We soon learned, however, that their motives were more complicated than this, and sometimes more desperate.

Take your average business man. I'm not talking about a major corporation here, but an ordinary guy who's trying to break into the business, or who's struggling to keep his head above water. This guy needs some heavy equipment to stay competitive, say, but his balance sheet isn't all that strong. In fact, when you study it you realize he can't really handle the extra expense of paying for the equipment outright. Since he's struggling already, he certainly doesn't want to show this debt to show up on his balance sheet. What's more, he can write this equipment off in half the ordinary time with a lease, and that saves him money too.

Then, too, there are the instances where a company's credit simply can't support the usual avenues of financing, the straight purchase or the installment plan. These people come to us not because we offer them such good terms. They come to us because we're the only game in town, the only ones who can offer them terms of *any* kind.

So you see, as we got into the business we saw many, many reasons why a customer might choose to lease. After a while, in fact, to tell you the truth, it got so we didn't believe anything a lessee told us about why he was leasing in the first place. We looked at the guy's balance sheet, and saw all kinds of quirky things. There were other circumstances like the ones I've described.

But we never said anything, and always let the guy save face. Why should we? If we got paid—and we almost always did—that was our bottom line. In fact, I take pride today in the fact that we floated a lot of little companies that might otherwise never have made it.

I recall one major private company—I won't mention the name—that was to go public.

In order to go public, and in order to woo stock purchasers, this company needed some impressive tangible assets. So they announced to the stock-buying public that they were currently refurbishing their plant with the latest and greatest in state-of-the-art heavy duty equipment and machinery.

This company then went out, bought carloads of new equipment for their plant—about $500,000 worth of it, to be exact, which was a heck of a lot of equipment. Instead of paying for all of it outright they *then leased* it directly from us.

Of course, this transaction did not appear on their balance sheet—other than as a note listing that they were maintaining a certain amount of rental equipment. Over the next three years the company then paid off this debt, their investors got all their dough, and everyone was happy.

This was an extremely clever ploy, I thought. Yet it was just one of many like it, where a company used our leasing option as a basis for launching an otherwise untenable or even impossible commercial idea. Some of these companies, I should add, eventually went on to become multi-billion dollar businesses.

Another case in point comes to mind. When things in the business world are expanding and growing, leasing is always a great deal for everybody. There was, for example, a small group of retail shops known as "White Front Stores" founded by two clever guys.

One day these clever guys came to see us. What they

wanted to do was establish a chain of retail stores. In order to float the whole thing and furnish their stores they needed to lease a large amount of fixtures.

"How much are your fixtures going to cost?" I asked. "I have to know so I can get a financing commitment with our banks."

Approximately $150,000 per store, they told me.

That's a lot of fixtures, I thought to myself. How many stores can these guys possibly build in a year? Remember, it's still 1950, only a few years after Levittown. People didn't think in terms of large chains or massive retail constructions at that time. If you were an eager retailer you started with a single store, then maybe you built another, then maybe three or four more over the next four or five years. If you were lucky.

"How many stores are you guys thinking of opening?" I asked.

"Forty stores a year," they said without changing expression.

I almost fell off my chair.

It was an exceedingly bold plan, and in retrospect a visionary one. There was only one problem from my standpoint. As lessor I'd have to find the financing to buy them the fixtures.

Already, understand, I'm on the hook for more than $6 million out of pocket, and the net worth of my company is no more than $5 million. I'm taking flak from everybody about this—the bank, the Wall Street people. How can you get yourself in so deep? they're hollering at me. How can you do such a terrible thing?

So what happened—and only someone in an entrepreneur's position has the flexibility to do these things—I got them their fixtures anyway, and these guys built their stores. As it turned out, they raised the money for their building mortgages from Massachusetts Mutual Insurance Company. After about a year I went back to Mass Mutual and told them: Look, you have a mortgage on these stores. Why don't you take over the fixtures too, since the stores are all doing so well? They agreed, took over the fixtures, and it worked out very well for all of us.

It was timing, It was luck. Every day there was another reason for doing what we did. Sometimes we made mistakes, sometimes what we did seemed silly. But the timing was right, and it mostly worked out. The things we did then, you can never do again today. The timing was right.

Growing—and Growing Excitement

Growing is an opiate. A stimulant. An aphrodisiac. The greatest thrill ever experienced by man or beast. The finest brand of champagne. The most delicious caviar.

This, at least, is the way we looked at it in those days when our boundaries were pushing out, our cash flow increasing, our business ballooning.

It was growing so fast, indeed, that we began to realize that if we were going to continue to expand we'd need additional sources of financing.

We'd been a three-person show up till then, of course, and we were dying to keep it that way. But at a certain point, we knew, this arrangement would stop being cost-effective. We needed personnel now if we were going to continue to grow. Sometimes you have to spend money to make money.

So first we found Dot a bookkeeper.

Then we hired a real live secretary for Mel, something we'd never dreamed of in our old Mom and Pop incarnation.

Finally we even got me a secretary.

This was the big time, all right. Next we hired a file clerk, and soon after that several employees to cover home base for Mel and me when we were on the road.

Piece by piece we were building an organization, and a business. And what fun it was, what great fun. . . .

Catching Up

Of course, we still owed a considerable amount of money to the factors, Walter Heller and James Talcott. We were still paying them back every month at an extraordinarily high rate of interest.

On the other hand, we never forgot that without the help of these companies we would never have built up our business and made it as far down the line as we did. So we didn't begrudge them their 16 percent a month, even though we could now go to the banks and borrow at 7 percent for other deals. We were prepared to let the portfolio of leases assigned to the factors eventually pay themselves out. Most of them, as luck and time would have it, were almost up anyway. A majority of them had less than two or three years to go.

It was nice to know, of course, that if we ever needed a great deal of money in a very great hurry we could also return to the factors. Having paid off our debts through the years with such punctuality, we were on excellent terms with both Heller and Talcott and they were more than happy to oblige. But our factor days were over, really, and from now on all new leases would be financed through the banks.

This shift from factor to bank called for a lot of other modifications within the structure of our offices as well, and it especially shifted Dot's position.

We had people in our office now who could do the bookkeeping and the letter writing and answer the phone. Now we needed somebody who the banks could trust and work with.

Dot was our woman. She now began to layoff the leases herself, gather them as they came in, periodically put them into a portfolio, then deliver them to a bank. She also began to forge personal relationships with key financial people at a number of banks in the city. This, as we will see in a later chapter, put us in strong strategic position down the line.

Dot's shifting role also helped for present reasons too.

Because once we went public and started spending real money, we owed every bank in the city—Chase, Manufacturers Hanover, Bank of New York—the works.

We'd go to bank A. We'd arrange for a loan. Then we'd quickly use up all our credit.

We'd go to bank B, start the same process, and quickly stretch to our limit again.

Banks C and D followed, and more after that. Sometimes it seemed as if there wasn't enough money in all New York City to pay for our deals.

Every time we reached the limits of our borrowing, which happened all the time with the large deals we were cutting, we'd have to find yet a new source of financing. This is where Dot shined. She knew the bankers, knew their wives, knew their personalities, knew how to push them to the limit—nicely. She was working the "inside," as it were, and her labors quickly paid off.

Yet despite the fact that we were growing so quickly, and playing in such a rarefied atmosphere, I don't think any of us ever forgot that we were a family business.

And we loved it that way. It was a hands-on deal, and this made us feel in complete control. The thought of hiring outside salesman or professional marketing people never crossed our minds.

We had no idea where things would ultimately go, of course, We simply waded into the stream with our eyes open, and let the waters carry us where they would. Always, it seemed, there was a new project coming up, a new challenge, a new twist, a new way of doing things. I don't believe we ever had a master plan behind it all. I don't believe we ever sat down and figured out exactly where we wanted to go. The modus operandi just developed on its own, you could say. We did the best we could every day, and every day we learned something new.

A Very Unique Position

As a result of stirring the pot we found ourselves in a very unique position. Our procedure was like this: we'd sign up a manufacturer and become his leasing agent, or arm. We would supply him with copies of our leases. He would sign the leads. Then all he had to do was call us and ask for the dollar amount, give us the number of months involved in the deal along with the cost of equipment, and we told him what the monthly rental would be. In both cases this was an established figure, since the manufacturer produced only certain types of equipment and we had a rental rate on each type. When the manufacturer's salesman got the order and had the lease signed, he would then return the leases to the manufacturer, who would forward them to us, and we would pay 30 days after the equipment was shipped, delivered and accepted.

On this schedule, our company incurred very few expenses. We had low sales costs, a manageable travel budget, and a tiny staff. Advertising was kept to a minimum. Instead, we got the word out by periodically writing articles for trade magazines explaining the advantages of leasing. People read these articles, became interested, and wrote to us, wanting to know more. Basically, our product sold itself. Soon we had customers across a national platform including places like Puerto Rico and as far away as Hawaii.

It was a bright new kind of business, and of course one day the inevitable began to happen: other leasing companies began to spring up and threaten us with competition. This should have been intimidating. But we had the edge. Why? Because most of these new companies specialized in certain kinds of products. We, on the other hand, would lease *anything*.

What do I mean by this?

Well, someone once asked me for a list of the items we leased in these early days.

I sat down and wrote it out. It's far from complete, but here's how it looks:

> Machine tools
> Office equipment
> Forklift trucks
> Lighting fixtures
> Air-conditioning units
> Over-the-road tractors and trailers
> Precision equipment
> Manufacturing equipment
> Store fixtures
> Etc, etc, etc.

The point is that we didn't limit ourselves, didn't specialize, didn't settle into one field. As we grew, there always seemed to be another area where leasing would be helpful. The world, it seemed, was screaming to be leased.

The New Toy

Before we knew it, the two years allotted to us by Sutro were over. Sutro was extremely happy with the financial statements we showed them, and announced that we were ready to go public, just as they had promised at the beginning of the deal.

Suddenly we had a new toy: Wall Street.

Right away we all got involved in the process, and started asking Mr. Florzheimer questions about how Wall Street worked and how we could make our stock move once it was issued.

Always a practical man, Mr. Florzheimer chuckled, nodded, then politely told us (in so many words) to mind our own business and leave the Wall Street wheeling and dealing to him.

Though it was a bit of a disappointment at first, over time we learned that Mr. Florzheimer was right: that we were in the leasing business, he in the money business, and never the twain shall meet.

Since Sutro was our major stockholder, it was agreed that they would find a Wall Street house to underwrite our original public offering. After some searching, Burnham and Company was selected.

Tubby Burnham, the principal of Burnham and Company, was in charge, and was working on how to best get the issue out. During this time he and I met on many occasions. With the experience of both Sutro Brothers and Burnham and Company, we came up with what I still think is one of the great concepts of a small company going public.

Here's how it worked: At this time — and before we went public — one-third of the stock was owned by Mel and his family, a third by our family, a third by Sutro Brothers. Obviously, if we were going to sell stock to the public we would each have to reduce our stock holdings accordingly.

But Burnham and Company was smarter and came up with what they called a "unit plan." In order to buy one hundred shares of National Equipment Rental at, say, $5 a share, you had to purchase two bonds, each in the amount of $1,000, or $2,500 for the unit. There were warrants attached to this bond which could be exercised at a later date.

Doing it this way, National Equipment Rental gave up very little stock, and at the same time acquired a substantial amount of funds that we quickly put to work.

To our delight, the issue sold out immediately. Our stock began to move.

Can you imagine the excitement in our family when we saw the first 100 shares of stock come over the tickertape?

We were all present on the floor of the American Exchange when it happened. The transaction took place and NER went over the tape at the asking price: a big $5.

Our timing was perfect. Our business was flourishing. And our bank lines were increasing to meet our needs. It all seemed to be happening so fast, yet with all due respect, we had a solid foundation. Our past experiences allowed us to handle the situation and not be carried away by it.

We were on our way.

Chapter 15

❧ ❧

IN BUSINESS, OUT OF BUSINESS, AND IN BUSINESS AGAIN

Mel

I must open this chapter with a sad and necessarily brief remembrance.

During the first flurry of activity that took place while we were selling NER, my beloved brother-in-law, Mel, passed away.

There's not a lot I can or wish to say about this angelic man. Ordinary words fall short. Only that he was the best of friends, the most able of business partners, and the closest of relatives.

From the start Mel never quite understood or agreed with this new-fangled thing called leasing. Coming from the old school where you bought your own equipment and kept your money in the bank, he always wondered why anyone would want to lease a business machine when they could just go out and buy it.

But here's where the man shined. Even though he didn't agree, his attitude was easy and tolerant.

"If you want to try it," he'd say, "let's try it. I'm behind you a hundred percent *whatever* you do."

Once Mel committed himself you always had his complete support and backing. That was the kind of man he was.

I miss him every day of my life.

A Brief History of Leasing

We were on our way to big things. Bigger things than I could have ever imagined.

And yet . . . and yet . . . through all the joy of going public, of making money, of seeing our business grow and expand every day of the year—through it all, ironically, we were also sowing the seeds that would cause the death of our cherished creation, National Equipment Rental Company. Little did we realize at the time that, as we labored to build our company with blood, sweat and tears, our labors were also setting the stage for its final demise.

⊶ ⊶

Let's orient ourselves a bit.

We've mentioned the reasons in earlier chapters. But it won't hurt to review.

First, there's fact that with a lease you depreciate your equipment in three years rather than seven.

There's the fact that by using leased equipment you do not require a large outlay of cash on-the-line to start up a business.

There's the fact that you don't need to go hat-in-hand to a bank for your money.

There's the fact that if you lease X-dollars' worth of machine equipment, these costs never show up on your balance sheet as a debt, thereby giving you a healthier balance sheet when you need it.

And finally there's the fact that a lot of amazing new machinery was pouring off the post-war assembly lines in the early 1950's. Items like the forklift, for instance. Today such machines are common fare at any factory. During the post-war era, however, the forklift was a sensational new invention and every business that handled heavy equipment wanted one.

To buy even one forklift was an expensive proposition, and for small companies on a limited budget it was financially out of the question. But to lease a forklift, and to pay it off *over time: ah!* that was a different matter entirely.

These and several other benefits, I believe, made leasing stand out as a powerful option in the business community. As the years passed more and more people availed themselves of it. If you ask me, however, the bottom line to what makes leasing so attractive was simply human nature.

That is, it's psychologically easier to spend small amounts of money over an extended period of time than it is to plunk down a huge sum all at once. Even if you end up paying a bit more money over the long run, as with a bank loan or credit card, the means justify the ends.

This, I believe, is what clients liked most about our deals, and what ultimately made leasing so popular. I'll even go one step further. Note that from the years 1950 to the present time, leasing has allowed vast numbers of aspiring entrepreneurs to launch their business on a shoe-string, and to make a financial go of an otherwise unaffordable and untenable enterprise.

Thousands, perhaps hundreds of thousands, of small businesses have followed this course, using leasing as a bootstrap, a fulcrum for making something out of nothing, then growing their business to great size—sometimes mega-great size—all because they were afforded a chance that the banking establishment refused to give them.

This influx of energy and industry, in turn, has been a vitamin pill to the American business community for many decades, and our economy has become richer and stronger because of it.

I'm not taking credit for America's industrial triumph of the past 50 years. But I would like to point out in all humility that leasing has been one of the primary financial forces responsible for the great post-war economic boom—a boom that, in a sense, continues to perpetuate itself even up to the present day.

That's just to set the record straight.

Killed By Success

Now let's go back in time a bit, to the year 1967.

National Equipment Rental Company has gone public by now. Business is growing at a steady pace, and stock is selling for a respectable $10 to $12 a share, as listed on the American Exchange. Dot, Mel and I own about a third of these shares, and the public owns the rest.

Then suddenly, for reasons I still cannot entirely explain, word gets out on Wall Street that leasing is the new investment. A friend of mine at Leasoco follows up by coming out with a public issue, and in 12 months National Equipment Rental Company's stock doubles more than *ten times*.

By December of 1967 our stock is valued at $125 a share, and NER is voted "stock of the year."

Now I loved National Equipment Rental Company. It was my baby, my toy, my pride and joy. I enjoyed every moment of watching it prosper and grow.

At the same time, I knew the time had come to sell it.

Sell it! Just at the moment when the stock was taking off! Why?

For that very reason—*because* the stock was taking off.

And because I knew in my heart and my gut that the stock simply wasn't worth the selling price. Something had to give, and I didn't want it to be the Silverman family.

Our philosophy at National Equipment Rental Company, you see, had always been: slow and steady wins the race. Don't try to make the big bucks in five minutes. Don't go for the home run every time. Get on first, then get on second, then get on third. Build something small and real, and work up from there. That's still our philosophy today.

Yet on the other hand, it's also necessary to stay alert to the winds of change, to read the signs of the times, and to recognize when your company's stock is overvalued. Remember, by law, being an insider, I wasn't allowed to sell my own stock, or very little of it—one percent every six months, in this case, which was tantamount to nothing at all. This meant I couldn't just slip gracefully out the back door. I also knew every nut and bolt of my company, and I was entirely certain that we were dealing with a bubble market here that was about to burst. Probably soon.

So what do you do when you're riding on a plane that's soaring into the air, but that's carrying a bomb about to explode.

You bail out.

The Golden Parachute

Of course, selling a company has a human component to it as well as a financial one, and this was our first concern. Over the years we had acquired a great deal of experience, not only in business but in matters of personality as well. This meant that we had weeded out the deadwood from our company's staff, and surrounded ourselves with a number of loyal, hard-working employees, all of whom cared almost as much about the business as we did.

Would selling National Equipment Rental Company mean that these people would lose everything they had?

Not at all. Because the one thing I had *insisted* on when National Equipment Rental went public was that each of our employees receive a substantial amount of options on any of our stock at $5 per share.

Thus seven years later when our company was put up for sale, this meant that every employee who participated in the option deal—and this was all of them—profited enormously.

It also meant that we could divest ourselves of National Equipment Rental Company in good conscience. A majority of our people were already at retirement age, and were ready to move on. They left the business well heeled, with a large life savings to show for it, and thanked us every inch of the way.

Through the years we have kept in touch with many of these people and still hear from them by phone and letter—how their lives have changed, their children grown up, their fortunes prospered.

One of my fondest memories is of the farewell dinner we held for our staff on the eve of selling the company.

Each employee that night stood up at the banquet table and recounted experiences he or she had at National Equipment Rental. Many employees told humorous stories. The room was filled with laughter and good fellowship. We sat there beaming. When the staff finished their talks and toasts, we thanked them for their love and loyalty, and told them we would never forget them. It was one of those rare moments in life, a mutual admiration society, a love feast, when everybody in the room knows that everybody else was here as their booster, their ally, and their friend.

And so we moved on with the sale of the company.

The Deal Made in Hell

At first it seemed like a deal made in heaven.

It was 1967, year of the Horse. National Equipment Rental Company had just gone into merger negotiations with Flying Tiger International.

The keystone of our agreement was this: Flying Tiger would purchase National Equipment Rental for $7 million. I would then stay on board for five years as a full-time consultant. In this capacity I would provide Flying Tiger with the full extent of my knowledge and expertise in the field of professional leasing

The deal went through and everyone seemed delighted. We signed the contracts, shook hands, slapped backs. Everything was hunky-dory. But almost immediately dark clouds began to appear on the horizon.

For starters, Flying Tiger moved National Equipment Rental from Queens to 120 Broadway in Manhattan's financial district. Here they staffed the offices entirely with their own accounting, credit, and secretarial personnel. They wanted, they told us, to eliminate all traces of National Equipment Rental's mom-and-pop image.

Fair enough, I guessed.

A few months passed, and it became even more apparent that Marty Silverman and the management at Flying Tiger did not share a common business philosophy. In fact, my education was now about to begin concerning the ins and outs of a large, fly-by-the-seat-of-your-pants, grab-it-and-growl kind of business corporation.

●✦ ●✦

The first thing I learned was that the name of this new business game — perhaps the only name — is volume. Hire more salesmen, Flying Tiger demanded. Double your profits. Speed it up. Take whatever credit risks you have to. Get those leases out and selling—now!

This new modus operandi, I admit, took me by surprise.

Next, Flying Tiger gave National Equipment Rental $35 million with instructions to put it out in six-month leases. True to their name, Flying Tiger then hired a group of tigers as salesmen to write these leases.

In retrospect, I can say that I have never beheld such a collection of hungry, ruthless human beings. By sending these salesmen out to hawk leases, the field was becoming like a predatory animal loose on raw meat: blood, blood, blood!

During this period I also watched the credit relationships I had worked so long and hard to cultivate at the bank crumble and dissolve. Flying Tiger's credit manager was a reasonably aggressive man. But when he saw the kinds of shaky deals his salesmen were bringing in he nixed a large number. This put the salesmen in a dither, and they complained to management that the credit manager wasn't giving them the full support they needed—and deserved.

One day the credit manager walked into my office literally wringing his hands. "They're crazy!" he kept repeating. "Wacko! Out of their minds! No one can take risks like this and build a solid business!"

A vicious circle soon arose: the leases got riskier and riskier; the credit more and more tenuous; the management more and more frantic.

And worse: our portfolio soon became riddled with leases on places like bowling alleys, motels, taverns, amusement parks, all high risk investments. Many involved unsavory and even quasi-criminal elements. Flying Tiger, meanwhile, hired several lawyers to handle the litigation that now started pouring in. They then added a collection department, an entirely new arm to the business that we and most other leasing companies had never dreamed of.

Faced with these shoddy policies, Flying Tiger's credit

manager finally resigned. He would rather leave the company, he told me, than deal with cheesy clients and risky credit. It was not just bad business, he insisted; it was a question of conscience as well.

I agreed.

After a while I could no longer stand around and silently watch the craziness either. Soon I was arguing with Flying Tiger's people on a daily basis, and playing gadfly every chance I could get. My relationship with them sank to zero within a matter of months. By the end of the year 1969, to my horror and chagrin, National Equipment Rental was losing most of its credibility and was becoming the laughingstock of the leasing community.

Disgusted, baffled, broken hearted, on December 31, just a few years after the sale of National Equipment Rental, I went to Flying Tiger's executive offices and laid my cards on the table.

Look, I said, you hate me.

And look, I said, I hate you. We've got a mutual detestation society going here. I can't stand the way you do business; you can't stand the way I do business.

Instead of torturing ourselves for the remaining two years of our contractual agreement, I said, let's call the whole thing off. You go your way, I'll go mine. No hard feelings.

Then I offered them a sweetheart proposal.

I would refrain from enforcing the balance of my two-year contract, I said, and would walk away from it cold, right now, this very moment. They wouldn't owe me a penny.

I asked for only one concession in return: that Flying Tiger allow me to reenter the leasing business at my own time and my own discretion, though in an area of leasing totally different from their own. I would not write leases on taverns, amusement parks, airplanes, or anything else that they were currently handling. I would carve out my own niche, I assured them, and never the twain would meet. I would give them a full guarantee of this in writing.

This was an offer Flying Tiger International could not refuse. We parted the best of enemies.

An Amusing Interlude

There was one amusing story connected to my divorce from Flying Tiger that I still chuckle at when I think about it today.

During the time when Flying Tiger and I were going our separate ways, and Dot and I were planning our own new company, it happened that I was simultaneously negotiating a $5 million deal with a company in San Francisco, the Freedon Corporation, to purchase their entire lease portfolio. Time was of the essence on this deal, it turned out, and all papers had to be signed no later than December 31, 1969.

Now Flying Tiger was well aware of the time constraints involved in this arrangement. But they also knew that Marty Silverman and Flying Tiger would soon be parting ways. This gave them pause. Could I be trusted to negotiate with Freedon?

Perhaps. But perhaps not. In actual fact, they had little choice in the matter. Freedon was an old client of mine and I knew the CEO of the company quite well. Flying Tiger was waffling over whether or not they really wanted to be part of this transaction in the first place, and I was a good middle man to represent them.

Finally Flying Tiger hit on a scheme: They would allow me to negotiate with Freedon, all right. But I could only do so in the company of one of their executives, in this case a VP named Fred Something-or-Other. If Fred approved the deal, then Flying Tiger would go along with it. If not, not.

You can imagine my chagrin.

I was a big boy by now and had been negotiating deals with Freedon and hundreds of other companies like them for years. Suddenly here I was, being asked to bring a chaperone along with me to make sure I did everything right.

No one, including the CEO of Freedon, was happy with this foolish arrangement, but time was running out, so we went ahead anyway and set up a meeting at Freedon's office for December 18. Fred and I flew out to San Francisco on the 17th, proceeded to the Mark Hopkins Hotel, and checked into separate rooms. We agreed to meet next morning at 7 o'clock, have breakfast, and take a cab to our 10 o'clock appointment at Freedon's offices.

❧ ❧

Next morning comes. It's 6:30. I call Fred's room.
No answer.
I go across the hall and knock on his door. Still no answer.
This is odd.
Taking the elevator downstairs, I ferret out the hotel manager, and explain the situation: we have a do-or-die business meeting with a major company in a few hours and I can't find my business associate.

The manager becomes concerned and immediately has Fred paged all over the hotel—in the lobby, the bar, the restaurant.

Still no Fred.

Finally the manager uses a skeleton key to get into his room. The whole time, of course, I'm thinking the worst. Fred has been kidnapped. Fred has had a heart attack. Fred is dead.

But no, not at all. Not only is Fred not dead. Fred hasn't even been in his room. It's stark empty—no bags or unmade bed or rumpled towels in the bathroom—nothing.

By now it's 8:30 and this whole affair is starting to feel like a bad science-fiction movie. At the same time, however, I have a critical meeting to attend and I figure, what the heck, if Fred isn't here then I'll just have to go it alone.

Which I do. At the meeting my old friends from Freedon learn that I'm leaving Flying Tiger soon and am starting up my own company. They are delighted at this news and offer to sell me the portfolio directly. Fine. We make a deal.

After the meeting I hang around San Francisco for a few days renewing old acquaintances and advising associates of my new situation. Not once during this entire time do I see hide nor hair of Fred.

Finally I return to New York. Here I head to Flying Tiger's offices and sure enough, there's Fred sitting in his executive office bright eyed and bushy tailed.

What's going on?

Well, believe it or not, it seems that my erstwhile business partner had met an attractive young lady the first night we arrived in San Francisco, and that he had never left her side (or her apartment) the entire time he was there.

End of story.

Now one might suppose that Flying Tiger would be bothered by this extraordinary bit of irresponsibility. But no, not at all. Fred wasn't even reprimanded, and he was to stay on at Flying Tiger for many years to come.

So what really happened?

To this day I don't have the slightest idea. Perhaps Flying Tiger didn't really want the deal. Or perhaps they didn't have the money and this was their odd way of backing out. Was it all a set-up? Your guess is as good as mine.

What I did know was that shortly after this incident I left Flying Tiger forever with a brand new leasing company, a brand new $5 million portfolio with Freedon Corporation, and a brand new contract with the same company to handle all their future leasing business.

Thank you, Lord. Thank you, Flying Tiger.

And thank you too, Fred.

Different Name, Same Business

It's the early 1970's and the techno-economic landscape is changing every day. This change is powered principally by a single new force: the electronic revolution. Although it's not widely realized today, even during the early 1970's sophisticated electronic machinery of all kinds was being manufactured for office use and a new generation of office machines was already changing the way business was done in America.

Here we're talking cutting-edge electronic postage machines, stamping machines, keypunch machines. Electric typewriters were becoming standard equipment and were replacing manual typewriters in every office around the country. During the mid-1970's the IBM's Selectric introduced the self-correcting typewriter, and this ground-breaking invention changed the secretarial landscape entirely. It's difficult to understand the impact such machines had on office work today. No more hand-erasing, no more rewriting entire pages because of one mistake, no more White-out and eraser tape. The machine did it all for you. Everybody wanted one.

Just like everybody wanted one of the new Xerox machines too. Introduced by the Xerox Company in the 1950's, these marvels of science were becoming standard operating equipment in the early 1970's, and wonderful improvements were being made each day in both speed and clarity of image. Gone now was the yellow paper and the reams of carbon copies. If a company didn't have a Xerox copier they weren't really in business. Every office not only wanted one but needed one. The concept we take for granted today, of falling behind the competition electronically, really began in the 1970's.

Finally there was greatest revolution of them all: the personal computer.

This bonanza also started sometime in the early 1970's. Yes, the 1970's. Though most people believe that desk-top computers became popular in the mid-1980's, many offices and small companies were already using primitive versions a decade earlier. In 1975, for example, many large law offices were writing all their documents on a dedicated word processor known as a Viadex. It didn't matter much that the machine took up a quarter of a room or cost a mint. The work it churned out, and the speed it did it in more than compensated for the size and cost.

The electronic revolution was, in other words, in full force. Yet despite the boom, few leasing companies were handling these new machines. Why?

Again, because most of these companies were looking for the big score—the airplanes, the IBM mainframes. Everyone wanted to make a lot of money fast.

For this reason we decided to take a different route. Instead of going for the big kill we'd concentrate on the small office-machine manufacturers that were just then producing exciting new and innovative products. We'd handle the ten thousand dollar deals, we decided, rather than million dollar deals. But we'd do a *lot of them*.

Of course, there was the question of what to name our new company. Here, as it has happened so many times before in my life, Lady Luck stepped in. During the 1930's, it seems, a major New York State utility company named North American Corporation was declared a monopoly by the government and was systematically broken up.

It took 30 or 40 years to accomplish this task—there were many parallels of this breakup to that of AT&T—but by the 1960's all that remained of North American, legally speaking, was its name.

As it turned out, two lawyers ended up owning this name, and one day they called on me with a business proposition.

I listened carefully to all their ideas and found them utterly untenable. There was, however, one thing they did have, that I liked: the name: North American.

Look, I said, I'll tell you what I'll do. Let me buy your company's name, North American Corporation, and you go sell the rest of your assets to someone else. It's like free money.

We dickered around for a while and finally made a deal. For the sum of $3,000 I purchased the name of a business that was once one of the largest and most influential companies in the United States.

It was, we all agreed, an auspicious beginning.

Start Up Costs

Now we have the name, the product, the business — and we're in business.

We're also doing things the way we like to: mom-and-pop style, no frills, tablecloth spread out over the mahogany conference table, and everything on a small, personal basis.

This time, however, there are differences. We don't, for instance, have the start-up hassles we'd experienced in the beginning. In those days we would create a portfolio of leases and periodically discount them at a bank. That, as you know, is how we got our cash. It was a simple business then. I put out long-term money and borrowed it short-term. I borrowed for a year but I rented a piece of equipment for three years. So it took me three years to get my money back and make a profit.

This meant, in turn, that I periodically found myself out of cash and forced to borrow more. In the National Equipment Rental days we accrued tremendous amounts of debt this way, all of it secured by the equipment, yes, but debt nonetheless.

Now, however, in the early 1970's, things are different, primarily because of the $7 million we've received from the sale of our company. No longer do we have to hock every piece of paper we can find. We don't owe anyone a dime. That's a good way to begin a business enterprise, believe me.

Then there's the fact that we've been in the leasing business for 20 years, and that during this time we've maintained an immaculate credit record with every one of our banks and creditors. Despite the fact that Flying Tiger did its best to ruin us, the lenders understood what had happened and they knew we were still solid citizens in the credit department. In fact, the banks trusted us so thoroughly that in the future when our new company reached its peak in the 1980's there was a time when we actually owed the banks more than *$100 million*—and all of it entirely unsecured.

How is it possible for a small leasing company to owe so much money unsecured?

Our formula was as follows: We cultivated a number of banks. We always paid our debts on time. We kept a ten percent balance in the bank against what we owed. And most importantly, we never borrowed more than $5 million from any one bank. There was even once a time when we were in debt to 20 banks across the country and had a perfect balance sheet with all of them. And if, theoretically, a bank got uncomfortable with our relationship and wanted out—this never happened, by the way—we'd be able to say to them, look, you're unhappy with our deal, so why don't you step out of line. We'll pay you your $5 million, and if and when you want to get back on board in the future we'll be here.

That was the way we did it. Simple then, but today there's simply no way a company could operate in this same fashion.

Why? In my opinion, at any rate, there are no real bankers anymore. There's a collection of very nice men and women who go to Harvard Business School, yes, and who all own MBA's. But none of these people have any real power or independence. The banks that hire them keep a tight hand over everything they do. Today if a major company wants to put together a big deal they have to gather a consortium of banks. That's how it works. This, plus the fact that the personal element has gone out of banking as well.

For example, from 1950 to 1980, our company maintained close ties with bankers at more than 20 banks. We visited the executives at their banks at least once a month. We sent them constant information. And updates, and we responded immediately when they made a request. On top of this, we cultivated personal relationships with many of these administrators, and a few became close business friends.

A tremendous backlog of mutual trust was thus built up over the years, and the banks were always willing to take a chance on us. Since our company made a lot of money every year, the banks made a lot of money every year too. And since the banks are in the money-making business, they become increasingly willing to oblige you on your next deal.

•→ •→

At any rate, we decided to go into what appeared to be this fertile new leasing territory, the office machine business. Soon we were leasing a large inventory of items like Xerox machines, IBM typewriters, and data processing equipment. We would rent anything a client wanted, provided he lived up to two criteria.

One, that his credit was good. And/or two, that the equipment we rented to him could be readily resold. If a customer met these standards we were always willing and happy to do business.

Of course, since we were working in a relatively new field, we had to do a good deal of scouting in the boondocks for interesting new prospects. Here we discovered that all across the country little elves were busy in their workshops turning out marvelous new electronic gizmos, all of them in some way related to the electronic revolution that was just then beginning to sweep America.

One day, for example, I got a call from a company named Sycor in Michigan. Sycor was a tiny computer manufacturer run by a likeable middle-aged business man named Sam Irwin. In our first conversation Mr. Irwin informed me that his outfit was producing a jim-dandy new computing machine that he felt certain was going to revolutionize the way business was done in this country. Would I be interested in coming out to Michigan and having a look?

One takes such claims with a grain of salt, of course, except for the fact that recently, Mr. Irwin told me, Sycor had made a deal with the giant Union Carbide Company for a number of these new machines. At this point in the deal Mr. Irwin needed someone to help out with the leasing. Would I come out, take a look at their operation, and if I liked what I saw, handle the deal?

What made his machine so different from ordinary mainframe computers? I wanted to know.

Sycor's computer, Mr. Irwin explained, was not constructed with the usual mechanical parts or even with a lot of cumbersome transistors. It was a whole new concept in electronics, he said, composed of a number of miniature chips and components so small you could hardly see them with the naked eye.

It all sounded like Buck Rogers to me, but Irwin insisted he was for real. And since this new device was so small and compact, he went on, it could easily sit on an office worker's desk. No more taking up half a room in the basement of one's office like most mainframe computers did.

"Who knows," Irwin added, "maybe someday in the distant future every person in every office in America will have one of these machines on their desks."

"Maybe," I answered, thinking this guy was sounding a bit manic.

"They might even have them in their own home too," he added with a laugh. "Every family their own computer, *ha, ha!*"

Ha, ha, indeed. In retrospect, I realize that what Mr. Irwin was describing to me in that conversation was a piece of history that would soon shake the world: This man was currently building one of the world's first desk-top computers.

◗ ◗

Like the early days of the Apple Company, Sycor's operation, I could see as I pulled up to their offices, was basically run out of a garage.

It was a large garage, I grant you, and a glorified one but a garage nonetheless. Don Simon, who had been on my staff at National Equipment Rental for many years, made the trip to Michigan with me. I still remember the two of us walking around Sycor's plant, looking at all the happy workers busily assembling components, soldering connections, packing machines into cartons, loading the trucks. It was all so very organized, so very professional. Yet there was also something strange about this whole operation that puzzled me, something unnatural that I couldn't put my finger on.

After we'd been given the grand tour of the plant for an hour or so by our host, Mr. Irwin, Don Simon gave me the high-sign and pulled me into a corner.

"Marty," he said under his breath. "Do you notice anything strange about this place?"

Yes, I replied, but I couldn' t say what it was exactly.

"I'll tell you what it is," Don said. "It's all too perfect and pat. If you ask me I think half these employees are shills. Ringers. The boss has brought them in just for our visit."

I looked at the rows of happy workers again and sure enough, this was exactly what I'd been feeling in a subliminal way. The whole place had a simulated quality about it. It was more like a stage set than a real working factory; sort of like the model communes the Chinese Communists used to set up on an ad hoc basis to impress visiting dignitaries. To this day I'm convinced that Mr. Irwin had hired a gang of locals to come in and sit there at their desks looking industrious, just to make a good impression on these big-shot money men from New York.

At the same time, however, I must admit I was also deeply impressed by what I saw at Sycor. Not so much by the puny plant with its bogus air of activity, but with the product itself, the computer. Compared to today's machines it wasn't much more than a glorified calculating machine. But by the standards of the day it was a blooming technological miracle. Here it was, a table-sized square of metal and plastic putting out more computing data in ten minutes than a Univac machine of a generation earlier had produced in an hour. And a Univac machine was approximately twice the size of a spacious living room. Whatever number of people actually worked at Sycor, I thought, this company is turning out a great product.

We went into Mr. Irwin's office, sat down at his conference table, and discussed the terms of the deal. Don and I explained that the actual selling price of his equipment had no meaning to us. The only thing we were interested in was what the monthly rental would bring us on any single piece of equipment. Thus, for example, if a piece of equipment had a list price of $10,000, I explained, but to be competitive it had to rent for $300 a month, the most we as leasers could pay Sycor for such an item would be $7,500.

Mr. Irwin thought this over and allowed that it sounded fair. If this deal could get him an increase in volume, he said, he could work with these figures.

I replied that any increase in volume would be up to him. But that obviously the more machines he got into the marketplace the better his chances were of success.

At this point Mr. Irwin asked: "How much of my equipment would you be prepared to buy in any one year?"

"How much would you like us to buy?" I responded.

The biggest number he could think of was $3 million.

"Okay," I said. "Three million. No problem."

I thought he was going to fall off his chair.

"But," I added before he floated away entirely, "if we're going to help your company grow and prosper this way it seems reasonable that you should also allow us to participate in your profits."

Sycor was a public company listed on the NASDAQ exchange, and their stock was selling at approximately $4. I told Mr. Irwin that in return for taking a chance on his new and, frankly, risky business I would receive a certain number of warrants on his stock at $4 apiece. A warrant, I should add, is a guarantee giving one the right in the future to purchase a given stock at a predetermined price, even if the market value of that stock has risen higher than the warrant's original value. Thus, if I pay someone $4 a share for a warrant on their stock, and this stock goes up to $10 a share, I still have the right for a certain period of time to buy that stock at $4.

When there's no pie to share, everybody's pleased to give you a big heaping slice. Mr. Irwin agreed to our request, we shook hands, and everyone at the table seemed delighted with the arrangement. We said goodbye and flew back to New York that same afternoon. (I recall my grandfather telling me years ago that once you make your deal, get yourself the hell out before anyone changes his mind.) Upon return we immediately wrote Sycor our usual three-paragraph letter of agreement spelling our leasing terms in the most simple language possible.

Paragraph one of this agreement outlined what we were prepared to do; paragraph two outlined what we expected our leasing partner to do; and paragraph three outlined what we and our partner would do together.

Mr. Irwin promptly signed the letter and returned it to us, and we forwarded him copies of our lease plan, suggesting that his salesmen take these leases with them into the field when they made sales calls. This way if the prospect agreed to use the equipment they could sign the lease form on the spot and expedite the deal.

◆→ ◆→

The arrangement with Sycor was the first of many such deals that North American Corporation made during the early 1970's with fledgling computer companies all across the United States. It was like throwing stones into a pond: word quickly spread among small electronic manufacturers all around the country, and especially among the computer manufacturers, that Sycor had found a leasing company to handle non-full pay-out or 90-day cancelable leases.

Not long after our trip to Michigan we received a call from the Datapoint Corporation in San Antonio, Texas. A man by the name of Mike Farraty introduced himself and informed me that he manufactured a small computer similar to Sycor's. Would we be interested in coming down and looking at their operation; and perhaps, if we liked what we saw, in leasing their product? Or did we have an exclusive arrangement with Sycor?

I explained that we did not make exclusive agreements with any single manufacturer, and that we considered ourselves a bank, open and available to all qualified investors. In short, we would lease anyone's equipment at any time and any place, provided they met our terms.

Several days later we arrived at the San Antonio airport. Mike Farraty met us and drove us to his plant.

The Datapoint Corporation, I must say, was a good deal more impressive than what we had just seen in Sycor. There were more people at work here, more wheels and whistles turning, and a whole lot more product pouring off the assembly line. Plus the fact that neither Don Simon nor I sensed anything artificial about this operation. It was the McCoy.

Selling Datapoint on our leasing concept was even easier than Sycor. We explained our deal to Mr. Farraty, how it worked, how it provided for all parties involved. His response was that the deal sounded fair, and that he would like to start working with us right away.

As it turned out, Datapoint already had some leases in place, and we agreed to take them over under our regular conditions.

And so we were in business again. First Sycor, then Datapoint, then a string of other small computer companies that followed one after the other like dominoes. After a while we didn't have to negotiate each deal with each new manufacturer. Through hearsay, the companies knew how we operated and the simple fact that they invited us to visit them meant they were willing to accept our terms.

And so we took it step by step. There were no quantum leaps in the growth of North American; just as there had been none in National Equipment Rental. We just kept slowly adding new companies, new clients, new business. As our portfolio grew, our bank clients grew along with them. After a few turns out of the starting gate, we got to know more about what the computer industry was all about, and exactly how its needs and ambitions were prioritized. A standard leasing formula was soon established, and we stuck with it for years to come.

Before too long we were affiliated with 25 or so computer companies across the United States. As far as I know we were the only leasing business in the country working in this area, which meant that competition was not a problem. Our modus operandi was the same with each manufacturer: we would visit the company, check them out, do some research. and if they looked good we'd make a deal and receive a certain number of warrants. Within a few years time I owned a potential piece of most of the young up-and-coming computer companies in the United States.

New Company • *New Era* • *New Ball Game*

As I said earlier, the very nature of the leasing business had changed dramatically since we started in it 20 years before. What did this mean in practical terms?

Several things. First, that we had to explain to the banks what these changes were all about, and how they affected our new credit needs. The trust and credibility we'd built up over the past years was invaluable to us now.

You may recall, for example, how difficult it was for Mel, Dot and me in the early 1950's to educate the banks concerning the concept of leasing. Time and again we tried to impress on them the fact that companies did not need to own their machinery to run a successful business, and that most companies simply needed the use of certain pieces of equipment for a limited period of time. It took us half a decade to teach our creditors this very basic lesson.

In the early days, as well, clients signed three- and five-year leases, attempting to stretch out their payments as long as they could. This was especially fortunate for us because we had such leases to pledge. and the banks felt secure knowing they had both a receivable on lease and the equipment itself. This combination of receivable and tangible asset made it possible for us to borrow in those early days. In fact, without this combination we could never have put leasing on the map.

Now it's the early 1970's and the complexion of American business practice has changed dramatically. Across the country hundreds of little leasing companies were springing up like mushrooms. All of them had realized by now how lucrative the leasing business is: you simply buy the equipment, borrow from the bank, lease to local customers, collect the payments. All this can be done from a small office with a minimal staff and almost no overhead.

The secret was out.

Thus, at North American we decided to go about the

financial side of our leasing plan in a somewhat different way from the others.

I won't bore you with the details of how we changed our leasing policies or modified our standards. Suffice it to say that in the old days of a 36- or 60-month lease, we were exposed for the full 38- or 60-month periods. Now under our new leasing agreement, our greatest exposure was for 25 months; that is, in 25 months we recovered all our costs and still owned the equipment, which we could then return to the manufacturer if we wished.

The banks liked this.

And yet, they were cautious. As usual. Not only did they have trepidations, but they had pretty much the same trepidations they'd had 20 years earlier.

So what did we do? What we had always done. We nursed the banks along. We lunched with the executives. We called them every chance possible. We explained to them in painstaking detail how our new leasing agreement worked. We attempted to make the banks feel secure, and we proceeded to accomplish this difficult task step by step by step.

As before, it wasn't easy.

There was, for example, always a particular person on the executive staff of every bank, the one who invariably asks "But what would happen if. . . ." That's what this person always says: "Well, gentlemen, I see the point you're trying to make. And it's a good one. I'm almost convinced. But just tell me: what will happen if. . . ."

He would then proceed to elaborate some obscure problem, the solution to which was known only to God Himself. The only answer we could come up with to such questions was the dependability of our reputation and the reminder that up till now we had done exceedingly well by our creditors, adding significantly to their wealth over the past 20 years.

●► ●►

As the months rolled by and as we struggled to get North American off the ground, Dot and I recalled that at National Equipment Rental we had maintained an especially strong relationship with several banks in Philadelphia, namely the Philadelphia National Bank, the Fidelity Bank, and IBP.

Since these banks were relatively close by we contacted them and attempted to renew our relationship. First, we prepared a balance sheet. Since our company was no more than six months old, all we could show at this point were assets and liabilities plus a surplus of $2 or $3 million.

Then we telephoned our friends at these banks, set up appointments, and took the train down to Philadelphia to visit all three of them.

Our associates at the banks were all very eager and friendly, as we'd hoped they would be. They were immediately intrigued by our new approach to leasing, and wanted to know when we would be prepared to start a relationship.

They were a bit taken back, I think, when we told them: Right now. Okay, they laughed—right now.

They then gave us a set of papers. It was understood that we would fill out them, send them back, and each bank would then say yea or nay to a million-dollar line of credit, completely unsecured except for our own personal guarantees. Before we left Philadelphia all three of our banker friends had made it relatively apparent that we had a strong chance of getting what we needed.

How happy Dot and I were on that train ride back to New York City. Once again we had the old thrill of the deal. And the fact that we were borrowing unsecured—what a luxury! What a dream! How comfortable we felt dealing with these same banks that years ago had barred their doors to us What a joy it was to feel so free. We had no intention of building a huge company with hundreds of employees now. All we really wanted was to be together and enjoy everything we did. There was no question in our minds that we would make a good living. We knew we would. We had money in the bank and that nest egg made all the difference in the world. What we wanted at this point was to simply enjoy each other, our family, and our work. We held hands as the train clattered on. We chatted, we giggled, We hugged. And we looked together toward the future. We were both so grateful.

I daresay, however, that neither Dot nor I nor any of the nice fellows we met with that afternoon at the banks would know that some day we would be into these three banks and a many others like them not for a million dollars or even ten million, but well over $100 million.

And when it finally happened neither the banks—nor we—would bat an eye.

Wrapping It Up

What of all the small computer companies we bankrolled during the early 1970's?

Many of them either went on to become enormously successful businesses in their own right, or were bought up at fancy prices by far larger firms.

Sycor, for example, grew in leaps and bounds, and eventually merged with Northern Telecom. Today their stock is worth dozens of times the amount of the warrants we received.

Some companies, on the other hand, perhaps as many as half, fell by the wayside, making us little or no money at all on their warrants.

A majority of these companies, however, were firmly riding the electronics fast track, and many of them went on to either become huge corporations in their own right or to be bought up and merge with bigger companies. In both cases the warrants we purchased at such reasonable prices when these companies were just getting started paid off with gratifying consistency.

With the Sycor and Datapoint deal in place and a line of other small computer manufacturers anxious to come on board, we thus closed out the business year of 1971.

It had been a good year.

We had once again established ourselves in the leasing business. Our new staff, like our old one, was small, mobile, and dedicated. It consisted of Don Simon, my associate and administrator; Georgia Henry, my secretary; and of course Dot and me. All we needed beyond this tight little crew was an accountant and bookkeeper to take care of the mail.

That was it. We traveled light, and Dot once again set out to keep the banks happy and make sure our credit prospered.

During this time we also adopted a new slogan: "We do when others don't; we will when others won't." No frills, in other words. No French antique furniture in the waiting room or Fifth Avenue addresses. Just good, honest leases for people who needed them.

And so gradually, stepping stone by stepping stone, we grew.

What we didn't realize in these early years when we were getting North American off the ground was that a bonanza was coming our way that would make everything we had done up till this moment seem almost like nothing at all.

❧ ❧ ❧

Chapter 16

❖❖ ❖❖

THE BIG ONE

Over the next several years at North American our leasing business grew at a brisk rate, due mostly to our success with the new line of office equipment and computers.

Over time, however, a curious problem arose: a growing number of the electronics companies we were dealing with had increased their business with the Federal government. There was nothing unusual with this fact in and of itself, of course. By now the government had come to recognize the tremendous value of computers for streamlining their record-keeping, their accounting, and dozens of other functions. Agencies like the IRS, the Department of Commerce, the CIA, and many others were ordering large numbers of powerful computers, and we were usually the lessor in such deals. The problem lay in the government's methods of doing business.

In plain terms, this meant that if a company—say Sycor—leased their computers to a government agency, the government insisted on paying Sycor the rent directly. Since we purchased all our equipment, this was not an entirely satisfactory deal for us. To adjust to this pesky wrinkle, we formed a separate division of our company called Federal System, Inc., that was designed to represent all the manufacturers servicing the government with leased equipment.

Now the United States government is the largest bureaucracy in the world, and one of its many bureaucratic snafus is that it required us to pass through what it called an "Assignment of Claims Act" before it would pay rent to us.

As for how this act works, suffice to say that since we as lessors were considered middlemen by the government, the government would not recognize us as a separate business entity. And hence wouldn't pay us until we had filed a claim and gone through an inordinate amount of paper work for each and every transaction that took place.

Given our size and time constraints, such a demand was basically impossible. There was just too much business being written to operate this way. The only thing to do was to pay a visit to Washington, and talk with the authorities directly.

And so, one fine day, with my best suit on and my Purple Heart conspicuously pinned to my lapel, I visited our nation's capital. Here I met with several quasi-reasonable individuals, and I explained my situation to them.

As always, the government was a decade or two behind in their business savvy and still didn't understand how the principles of leasing really worked. I spent several hours patiently explaining the dynamics of this "new" system, and eventually I got my point across.

What I told them was, look, it's impossible for us as a leasing company to file a claim every month for each of the 20 or so manufacturers we represent. So could you—would you—permit us to form a second corporation that will go by the name of Federal Systems?

They were inclined to agree with me. Other larger corporations at the time operated in more or less the same way. Why couldn't we?

If, for instance, General Motors leased the United States government 10,000 cars, it didn't bill them as "General Motors," but as a separate subsidiary they referred to as G.M.

Federal Systems. Doing things this way was less confusing for the feds, as well as for us, and they happily went along with the concept.

At any rate, the people I spoke with admitted that my request was reasonable, and they agreed we could form our own separate corporate branch of North American to service the Federal government. From then on we were able to bill all government agencies directly for the rent on equipment leased.

Our volume of business with the government eventually grew to $100 million. And now that the government was our lessee, the banks were always eager to supply the funds.

I sometimes wondered just how much the banks would have given us on these leasing deals. Two-hundred million? A billion? Who knows? For all its bureaucratic, cumbersome ways, in the long run the United States Government was always our best lessee!

The New Wild West

And so our business grew.

Of course, it wasn't always the easiest thing in the world to walk into a business office cold and sell them on the idea of leasing a computer. Most companies had been doing their bookkeeping and inventory control with pencil and pad and accounting machines for years. Now we arrive and explain that to improve their accounting practices they must update their system with computers.

Their reaction was natural: We're happy with things as they are. If it ain't broke, why fix it?

As might be expected, a majority of this resistance came from the accountants and bookkeepers themselves, the old timers who'd been working with antiquated equipment for years. These fellows were not eager to learn a new technology, especially since they didn't believe that this new-fangled computer could really do the job that quickly and well.

And remember, these early computers were primitive clunkers compared to today's sleek machines, with plenty of bugs and glitches. Sometimes a company would take one of our computers on a trial basis, only to have it eat up all of their data during a critical number-crunching operation.

Over time, however, through the 1970's and into the 1980's, companies both large and small began to see how powerful these new machines could be, and to realize that it was only a matter of time before the entire world became computerized.

Fortunately, we had hitched our wagon to the right star.

◆▸ ◆▸

The mid-1970's was a time when big investors were beginning to become v-e-r-y interested in fledgling computer companies, and in their potential. Before long, fortunes were made and lost by investing in small computer manufacturers.

The Vydec Company, for example, which manufactured a dedicated word processor, was growing in quantum leaps. As they expanded they required increasing capitalization. Finally they went to the Exxon Company in New Jersey for financial backing. Exxon liked what they saw and agreed to provide the needed funds.

But the going was tough for Vydec, and each time they kept returning to Exxon for more money. In turn, they gave Exxon more stock.

Eventually the founder of Vydec realized he had given away so much stock that he was now a minority stockholder in his own company. He was breaking his back to build up a business that was no longer his own. So he sold out to Exxon completely. Exxon, meanwhile, being an oil company, had no real understanding of how to market this new instrument. And so, in a few short years the once-promising Vydec Company was history.

The other side of this gold rush mentality was a company called Lexitron.

Lexitron manufactured a special dedicated computer that was "hard wired;" that is, electronically constructed to perform one or two specific tasks and no others. Modern computers, for example, can perform endless functions—play games, word process, crunch numbers, whatever. But Lexitron's machine was limited to its own circuitry. And thus its owners believed, its future was limited too.

Then along came Raytheon who took one look at Lexitron's machine and determined that they could upgrade it to perform a variety of different jobs.

"Impossible!" said Lexitron's owner, and he paid no attention.

Raytheon then proceed to do exactly what they promised, redesigning the unit. Subsequently, they acquired Lexitron, and produced the new machine for many profitable years.

It was, in short, a kind of Wild West atmosphere where many a canny entrepreneur sensed in his bones that innumerable fortunes were about to be gained and lost with this strange new invention called the computer chip.

None of these fortunes, however, would be more generous, vast, or remarkable than one in particular about to be made in the burgeoning field of telecommunications.

And thereby hangs a tale.

Enter the Irresistible Force

It's 1974. Business is growing and I'm feeling good about our future at North American. One day I get a call from a pleasant-sounding fellow named Bill McGowan. He'd like to make an appointment with me right away. He says, Come over and talk about the possibility of North American writing leases for him.

"Sure," I say. "Where are you?"

"Illinois," he answers.

Now this was surprising. From the familiar way he's talking I thought he was just around the corner.

A few days later this fellow McGowan saunters into my office, and introduces himself, along with his financial officer, Wayne English. Though he has a certain amount of polish and a good deal of business knowledge (he was, it turned out, a Harvard Business School graduate), I could tell right away that beneath the veneer lurked a street fighter all the way, a coast-to-coast trucker type full of will and moxie, who was going to charm the pants off you with his Irish sparkle, all right, but never—*never*—take no for an answer.

"So what can I do for you?" I asked him pointblank after some friendly small talk.

My new friends, it turned out, ran a small telecommunications company in Illinois that maintained a line of microwave towers running from Chicago to St. Louis. If their company could acquire one of the new PBX (Private Branch exchange) switches just coming onto the market, McGowan explained, they could increase their customer base from the present 6,000 clients to at least 12,000. A PBX switch, I should explain, was a large telephonic device that was just becoming popular with businesses across the country. In essence, it allowed a single company, or even a chain of a company's satellite offices, to tie all their phone lines together into a single mini phone center.

This switch, McGowan announced, would cost $750,000.

He wanted us to arrange the purchase, and lease it back to him.

Sounded interesting. But why was he coming to me? I wanted to know.

"Where does the phone company figure into the picture?" I asked. "Why don't you just go directly to AT&T?"

McGowan and English both smiled.

"Well, you see," McGowan replied, not without a touch of pride in his voice, "We're an independent carrier. We're presently in competition with AT&T."

Competition? This tiny outfit wanted to compete with the largest company in the world?

Then in the back of my mind I remembered: Over the past decade several small companies had been battling Ma Bell in the courts to break her monopoly on telephone service. I remembered that the FCC finally ruled in favor of several of these small operators, and that it was now technically possible and institutionally legal for a small, independent carrier to go head-to-head with AT&T.

I asked my visitors if they had brought some financial information with them, which of course they had. Glancing at their company's balance sheet and financial statements, it became quickly apparent that they owed money to a large list of creditors and banks, *and* had limited assets—no equipment, no machinery, no nothing.

"You're in a very capital-intensive business," I remarked to them after perusing the statement. "Where is the cash flow going to come from to run this company, and to pay our rental?"

McGowan shrugged and smiled his broad Irish smile at me. "We have all kinds of financial people interested in us right now," he said. "We'll get the job done."

Then he leaned back in his chair.

"Imagine," he said, "if an independent carrier like ours could capture just *one percent* of AT&T's business. *One percent*. That niggling little amount would be enough to make all

of us very rich men. And now that the FCC has ruled for deregulation, it can be done. Why shouldn't we be the ones to do it?"

Now one of the things on which we prided ourselves at
North American Corporation was that we rooted for the under-
dog and were ready to go out on a limb for a gutsy new business. I liked this guy, and I liked his vision: David and Goliath.
Jack the Giant Killer. Take on the largest, toughest, meanest
company in the world single-handedly. And do it, what's more,
without any money or assets, with, in fact, nothing but persistence and will power. Of course, In the past few years, I knew,
other companies had tried and failed at the same challenge. But
all that had been before deregulation. Theoretically what
McGowan was saying was true. You could go head-to-head
with AT&T. But with his minuscule bank account and total lack
of assets, could he really do it?

I asked him who manufactured the PBS switch.

Danray, he replied, a Dallas-based company run by a
dynamic CEO named Jim Nolan. We then began to brainstorm
on how his equipment could be purchased.

After a long discussion, Jim Nolan agreed that a deal
could be arranged.

We agreed that North American would pay $35,000
with our purchase order. The balance would be delivered after
we received two years' rent. McGowan's company would also
pay us $16,000 a month for the lease with money earned from
the increase in business that the new switch would presumably
generate—the hypothetical 6,000 new customers. By working
with these figures, we calculated, North American would
receive an income of approximately $200,000 a year.

Sounded good on paper.

But there were plenty of potential pitfalls.

Could we afford the risk? Should we take the chance?
What would we do if McGowan's business *didn't* double, as he
planned? What if he went down the tubes instead? Obviously
if McGowan defaulted, Danray would repossess the switches,

and our exposure would be something around $350,000.

Though I raised these question several times and never received an entirely satisfactory answer, McGowan and Wayne English were so full of confidence—no, not confidence, *certainty*—that their enthusiasm was infectious. It was apparent to me that these men were determined to succeed. The best word I could come up with for both these men, and specifically for McGowan, was a word one reserves for special kinds of people: *visionary*. McGowan was, I believe, a man with one eye on his pocketbook, yes, but with the other on a star. It's difficult to say no to such men.

I decided to call Jim Nolan, to see if he would participate with North American on some basis if we purchased the switch. In our discussion I suggested that if Danray, the manufacturer of the PBX switch, would cooperate with us in this deal we might be able to figure a way to swing it.

McGowan had worked with Nolan before, he said, and the two of them had maintained a warm relationship through the years. Nolan would be predisposed to making the deal, McGowan assured me, especially if I could *just* nudge him along a bit.

◆▸ ◆▸

I called Nolan on the spot, introduced myself, and told him I was here in my office visiting with two new friends, Bill McGowan and Wayne English. All three of us were trying to figure out a way to purchase one of his PBX switches, I said, and lease it to McGowan's company for five years.

Jim Nolan and I both agreed that there was a lot of risk involved in this deal, but that the prospects were intriguing. Nolan seemed like a bright and savvy fellow, though sophistication alone was not necessarily enough in his business. As it turned out, Jim Nolan eventually built Danray into a prosperous business, and eventually sold it to Northern Telecom. Northern

Telecom went on to became one of the largest manufacturers of switches in the world.

My first question to Nolan was this: If McGowan's telecommunications company defaults on the lease, how much help can I expect from you in remarketing this piece of equipment?

Nolan's response was immediate and frank. He explained that a PBX switch was a highly specialized piece of equipment, and that the commercial market for it, though potentially enormous, was still relatively limited at the present time. On the other hand, he said, if we ran into trouble he would certainly give his best effort to help bail us out.

Fine. He was a man of his word, of this I was sure. Yet in business this "best efforts" guarantee, along with a dime, usually gets you a fine cup of you know what.

So I took another tack. I asked Nolan if he would be interested in participating in some of the risk.

He wanted to know what I had in mind.

Well, I said, suppose I agree to pay you $500,000 for the switch when it's installed, then pay the balance of the $250,000 in a non-interest bearing note due one year from that date.

He said he was listening.

I told him that his only real gamble in such a deal was whether or not he would make a profit on the switch. He would, after all, have his $500,000 safely in hand which represented, I was sure, more than the cost of manufacturing.

Nolan thought about this for a moment, then replied that the proposition sounded interesting, that he'd consider it, and that he'd get back to me soon.

On my end I reasoned that North American would lay out $500,000 for the switch and collect $200,000 at the end of the first year. If McGowan's outfit defaulted, our total exposure would still only be $300,000. And if they didn't default, the $200,000 we collected could be repaid to Danray, along with another $50,000. We would then own the equipment completely. Such an arrangement would increase our yield, reduce our risk, and launch McGowan's company into a new dimension of success.

After Nolan hung up McGowan and I discussed the matter further. The more we talked the more feasible the deal seemed. Nolan would probably go for it, we both agreed. Like McGowan, he was trying to get his operation off the ground; and like McGowan, he needed all the cash and distribution he could find.

So far so good.

I then informed McGowan that if my company was going to take a risk like this one, we would have to receive a certain number of warrants on their stock as consideration.

McGowan said that this sounded reasonable. The only question was how many warrants were we talking about, and at what price? I suggested that we determine these details after he received the equipment and the leases were all in place. He agreed.

We chatted a bit more, and by the time our conversation was over everyone was relaxed and enthused about the new relationship between North American and this bold new telecommunications venture. We all shook hands. McGowan and English started for the door.

"Wait a minute, you guys," I called out to them, almost as an afterthought. "I completely forgot to ask you—what's the name of this new company of yours?"

"Well," McGowan answered, beaming that Killarney smile at me across the room,"for the present we're calling it Microwave Communications, Inc.—until we can think up a better name."

He tipped his hat, turned, and left.

Microwave Communications, Inc., huh? Rather a long and cumbersome, name I thought. But, of course, if you abbreviated it, it wasn't that much of a mouthful.

In fact, it sort of rolled off the tongue.
Just say it: MCI.

An American Success Story

Where had this fellow McGowan come from? Why and
how was he attempting such a ridiculously impossible feat:
competing with AT&T? Who would dare to do such a thing?

The story is worth a moment's telling.

It begins in 1962, in Joliet, Illinois, where an ex-farm
boy mobile radio dealer named Jack Goeken and several business associates have just set up a branch dealership in
Springfield, the state capital.

One of the most heavily trafficked trucking routes in the
mid-west runs by their new office, the stretch between Chicago
and St. Louis, a run of road just under 300 miles long dotted
with dozens of industrial sites and important delivery depots.

One day Goeken gets it into his head that if he builds a
set of relay towers along this route using his mobile radios, he
can tie the two cities together over the airwaves without having
to rely on the local telephone company. His plan is to install
radio repeater towers 30 miles apart all the way along the
Chicago-to-St. Louis route (the average range of a mobile radio
at the time was about 15 miles in either direction). This network will allow truckers making the run to communicate with
one another, he figures, and more importantly, with dispatchers
both in Chicago and St. Louis.

Great idea. But there's one problem. The Iron Mother,
AT&T, doesn't tolerate *any* telecommunication competition, no
matter how small or niggling. And this includes a tiny string of
radio towers in the middle of the sticks.

At the same time, however, Goeken senses a sea change
that wasn't there even a year or so earlier. Business firms across

the country, he notices, are becoming increasingly aware of the new cutting-edge telecommunication technologies that are just now starting to come on the market. And yet AT&T, the great conservative dinosaur company, is doing little or nothing to exploit these new technologies or to get them into the hands of the general public. Indeed, in certain ways AT&T seems *opposed* to the new opportunities in telecommunications, and a lot of companies are growing increasingly discontent.

These rumblings are quiet ones, of course. It's still the1960s. Who, after all, is going to oppose Ma Bell? At the same time, the climate is becoming increasingly ripe for someone to give it a try. And as fate would have it, this someone is to be Jack Goeken.

And so, against all odds, with no money, no assets, no credit, and no credibility, Goeken does something totally amazing: he files a legal suit against AT&T before the Federal Communications Commission. Being a taxpaying businessman, Goeken maintains, he has a right to set up his radio towers anywhere he likes.

Now for Goeken, understand, this battle is not just a matter of money. It's based on common principle. As an American, he insists, he has a God-given right to establish his own communication business, even if it is nothing more than a 300-mile string of mobile radios. What right does AT&T have, he asks, to stand in his way just because it's the biggest, and at that time, the *only* guy on the telecommunications block? Isn't America built on the notion of free enterprise and independent initiative?

Doing his homework, Goeken discovers that in 1959 the FCC has already heard the anti-monopoly complaints of a handful of American businesses, and has responded by allowing several of these companies to build their own internal microwave communication networks. Things are changing, he sees.

Goeken also determines in his research that, legally

speaking, AT&T has a *de facto* monopoly over the country's phone lines but *not* a government mandate. This means that technically all Americans are within their rights to compete with American Telephone and Telegraph any time the spirit moves them. It also means that AT&T's resistance to such attempts is fundamentally illegal.

Goeken now proceeds to raise the remarkably humble sum of $3,000 from a small group of friends in Joliet. In 1963 he then applies to the Federal Communications Commission in Washington for a license to become his own common carrier and to operate a microwave-driven communication system along the St. Louis-to-Chicago run.

For the next four years the case of Jack Goeken versus AT&T drags on, and during this time the gargantuan AT&T throws every bureaucratic snafu and legal dirty trick it knows at poor Mr. G.

But Goeken is an immovable object and irresistible force combined. By now he has become an authority on telecommunications law, and an expert at handling the FCC. He has also picked up several significant allies along the way — lawyers, entrepreneurs, financiers — who believe in his cause, and who are willing to bankroll his law suit the whole nine yards.

In the end, the FCC rules in favor of deregulation, as we all know, and by so doing they set a precedent in communication rulings, opening the door to any enterprise that wishes to set up shop as a common carrier. Goeken is then granted his license. He is now free to build his chain of microwave stations, and to challenge Ma Bell and any other telecommunications company as well.

But Goeken, it turns out, is a crusader, not an entrepreneur. It has never occurred to him that his little business could be expanded beyond the 300-mile stretch of his radio line, and that he could really give Ma Bell a run for its money. Not at all.

It's at this critical point, in 1968, that Bill McGowan steps into the picture.

Already a successful financial consultant with a nation-wide reputation for saving failing companies, McGowan is bored with the regular business routine and is in search of bigger game. Joining up with Goeken and MCI that same year, his visionary's eye is quick to recognize the fantastic financial potential in this operation. At the same time, he understands that Goeken's vision is limited, and that given the right spin, this business could go national and even international.

McGowan finally makes his proposal to a stunned MCI staff: why not go after AT&T directly and wrest away a piece of its $7.5 billion *long-distance business*? The way, he knows, has already been cleared legally, and others are already getting into the game. Why shouldn't we jump in too?

Within a year McGowan then goes both to monied friends and to major companies like Holiday Inn and Allen & Company. He soon raises $5 million, and begins to set up small microwave networks across the country similar to the one that Goeken established between St. Louis and Chicago. McGowan's hope is that one day he can tie these little networks together into a single mother company that rivals Ma Bell.

An impossible dream, of course—for anyone but Bill McGowan.

Struggling On

For the next three or four years we did business with McGowan continually, leasing MCI as much equipment as we could. McGowan, it turned out, had exhausted his bank line, and now leasing was his only alternative. During this time I watched as he weathered one financial crisis after another, keeping his head above the water, but only barely. By the time four turbulent years had passed, in 1978, MCI boasted that it had reached its promised goal, a customer base of approximately 12,000 clients.

What they didn't boast of was that they owed $33 million to a variety of creditors, and that they were tottering on the brink of insolvency.

For while McGowan had been busy putting MCI on the map, he was also busy borrowing, borrowing, borrowing, going from one bank to another, arranging shoestring deals, making promises, wheedling credit out of organizations that technically shouldn't have let him in the door. He also owed us, North American, a sizeable sum, and he was digging himself deeper and deeper into debt with the Bechtel Corporation, a construction company that was building many of the microwave towers that were already beginning to dot the American landscape.

Meanwhile, with McGowan playing for such high stakes and pushing the envelope, his partner, Jack Goeken, faded out of the picture. Tough and determined as they come, Goeken was a hometown radio salesman at heart; all this high finance and deep debt was over his head. Eventually he and McGowan cut a deal, making Goeken into a silent partner. By 1978 the Microwave Corporation of America was entirely McGowan's show.

Now what to do?

Here was a company hovering on the edge of unimaginably large profits, and at the same time of disastrous losses. Potentially MCI could earn millions of dollars for its shareholders, billions even, if it played its cards right. Great. But its numerous creditors were becoming more nervous and more vocal every day.

To make matters worse, MCI was presently deadlocked in a series of legal battles with AT&T, and this litigation was eating up a good deal of time and attention. Though all indications showed that MCI would prevail in the end, where was the money going to come to from till then?

McGowan's basic business strategy, what's more, though a brilliant one in retrospect, was vociferously questioned by many of his backers at the time. His notion was that we—meaning all his creditors—should look on MCI as a capital-intensive business and should value revenue over profits at this early stage in the company's development. Keep pouring money into microwave networks, McGowan demanded, keep leasing equipment, keep building up a customer base, keep selling services, and do so for several more years. At the end of this time, he promised, once the legal details are cleaned up, and the company stands on solid economic footing, the profits will flow like Niagara.

There was only one problem: how *to get* the company on a solid economic footing? Obviously a massive injection of fresh capital was needed if MCI was going to get out of debt and make a run for it. And where would this capital come from? By 1978 MCI had done all the borrowing it could do.

The answer Bill McGowan came up with was simple and direct: go public.

Going Public

The deal had to be carefully structured, and all MCI's major creditors—five banks, Bechtel, us—were involved.

Allen & Company, a venture-capital broker, agreed to underwrite a $30 million issue for MCI to get the ball rolling. It began with a cumulative convertible preferred stock. The concept was that $15 million of the issue would go to pay off a portion of MCI's debt. Allen & Co. would get $2 million for underwriting the deal, and the remaining millions would be used by MCI as working capital.

In the process, since they were running with a deficit net worth, MCI's balance sheet would also be restructured. To do this, Bechtel and North American both agreed to convert $3 million of MCI's debt into preferred stock, thus removing $6 million from their negative balance sheet.

So far so good. Next came the problem that up till now MCI had given out millions of warrants. It was agreed that all investors would dispose of 75 percent of these warrants, and that they would be replaced with new warrants valued at ten cents apiece.

Things were starting to fall into place now, and MCI's balance sheet was beginning to improve. Where Microwave Corporation Inc. had previously been running with a deficit net worth, these innovative changes gave it a positive net worth. The improvements would definitely improve the sale of the issue. We all started getting excited.

Then, as it often happens in such deals, one of the banks started to get difficult.

The First and Last of The First of Boston

It was the First of Boston.

They suddenly declared they were tired of carrying so much high-risk debt for MCI. They had no faith in the company's future, they told us. They wanted out of the deal entirely and immediately.

How to handle this one?

Psychologically speaking, when one member among a group of creditors gets panicky and wants out, this riles up the other banks like blood in shark-infested waters, and makes them wonder if they're going to get their rightful share.

In this case, MCI's other creditors were all major banks including the First of Chicago, Continental Bank of Chicago, Manufacturers Hanover, and First National City Bank. Perhaps the First of Boston knows something we don't know, the banks started to think. Perhaps we're in this thing too deep! Maybe it's time to bail out while we still have our skins!

A chain reaction threatened, and the situation, so promising just a day or so earlier, began to unravel.

It was decided that we should call a meeting and determine whether we could persuade the First of Boston to change its mind. Since we were also a major creditor, I was invited to sit in at the table with the banks. At the time I had approximately $5 million worth of leases out with MCI, and I stood to take a terrible drubbing if the banks did not agree to continue. What set me off from the rest of the fellows at the meeting, however, was that I was the only one there who was fully on McGowan's side.

Why?

First of all, because I liked the guy.

Second, because I remembered from my own experience how difficult it was to get a business started, and how problematic it can be to deal with banks.

And third, I really believed in what McGowan was doing, trying to buck the system and set up a new nationwide telecommunications network.

This doesn't mean, I should add, that I believed he could actually *do it*. That was another story entirely. Maybe he could, maybe he couldn't. But I liked the fact that he was trying.

At any rate, when the day for the meeting arrived, important vice presidents from five banks showed up, along with McGowan and Wayne English, CFO. We all sit down at the table.

This meeting, understand, was to determine whether or not this brash interloper, this Jack the Giant Killer, this Microwave Communications, Inc., that has dared to wrestle and defeat the great AT&T on its own private turf, would continue.

◆◆ ◆◆

From the start of the meeting things didn't look to bright.

It quickly became apparent, for instance, that the First of Boston was not going to budge from its position, and wanted out of this deal *no matter what*.

After going round the table a few times, the First insisted that the way to handle the deal was simple: all the other banks should buy them out. No problem.

The First then announced that it was prepared to sell its $15 million note for $13 million plus the thousands of warrants they held.

Immediately the feathers started to fly. All the bankers were hollering and howling at once like a group of school kids: Why should we buy *you* out! They were screaming at each other. Why don't you buy *us* out!

The argument went on in this vein for about half an hour, going nowhere; and again, I couldn't help but feel that I was watching a bunch of kids arguing over who gets the first turn at bat. At the same time, I was sitting there feeling gloomier and gloomier, not saying a thing, trying to keep out of the argument, but thinking the whole time that there's no way this thing is going to be resolved in a happy way, and I was going to get killed.

Then a strange thing happened.

Wayne English, MCI's CFO, turned to me in the middle of the melee and said in this hail-fellow-well-met voice, "Hey, Marty, why don't *you* buy out the First of Boston?"

I was flattered, of course. But I also felt like I was being placed on the hot seat.

"Love to," I said. "Only trouble is, I don't *got* $13 million."

Everyone laughed; and then in a half-joking way I added, "Of course, if any of you guys wants to *loan me* the money I might give it some thought."

Remember now, MCI owes me $5 million, and I'm dead

in the water if they go under. It's clearly in my best interests to keep them in business.

More chuckles. Then the spotlight moves away from me and the argument continues. A few more futile minutes pass full of childish bickering and bargaining, and finally five o'clock rolls around and it's time to close-up shop. The meeting is adjourned without having accomplished anything much. I go home feeling mighty concerned.

Then the next morning I receive a telephone call from Al Weiss, the VP from the Continental Bank of Chicago. Al asks if I meant what I said yesterday at the bargaining table— about buying out the First of Boston if the banks loaned me the money.

I told him I guessed I did.

We then talked at great length concerning the First of Boston's hard-nosed position and concluded that if the First did not cooperate in some way with the underwriting, MCI would surely fail. All the other banks were rooting for the deal to go through, Al assured me. They thought there was plenty of profit down the line for all of us. But none of them knew wanted to buy out the First of Boston. Al was particularly anxious for this underwriting to succeed, he told me, and from the enthusiasm in his voice I could tell he meant what he said.

Finally he came to the point: His bank, the Continental Bank, would loan us $8 million. The remaining $5 million, he suggested, should come from Bankers Trust which had supported us so many times in the past.

As Al well knew, my main contact at Bankers Trust at the time was a fellow named Clete Zinmeister, a tough character, a street fighter, but the type of guy who'd do anything in the world to help if he believed in you. Through the years Clete and I had forged a solid relationship, both on a business basis and a personal one. He was the man to see in such a deal, there was no doubt about it. The only question was, did I want to get involved so deep?

"Are you game?" Al Weiss asked. I could hear the anxiety in his voice.

I thought for a long moment. I thought about McGowan and Jack Goeken. I thought about the years these guys had put into trying to make a go of this bold and impossible adventure. I thought about my own personal struggles, trying to get my little company off the ground for so many years. And I thought about my $5 million investment.

"Sure," I said after a long pause. "Sure. Let's give it a try, Al. What do we have to lose anyway?"

"Not much," he answered. "No more than $13 million!" It was the laugh that broke the tension.

The Art of the Deal

That same day I telephoned Clete Zinmeister at Bankers Trust and spoke the magic words. We had a kind of code between us, you see. If a big deal was brewing I called him and said, "I'll bring the donuts, you bring the coffee, let's have a meet."

"How's tomorrow, eight o'clock?" he replied. "Usual place."

"See you then," I said.

Next morning I arrived at Bankers Trust, met Clete and his associates in front of the building, and we went downstairs to the basement coffee shop.

"I just got a call from Continental Bank," I told Clete almost before we were settled in our seats. "Continental told me I should ask you guys for $5 million."

Clete laughed. "Why don't you borrow it from them?" he asked. "From Continental?"

"Because," I answered, "yesterday I just borrowed $8 million from them."

The expressions on my friends' faces froze. This was big.

For the next hour I proceeded to explain the complexities of the MCI situation to them in detail. I told them about the First of Boston's hard-nosed position, and about Al Weiss's proposal. I told them about McGowan and the incredible potential of MCI.

At the end of this time Clete conferred quietly with several of his associates, then said he'd get back to me by three o'clock that afternoon.

At three o'clock he called, as promised.

Sure enough, Bankers Trust was in. They would loan me the $5 million. We had ourselves a deal.

➡ ➡

I immediately phoned the other parties and they, of course, were delighted with the news. It was decided that Wayne English could notify the First of Boston and tell them that Marty Silverman had agreed to buy them out.

Which he did.

Then a peculiar thing happened. Or perhaps not so peculiar when you consider human nature. Suddenly, the First of Boston got cold feet.

Silverman's buying us out, they no doubt said to themselves. What does he know that we don't know? What are those four other banks up to? How come this whole deal has turned around so quickly? What's going on that we don't know about?

The First of Boston began asking a lot of questions and finally started making noises about not selling at all.

You can imagine the reaction of the other four banks. After playing the gadfly for days and being a constant irritant to all of us, the First suddenly got coy: should they get out, or shouldn't they?

A flurry of telephone calls followed between all the banks—also a bit of cajoling and even, perhaps, some implied threats. The upshot was that in the end the First finally agreed to sell its position after all.

Immediately I telephoned the officer in charge of the First of Boston, and informed him in no uncertain terms that I did not want this deal to be mummified in red tape. I told him that my own company would draw up the legal documents, keeping them short and to the point, and that I didn't want any lawyers around at the closing to bring up hair-splitting problems that would blow the deal. All I needed from the First of Boston, I insisted, was a simple letter assigning all rights, titles and interest in the notes and warrants to North American Corporation for $13 million.

Miraculously, they agreed. They would write the necessary letter, they said. The only stipulation was that I show up at their office the next morning at ten o'clock in Boston with federal funds. Difficult to the last.

I telephoned Al Weiss at Continental Bank and Clete Zinmeister at Bankers Trust. I told them the time and date of our meeting with the First of Boston, and that they would have to bring federal funds with them. After we'd gotten over this big hurdle with the First of Boston, we all agreed, we'd iron out the paper work between us.

Next morning at nine o'clock we all arrived at the First of Boston's building. We downed several cups in the coffee shop, and proceeded to the First's main offices.

Right away things got hot. Smiles disappeared. Voices got louder, then turned harsh and intimidating. The Bank of Boston would have many millions of dollars of federal funds in their possession by approximately twelve noon that day. But who, the question came up, was entitled to today's interest for these funds?

I sat there quietly as the banks blazed away at each other, astonished that they would jeopardize such a sizeable deal over a single day's interest payment. What was this all about? Was it simply a smoke screen on the part of the First of Boston to back out of the deal?

The hostility in the room increased, and I died a thousand deaths thinking that the deal was going to crash after all. I couldn't believe that grown men would make such fools out of themselves over a few dollars.

It was only after the argument was resolved that I understood what all the fuss was about. The interest on the money passing hands that day was not $356 or $1,000 or even $5,000, the kinds of figures we think of when we think of bank interest. It was approximately *$18,000!* The fight, it turned out, had by no means been over nothing. That day I gained a new respect for the bankers' point of view. But since they had federal funds in their hands by 12 noon, the First of Boston agreed that no interest was due them for that day.

◆◆ ◆◆

The deal was done. North American Corporation was now one of MCI's banks. The rest was details.

First of all, the creditors and banks owned millions of MCI's warrants outstanding at prices ranging from $2 to $4. We all agreed to reduce this number to a total of 3 million warrants at ten cents a share.

It was also agreed that the First of Chicago, Manufacturers Hanover, City Bank, Continental, and North American would hold a certain number of warrants exercisable at ten cents a share up to the year 1985. The First of Boston, in turn, agreed to return to MCI the warrants they held; and MCI agreed to issue 350,000 warrants to North American at 10 cents per share, exercisable until May, 1985.

We were now ready to proceed with Allen & Company's underwriting, and the issue was ready to be launched. MCI received $28 million net of the $30 million from the underwriting. It could now reduce its debt and run the company with an ample amount of working capital. Fine.

Yet despite the euphoria over making the deal MCI was by no means out of the woods.

One Last Time

I couldn't believe it.

After all this wheeling and dealing at the bargaining table, after all the warrants that passed hands, after the First of Boston was paid off in full, there were still entanglements.

Serious ones, too. This I discovered a few months later when Wayne English paid me a visit.

What's the problem now? I asked, seeing that Wayne looked troubled.

W-e-l-l-l. . . It seemed that Allen and Company was ready to go public with the issue all right, but that MCI was having trouble getting its statement certified. Which meant that the whole deal, with all the work that had gone into it was about to go down the drain.

Why can't they get certified? I asked.

Because, he said, MCI was supposed to have at least $2 million tucked away in the bank, and this, he said, they didn't have right now.

Why? I asked.

Well, because they had an interest payment due on their loans coming up, and this was going to use up most of their available cash.

So here I was with egg on my face once again, $13 million into the deal, with my name on the paper, and now they were telling me the deal still wasn't going to happen. They couldn't get the bloody statement certified because they didn't have the cash.

"So go borrow it," I yelled at him. "You guys are good at that."

"I guess that kind of brings up the subject of why I'm here," he replied.

"Uh, uh! Not me again!" I shouted, amazed at the nerve.

"Calm down, Marty," Wayne replied. "I know you're into this thing up to your eyeballs. We just went to the Riggs National Bank looking for a couple of million dollars in lines of credit and they're interested."

"So what's the problem?"

"We need someone's personal guarantee," he replied.

"And that someone just happens to be me?" I said, feeling that I'd been here before.

Wayne smiled and nodded.

Now I'm already in for 13 million. What can happen to me? I ask myself. Two more measly million? What the heck. Might as well be ruined over 15 million rather than 13.

After a bit more conversation and back and forth with Wayne, I agreed that yes, once again I'd put my finger in the MCI dike, and save the company. I was surprised that we, as a very small company, could borrow $13 million while MCI was unable to borrow a measly $2 million more.

But I didn't complain.

❖❖ ❖❖

So, I acted as guarantor on the deal. The Riggs Bank gave MCI the loan, and the Bechtel construction company chipped in as well. My company, North American, received another 30,000 MCI warrants at ten cents apiece with a guarantee, plus plenty of preferred stock. And that December MCI went public for their $30 million.

Then two years later the *real* miracle happened.

In 1983 MCI, which by now had overcome most of its hurdles with AT&T and was becoming a major player in the telecommunications industry, Michael Milken of Drexel-Burnham agreed to proceed with a new issue for $500 million.

As luck would have it, MCI had just released its quarterly figures, showing their most successful quarter of all time, with $331 million in revenues, and profits of more than $90 million. This advance represented an increase of more than 10 percent over the previous quarter's earnings.

When many of the people on the Street heard about this they became bullish over the new issue. As a result the issue was heavily over-subscribed, and the offering was increased to $1 billion. This meant that North American Corporation and the Silverman family were holding countless numbers of MCI warrants and preferred stock.

We were rich beyond our wildest dreams.

❥ ❥ ❥

Chapter 17

◆→ ◆→

THE PHILANTHROPY BUSINESS

A Strange Dilemma

After the MCI deal went through and the returns from the stock dividends started pouring in everything changed.

Before MCI we had been a moneyed family. Now we were a rich family. Far richer than anything we had ever expected, ever needed, ever imagined, and perhaps ever wanted.

If this sounds falsely humble, I don't mean it in that spirit.

It's only that for years my people and my wife's people had always gotten along happily with the basic things in life. None of our tribe ever craved after yachts and mansions. This is true even today.

It's not that we're saintly or above it all, only that my wife and I had both grown up in hard-working households where we had learned to make do with what was there, and to like it. Living modestly was our style, our way of life, and after a while, if you live this way long enough, you get used to it. It becomes the norm, a habit and, I should add, a kind of protection from the temptations that arise when the money pours

in. As the saying goes, "From fancy tastes come fancy problems."

So here we were facing a dilemma. Where once we had
been one business among thousands of businesses, almost
overnight our bank account had swollen to epic proportions,
and we were suddenly ranked in the stratosphere of the multi-
millionaire.

We could put a certain amount of these profits back into
our company, it was true. But our business really didn't need it;
it was large enough and self-working enough now to prosper on
its own without financial injections from outside. And as I said,
neither Dot nor I had pretensions to the high life or to parlaying
the money that was just then rolling in from the MCI deal into
yet bigger and better business.

And there was another sea change going on too. A
change brought on by age and experience and a restlessness to
move on. Dot and I thought it was time to sell our company and
get out of the leasing business entirely.

Changing Times

Why abandon a lucrative and established company?
Why leave the goose that lays the golden egg? Especially since
our company had more or less started the equipment-leasing
business in the first place?

The answer in two words: changing times.

When we started in the equipment-leasing business our
competition was practically non-existent. For all intents and
purposes we owned the field.

What's more, for reasons that I still don't understand to
this day, it took other entrepreneurs a relatively long time to
catch on, to realize that leasing was the wave of the future, and
that they had better hop on the leasing wagon now while there

was still room in the business for the little guy.

But things change, as they must.

As the years passed it slowly became apparent to just about everyone in the business world that leasing an item—it didn't matter what item it was: car, computer, forklift—that leasing an item was a financially sounder strategy than purchasing it outright. All the work our company had done in the beginning to convince customers that it's better to lease than to buy was paying off now, in spades. Leasing finally caught on.

Even when the competition began to mount, however, our company held its own, mainly because we were willing to take risks that other companies turned their backs on. We could always find a way to cut a difficult deal.

When business computers first came on the scene in the late 1970's, for instance, no leasing company would touch them, and few businessmen would lease them. So we pushed all the harder and at the same time made an end run, going to the government and convincing them that leasing a computer was their best option. The result was that a majority of our business in the early 1980's was leasing computers.

Another example: Most people don't realize it today, but the plastic cards we use today to pay for just about everything only got their start in the 1950's. It started with the oil companies. They all wanted it to be as easy as possible to use their gasoline, so each company—Exxon, Mobil, Shell—started issuing special plastic credit cards that you gave to the attendant at the station after each sale.

Now this meant that every gas station had to have a device for the attendant to feed the card into and to process the transaction. It was all brand new at the time and they were struggling with how to make these machines as efficient as possible. One day a guy came to me who wanted to send 250,000 gas stations around the country this card-printing device for $3 a month.

I told him no way, you can't send out 250,000 bills for $3 every month, then receive the checks, process them, keep the records, and so forth and still make a profit. The guy left and that was that.

Two months later he comes back. Nobody will go for the idea, he tells me. Did I just happen to have any ideas?

I used to run a gas station, if you remember, and I knew how the whole thing worked: the guy from the gas company comes in with the truck when you have a tank full of gas and he empties his truck, then he comes in and I sign a ticket for him recording the amount of gas I've purchased. When the guy comes in he signs the ticket.

So why not add the $3 for the printer at this point, and let me, the gas station attendant, collect the money directly from the gas company, from Exxon or Gulf? This way you don't have to collect the money from a zillion different oil companies, you just collect them from the major oil companies at the end of the month.

The guy took the idea and ran with it. Eventually this is exactly the way the gas buying transaction was done just about everywhere.

Then one more thing happened. I have to laugh. If you were to sit down and try to think this scenario up on your own it would be impossible. But fate has a way of doing it for you. Now the oil companies, you see, started doing things this way, which meant they were receiving all these little pieces of paper back from the gas stations across the country, thousands and thousands of them each month, so many that it finally became impossible for the individual person to read all of them. To take care of this problem some smart person invented a machine called the optical scanner, a device that was specifically designed to read the company's bills.

Now as it turned out, these scanners cost $10,000 apiece, more than the oil companies wanted to shell out. So what did they do? They came to me. And I leased them the scanners instead.

What goes around comes around.

At any rate, that fact that our company was willing to go out on a limb and tackle the problems that the other ones didn't want to deal with is one of the major reasons why our company was able to keep its head above water even when the competition all around us became fierce.

But as I say, things change. Eventually the giants started moving into leasing field, the Fords and General Motors, and they immediately started changing all the ground rules, complicating things, pumping money where it shouldn't be pumped and getting cheap where they should have been forthcoming. The whole nature of the business altered within a few years, and after a while we wanted out.

So my wife and I sold off the leasing business we had worked for more than 30 years to establish and prosper. The deal was cut and dried, and really the only interest we maintained in it was that I was held on as a consultant for a few years after the sale was complete. Even this arrangement didn't work out very well, however. I felt like a fish out of water, and within a few years we had severed our connection to our old business completely.

We were now on our own again, starting over.

What Did You Do at the Office Today, Dear?

They say that medically speaking, when a person reaches retirement age and leaves the job he's been laboring at for 40 or 50 years, that person's chances of getting a stroke or heart attack increase by as much as 50 percent.

Why? Probably because that person has nothing much to do and dies of boredom.

Or at least that's what it began to feel like to Dot and me. Not boredom exactly, but a feeling that we weren't accomplishing things anymore and that we were out of the loop.

Every day when I'd come home from serving my time at the leasing company as consultant Dot would quiz me: What did I do in the office today? Who were we leasing to right now? Any new deals?

She, like me, needed new horizons.

Often in life people sit down and carefully work out a plan. They strategize a concept from here to there, from A to Z. Then they go about doing it.

This approach may do the job for some people. But historically speaking, it hasn't worked this way very often for me and for my family. Our approach has always been to simply get into the stream and let it carry us where it will.

And this is exactly what happened during this transitional time in our lives. After feeling like a fish out of water for some time, my wife decided to go back to college and take a course in Social Work. She attended the New School in lower Manhattan for a while, and there she met a certain Judge Otten who was just then serving as a Family Court judge. My wife told Judge Otten that she was looking for a worthy human resource project to become involved in.

Judge Otten, in turn, told my wife about how many people come into his court each day who can barely read and write. Their literacy level is almost nil, he confided in her, and it makes it that much harder for them to help themselves and their child.

One talk led to another. Until one day Judge Otten and Dot decided to do something about the illiteracy problem in New York. Forming a partnership, they founded a project that Dot would eventually became deeply involved in, and which was known as "Two Together."

The purpose of Two Together was to provide academic help to disadvantaged children from poor, inner-city areas. The main thrust was to help children with reading skills and to bring slow-starters up to speed in both their language skills and reading comprehension levels.

Today there are, of course, many reading programs in the schools. At the time though, Two Together was something of a pioneering venture. Many of the literacy programs in existence today throughout the United States are based on the model that Two Together helped establish.

Now as I mentioned earlier, Dot had a special way with banks and bankers, based on a combination of charm, knowledge, and persistence. Through the years our leasing business made constant use of her skills in this department as front woman for our financial negotiations. Because she was both cordial and straightforward, over the years she also managed to form personal relationships with a large number of important bankers in New York and other key cities along the East Coast. These men at the various banks trusted Dot and knew that when she gave her word to them on a deal it was always good. In all our years dealing with different financial institutions in the leasing business we were never once forced to delay a payment or renege on a deal.

Naturally, the banks liked this. And they liked Dot.

Dot visited a number of her banker friends, told them all about Two Together, and made them an offer they couldn't refuse. "I want to start a reading project to help illiterate children in this city," she told them. "If it works we can branch out, help children in other cities, make a contribution to education that will really count."

You have people associated with your bank, she reminded them, who have tutorial skills, and also some spare time during the day. "What I'd like to do is talk to these people about volunteering their time a few hours a week to work at Two Together. The plan is these people will sit down once or twice a week with a kid who was brought up in the ghetto, and who, for whatever reasons, never really learned to read very well—if

at all—in the first few years of school. The two will work
together academically, form a relationship, and in the process
both the child's social skills reading skills will be improved

"What I'd like you to do," Dot said, "is to give us a
room. Not on your main floor of course. But somewhere in the
back of your bank—there's always a meeting room or two in
every bank, isn't there? Lend us your volunteers and one or two
of these back rooms, and my agency will do all the rest."
Before long Dot had convinced several of her banking friends
that this was a worthy cause, and she was off to the races.

Two Together was a great success from the start. After
a year or so it boasted around 175 volunteers from all walks of
life, each of them working one-on-one on a weekly basis with a
single students. Dot helped find the kids for the program herself, and there was always a waiting list.

In the years that followed, Two Together helped put
thousands of disadvantaged children on the right educational
road. Ultimately the JCCA took the project over, and it's still
running today, as successfully as ever.

Working with this project had a powerful affect on Dot.
It made her aware of how much she liked public service, and
how useful one person could be in the world if she simply persisted. From time to time Dot and I began to discuss the possibility of going into the philanthropy business, and dedicating
our accumulated resources to help worthy humanitarian projects of all kinds.

Dot liked the idea. We talked some more.

Dot

Then in 1983 Dot developed cancer. Before the year
was over she had passed away.

It's impossible to describe the emotions that follow such

a loss. It's impossible to talk in any sensible way about the hole that's left when a person you have lived with and loved for decades suddenly vanishes. All the things you did together, your reliance on one another, the trust, the companionship, the plans and expectations and love—none of them are there anymore.

And then the question arises in the aftermath: how does one honor such a person, and such a memory?

From where I now stood in life it seemed to me that the most useful service I could render my wife, now that she was gone, was to continue her work, and to expand the small start she had made with Two Together until it became a full-fledged charitable organization dedicated to doing good in the world.

In the early 1980's the Marty and Dorothy Silverman Foundation was thus born, a charitable institution dedicated to providing financial help and organizational consultation to worthy programs of all kinds.

Of course, now that the idea had surfaced our work had begun. How does one go about starting a foundation?

Well, for starters it was the 1980's, and business in the United States was booming. The stocks we received from the MCI deal were growing on a regular basis, and were generating substantial returns. These revenues would take care of the financial side of our fledgling enterprise.

However, if one intends to start a foundation, certain guidelines are needed from the start. What were they to be?

After some thought, I came up with two basic rules that the Marty and Dorothy Silverman Foundation has abided by faithfully ever since its inception.

Rule one is that our task as sponsors is to simply get the ball rolling, to jump start the endeavor from point zero, then to step back and turn the controls over to others who are better qualified to run things than we are. We see the opportunity and supply the funds. Beyond putting the organizational and financial parts into a single package, and bringing the right people together for the right jobs, it has always been our policy never to became personally involved in the programs we launch. Laissez-faire is the name of our game—get the project on its feet, then let it run on its own.

That's rule number one.

Number two in an oblique way is related to number one. It says that whenever we made a financial donation to any organization—of whatever size—we wish to remain anonymous. Our policy is the same today.

Why anonymous?

Many people have asked me this question through the years. Usually I let them draw their own conclusions. One thing I do say about being an anonymous donor though is that it's a no-lose and often-win kind of deal.

Why?

Because every time an anonymous gift is made in this country, and especially in New York City, our foundation gets the credit. It doesn't seem to matter what the gift is for, or to, or how much—the Marty and Dorothy Silverman Foundation seems always to be acclaimed as the source.

Through the years, I daresay, our foundation has received more thanks and accolades for charitable work that we know nothing about, and that we were never involved with in the slightest way.

Once an anonymous donor gave the Albany Law School $75,000, and the calls of thanks from the school poured into our office for days. Another time the newspapers announced that our foundation was responsible for giving money to build some scientific device of some kind that I had never even heard of.

All this attention because we choose not to ask for attention. A strange irony. Yet as Maimonides says, the greatest charity is to give without expecting anything back, and without telling people what you've done. That says it all.

The Projects Unfold

The place to begin, we decided, was right here in New York City with the Einstein College of Medicine. Up to this time Einstein had very little presence in the field of psychiatry. So we arranged to give them a chair in psychiatry, something they sorely needed. We suggested that they seek out the single most outstanding psychiatrist they could find to fill it.

A world search commenced, and the college finally came up with a Doctor Van Prague from the Netherlands.

The doctor came to New York with his family, and for the next ten years filled the chair with brilliance and authority. Today Einstein is known for having one of the most outstanding schools of psychiatry in the country. So successful was he in establishing the psychiatry department at Einstein and a number of educational programs associated with it, that after his tenure was up and he returned home he was given a knighthood by Queen Beatrix of the Netherlands, and put in charge of the country's entire health and education program.

After the Einstein venture we moved on to what in many ways I think of as the foundation's crowning achievement.

Since the end of the war I had been active in various city armories and veterans organizations, and had generally taken an interest in the policies of our country's military. One day a committee of Jewish businessmen and veterans came to my office. For some time, it seems, they had been working hard to raise funds for building a Jewish chapel at West Point.

"Why not a synagogue?' I asked. "A chapel is for Protestants, isn't it?"

The army only knows one term for a house of worship, they told me, and that word is "chapel." So what we need, they said, is money to build a religious whatever-you-want-to-call-it at the Point. We're overdue, they said. There hasn't been a place for Jews to worship since the Academy was founded 184 years ago.

I thought for a moment. The men on the committee were all earnest, sincere and, I thought, a trifle over-serious about this matter.

"That's really a shame," I finally said. "Especially since the Jews played such an important part in the early days at the Point."

"What do you mean?" the committee chairman asked.

"Didn't you know? Half the members of the first graduating class at West Point were Jewish."

The man's jaw dropped. "You're kidding! That's not possible!"

"It is," I replied. "Absolutely. Want to know why?"

He did.

"Because," I said, quoting historical fact, "there were only two members of the Academy's first graduating class. One of them was Jewish."

Everyone laughed, and this eased the tension a little. Nothing in life is worth getting yourself too wrought up about.

I then told the committee what all of them already knew, that Jews have been trying to get a Jewish house of worship built at West Point for years, but that no one has been able to get to first base.

Look, I said, I've heard about all this. You go to this person, that person, raise a few hundred thousand here, spend a few hundred thousand there, and nothing gets done. What you need are a couple of substantial donations to get the ball rolling. Real money attracts real money.

We haven't really just come to you for money, several members of the committee said. We've come for advice: how do we get this thing off the ground?

If you want to build a Jewish chapel at West Point, I said, don't worry about money. The Lord will provide. Just keep at it and it'll get done.

We all shook hands and the meeting was over.

The next day a messenger arrived at my office delivering an artist's rendering of the proposed Jewish chapel at West Point. It was a beautiful little drawing, complete with landscaping and fine details. The caption beneath it read "The Lord will provide."

That broke the ice. From then on I began to meet with the committee on a regular basis, and we devised a strategy.

After a number of ups and downs, it was agreed that the Silverman Foundation would make a sizeable donation to the project to get things started, and that we would then work to generate additional funds from other donors. What that meant in essence was that I was now obliged to put the touch on other Jewish friends I knew to help out in this worthy cause.

I proceeded to visit a number of friends and to seek donations.

Every time I did they would ask me the same embarrassing question: just exactly how many Jews are there at West Point today?

I replied there are about 50 Jewish cadets, girls and boys.

That's not many cadets, would come the inevitable reply. And, the potential donor would invariably add, probably less than half of that number will actually use the chapel. That's only 25 students. Not really enough to warrant a whole building.

That was the usual argument. And my job was to overcome it.

I did this, along with other members of our committee, by pointing out to the potential donors what we considered to be basic truths in the matter.

The chapel, we told them, was not being built simply for worship. It was being built as a presence at the Point, a symbol of the Jewish tradition and spirit that was long needed in the military, and the absence of which should be both an embarrassment and a point of anger for all Jewish veterans who have served in this country's wars.

A chapel at West Point, we argued, in the small picture would be a place where Jewish cadets could gather, get to know each other, fraternize, feel at home in a largely non-Jewish environment. In the larger picture the chapel would become a national emblem for the Jewish people, a marker in stone for all to see that Judaism is part of the American military landscape, and that thousands upon thousands of Jewish boys have served—and died—in the American military since the day this country was founded. Jews from all over the world would come here and be proud.

Happily, many potential donors agreed.

Eventually the funding was raised and we were underway. An architect of note was hired whose credits included the design for the United Nations Building and Radio City, and work began on the chapel. Two years later the last stone was set in place.

Since that time thousands of Jews from all over the world have visited this spectacular building, and paid their respects to Jews who died in American wars.

Bar mitzvahs are now regularly scheduled in the Jewish chapel, along with marriages and holy days. Yom Kippur, Passover, all the Jewish holidays are celebrated. Locally, Jewish veterans hold their meetings here. Any person of Jewish extraction assigned to the post is allowed to use the chapel for ceremonies, and there is a day school for the children of West Point teachers and personnel.

The chapel likewise now has a full staff including a chaplain (read rabbi) of high rank who works with the Jewish cadets and accompanies them on field trips. Some Hebrew is also taught at the Academy.

In short, this building established a Jewish presence at the Academy that was sorely missing before. And it makes me proud. Though as I said, the Silverman Foundation traditionally gives money anonymously, in this case we opted to be known. If you walk into the lobby today to the West Point Jewish Chapel and look for the large donors plaque with the names of all the donors inscribed you will see our name there among the others.

Some things in life you just have to make exceptions for.

Postscript

I should add a PS to the story of building the West Point chapel, by the way.

After the chapel was built and furnished, a large official ceremony was held there, attended by a formidable number of military brass—generals, heads of armories, dignitaries of state.

Speeches were made, the tape was cut, champagne poured, congratulations all around. It was a spectacular occasion and one that I had been waiting to attend for many years.

Then later that day I returned to my office. There another framed picture exactly the same size as the original artist's rendering of the building was waiting for me in my office. Beneath this second picture was the caption: "The Lord Hath Provided!"

Both these pictures still hang in the spot of honor on my office wall. You can buy your Rembrandts and your Picassos. They're worth millions of dollars. But I tell you with all my heart that I wouldn't trade one of those pictures for all the Rembrandts and Picassos in the world.

Other Projects, Other Days

Since the West Point Chapel has been built the Silverman Foundation has been involved in a number of other interesting and, I hope, worthwhile enterprises.

In 1988, for example, officers from the Jewish Museum on Fifth Avenue came to me, announcing that the Warburg Mansion was being given to them to make into a museum, and that they needed about $60 million to float the whole deal. They had everything in place except for a $5 million guarantee.

Could I help?

I could. The banks all agreed that five million was indeed sufficient collateral. We said we would put up this money ourselves in the form of U.S. Government bonds with coupons to guarantee the loan. At the end of five years when the debt to the bank was reduced, the bank would release our collateral and everyone would get what they want—the Jewish Museum would have its building, the bank would make their profits, our foundation would get its money back plus the satisfaction of knowing we'd backed a worthy project.

Today the Jewish Museum is better than ever and continues to make its wonderful collection of Jewish books, manuscripts, and objects of art available to all who are interested.

Over the years the Silverman Foundation has changed and evolved like everything else, of course, and our particular emphasis has more and more focused on bringing aid and assistance to senior citizens.

Today many of the grants we make are to groups and institutions that help the elderly. The Brookdale Center on Aging, for example, that does so much good for so many senior citizens throughout the New York City area is a favorite project of ours. So is the Kosher Meals on Wheels program that supplies hot meals to handicapped and homebound Jewish seniors. Over the year we have worked closely with the Hebrew

Home for the Aged in Riverdale, Bronx, and with handicapped and abused children.

As a rule we don't go in for brick-and-mortar style projects; that is (with certain exceptions, as you'll see in the next chapter), we don't put up buildings. Our line of giving is tied in directly with help organizations, especially those in the field of education. Without education the people of this city and of this country never get into the stream of things. Each person born today must have a basic high school education and hopefully more to survive. So we like to give scholarships to minorities, to students with outstanding ability, to academic programs that educate the poor and disenfranchised.

As a public foundation we must give away five percent of our assets every year. Today because of fortunate stock investments the foundation has five times more than we started out with. Which means we can give away more and more money — which we do gladly. We wish we had more to give away.

Fortunately, we're also able to keep close tabs on our investments, and because of the nature of these investments we know pretty much to the penny what our income is going to be each year. This means we can make grants right up to our yearly profits, and this gives us a great deal of control.

Today my son Lorin runs most of the foundation's daily operations. All members of the family have a say in running things, I should add, but Lorin is top dog. Remarkably capable, kind, and far-seeing, he also has complete autonomy to make all decisions for us, and this is an unusual state of affairs in the foundation world.

When, for example, he attends meetings at the Grantors Association with other foundation heads from Rockefeller, Mellon, and the rest, the representatives there cannot make decisions on the spot. First they must check back with their board, and with the various heads of their institution.

But we have no outside director to tell us what to do

with our money. This means that in a room full of foundation executives Lorin is the only one who can make a fast decision. At times the other members turn to him just for this reason, because he can break a deadlock or a log jam just by saying yea or nay. That gives us an astonishing amount of flexibility and freedom in the foundation world, and allows us to move quickly when we have to.

At any rate, as time marches on we march with it.

Whatever worthy projects come our way we're always willing to give them a look, and if we think they will help the needy we're always ready to lend a hand. Through the years there have been so many wonderful projects that it would take me too long to name them. And as I said, building the chapel at West Point has given me more pride, perhaps, than all of them. At the present time however, a new endeavor is passing through the Silverman Foundation which is bigger, more important, and more gratifying, I think, than any project I have ever been involved with.

Save the best for last.

Chapter 18

◆→ ◆→

ALBANY:
A WORK IN PROGRESS

One Day Out of the Blue

One of the main features of the strange and never-a-dull-moment life that God has seen fit to send me is that of all the many deals and opportunities that have come my way, none has actually been my own personal creation.

By this I mean that each deal has, as it were, come to me. Not me to it. The only part I play in these episodes is to recognize the opportunity when it knocks, slip into the stream, then flow with the course of events as they carry everyone along.

For example, one day in the early 1980's out of the blue I got the urge to attend a lunch that was being given by the alumni office of Albany Law School.

More than forty years had elapsed since I'd graduated from law school. During this time I hadn't been in touch with them in any way.

Forty years is a long time between drinks. Yet I'd never forgotten how much that school did for me when I needed it most, and how the faculty members guided me along. Since the

MCI bonanza I'd often thought how nice it would be to help this worthy institution with a donation, though I had wondered how their finely tuned alumni seek-and-find machine had let a potential donor like myself slip through their fingers.

At any rate, one day the law school was giving this luncheon and reception in a hotel near my office. I thought to myself, what the heck, why not drop by, have lunch, maybe see a few friends from the old days, and learn something interesting.

So I go over to the hotel and I'm introducing myself around in the crowd, looking for a familiar face, trying to fit in. Pretty soon it becomes apparent that a lot of years have passed since my post-graduate days, and there's really nobody here who remembers me.

After making alumni small talk here and there in the crowd I make my way to one of the heads of the alumni office. I introduce myself, we chat for a while, I talk about my warm feelings about Albany Law, he nods courteously.

Then I mention that I'd like to make a donation to the law school for all it's done for me. The fellow smiles and says that's nice. He'll see to it that I'm put on the mailing list right away.

Well, actually, I say, I've brought a check with me. It's already made out. Who should I give it to?

I'll take care of it, he says, almost absentmindedly.

I hand him the check, and he glances at it.

"One hundred thousand dollars!" His eyes grow wide. "That's a great deal of money, Mr. Silverman! I don't know what to say."

He calls over several other fund-raising executives, and before I know it I'm the center of attention. By the time I left the party I felt as if someone had turned a spotlight on me full blast. Money causes a commotion wherever it goes.

In the weeks that followed the college processed my donation, then came to me with the big question: What did I want the money to be used for?

I reminded them that they were the experts in this area, not me, and that any notion they came up with was fine as far as I was concerned.

Still, they persisted. It was my money; I had the right to decide how it would be spent.

So I came up with a suggestion. How about putting the donation toward a new library?

No, they replied. A fellow named Shaffer who graduated from Albany Law two or three years ahead of me (and who was now head of Grand Union) had just overseen the building of a new library. Everyone was delighted with the structure, including Mr. Shaffer. Still, there was one other thing. Now that they had a new library the next priority was a building to house moot court. How did that sound to me?

Moot court. I remembered my own experiences at this challenging institution, this dress rehearsal for real legal life with its mock trials and debates with fledgling lawyers. I remembered my own adventures as a first-year man, then a second and third-year man, playing the part of a lawyer in a fabricated law court complete with judge and sometimes jury. I'd learned more in that real-life, real-time situation than I had in a dozen classrooms.

Sounds like a wonderful idea, I said.

Everyone was pleased. Shall we name the building after you? they asked.

I thought about this for a minute.

All I was really doing, I said to myself, was giving away money that the Good Lord had passed on to me for temporary keeping. A generation from today nobody was going to remember this guy Silverman. No one would recognize his name on a plaque. And besides, I hadn't played a seminal part in founding Albany Law, or in running it. In fact, I'd taken a good deal from this college. Now I wanted to give something back. How about the men who donated years of their lives to this school? I thought. They were the real heroes.

What about Dean Alexander? I said.

He, you will remember, was head of Albany Law School when I first applied, the man who helped me get accepted and who pulled more strings on my behalf than any poor young student had a right to expect.

"Why not call it the Dean Harold D. Alexander Moot Courtroom?"

Dean Alexander? Who was he? Nobody in the crowd seemed to remember.

But I remembered. I remembered very well. It felt good, really good, to get a chance to speak these words.

When the time came for them to build the moot court room I looked on proudly as they installed state-of-the-art facilities—computers, sound systems, closed circuit TV so that the students could see themselves plead their cases. As I watched the room going up and saw the huge portrait of Dean Alexander dressed in full robes set in its place on a center wall, I hoped that if the dean was watching it would make him proud. Without this good man's help my life would have taken a considerably different course. And, I daresay, a far less fortunate one.

A Terrible Problem

Several years passed. My children and I continued to run the Silverman Foundation and to enjoy the life which the Good Lord had made so bountiful.

Then one day in 1992 I got a phone call from my friends at Albany Law School. A terrible problem had come up, they said. Could they talk to me right away?

Experience has taught me that when someone tells you that he has a "terrible problem," and he wants to talk about this terrible problem "right away," this means only one of three possible things: money, money, or money.

Little did I know, however, that this phone call was actually marking the beginning of one of the most exciting and meaningful adventures of my entire life.

The Seed of an Idea

"We're too crowded," the Chairman of the Board of Trustees told me. "Too many students. We need to expand."

I listened and waited.

"But we don't know how to do it. We have absolutely no land left on our property to expand to. And the state is breathing down on our backs!"

In my day the school had an enrollment of 150 students. Today 750 students were crammed into the same buildings. The enrollment had quadrupled through the years while the actual size of the school had remained the same. How does one fit 750 young men and women into a group of buildings designed to hold a fifth this many?

Answer: you don't. Because of this overcrowding the New York State Accreditation Board was on their case. Reduce your student body, they threatened. Or expand your premises.

Or close down.

That was the problem the school faced, and it was clearly a real one. Was there anything I could do to help?

Now as it so happened, a small parochial school known as Christian Brothers Academy was located on the property directly adjacent.

Was there any hope they might consider selling us a few of their acres? I asked.

As a matter of fact, there had been rumors that Christian Brothers Academy was financially strapped, and that they might *possibly* be willing to sell off a small piece of their land.

Could I talk to them? The Board members wanted to know. Feel them out? See if they wanted to sell? Perhaps make a deal? All we need for our expansion is two or three acres, they told me, and we're in business.

A few weeks after this meeting I met with a group of clergy from the diocese of Lyncroft, New Jersey, that controlled the purse strings for the academy.

At first things seemed promising. Yes, the diocese very well might be interested in selling three or four acres. Yes, they very well might be willing to talk price. How much was Albany Law willing to pay?

Thus began one of the most frustrating three years of my business life.

On Tuesday my new friends were anxious to sell. Let's get to it right away.

On Thursday they changed their mind.

By Saturday they were back in the game. How much money did they want for their land?

They didn't know. They weren't sure. They'd get back to me.

Two months later. Are they still interested? Oh, very.

They think. But they're not sure. They'll get back to us.

A month later the deal is off.

A month after they're back at the table—let's talk.

And so it went.

After being toyed with this way for several years—yes, years—I came to the end of my leash. Tell me what you're really looking for, I finally told them, or the deal is off.

Then the truth came out. What the Brothers really wanted was not just to sell off three or four acres of academy land. What they wanted was to sell the *whole twenty-two acres* the Christian Brothers Academy stood on, then use the money to buy a new piece of land and build a new school.

Clearly the academy was failing. Every year it was getting fewer and fewer applications, fewer and fewer students. Costs were up, profits down. At one time the clergy taught without compensation. Now they were being paid. In short, the school needed a pile of money to start over again, and to keep their operation afloat.

So how much do you want for the whole parcel? I asked.

The Brothers parleyed for a while, then came up with a plan: We'll hire three local real estate agents, they said. Each agent will do an appraisal of the land's value. Then we'll divide their estimates by three, and set that as the price.

Fair enough. A few weeks later the appraisers went to work. They're top guys in Albany real estate, and between the three of them they come up with a price that seems to be in the ballpark—between $4.5 and $5.5 million for the entire parcel, complete with land, drill and athletic fields, and buildings.

So what's the final price? I ask. Do we split the difference?

No. They'd like a little more. Could I come up with a whole $6 million? they want to know. If I can, then it's a deal.

After some thought I told them that this was okay with me if it was okay with Albany Law.

But that's wasn't the end of it. While the diocese was drawing up the papers one or two of the Brothers had hired a fourth appraiser from Syracuse. This guy, it turned out, didn't know a blooming thing about Albany real estate, and after doing his appraisal he came up with a figure of $13 million for the twenty-two acres.

When I got wind of this I hit the roof. Not only had the Brothers gone against their word, bringing in a ringer though we'd agreed to go along with the price reached by the original three appraisers. But the ridiculously inflated price smacked of a put-up job if ever there was one.

In no uncertain words, I replied that they'd insulted my intelligence and that I would never accede to such a deal. I was flabbergasted that they would even suggest such a thing. We'd made a deal at $6 million, but now they were doubling the price and acting as if it was just business as usual.

It was the last straw. I told the fellows at Albany Law School that I was through negotiating, that I wanted out, that the Good Lord simply didn't want this deal to happen. Goodbye.

I folded my tent and went home, thinking that this was surely the end of the whole fiasco. Then, lo and behold, a few weeks later I hear from the Brothers. Mea culpa. Forgive us. It was just a mistake. We didn't authorize that Syracuse agent, somebody else did.

Who? The Pope? God?

No one knew. But the point was, they really *did* want to sell.

How much? I asked again.

They didn't know.

That's it! I said. That's the end! No more negotiating. I've been horsed around for three years, and that's enough horsing for any lifetime. I'm off for good.

End of story.

A few weeks later I got a letter from the headmaster at Christian Brothers Academy. It was a beautiful letter, really, courteous, insightful, to the point. He begged for one more chance.

"Give me thirty days, Marty," he wrote. "That's all I ask: just thirty days. At the end of this time I'll deliver the deal to you lock, stock, and barrel."

Then sure enough, a month later he's fought it out in the trenches with the others, and they've finally come up with an iron-clad deal. If I give them $8.5 million they'll sell the whole twenty-two acres. They'll do it right away, what's more, with no foot-dragging, and no more going back on their word.

What to do now? They're asking a $2.5 million more than the original offer—which, in turn, was a million dollars or so higher than the estimate they'd promised to go by from the appraisals.

Then I thought to myself: it's not my money they're going to use in this deal. Not in the long run. I'll lend the $8.5 million to the law school. We'll raise a bond issue through the state Dormitory Authority.

And anyway, over 25 years what difference will it make? What difference will it make whether I give them $6 million or $8 million? The Christian Brothers will get a new school out of it. A lot of kids will get a good education. And the law school will have its expansion room. Everybody wins. The good this deal generates will far outweigh the cost in dollars and cents.

I kept thinking about this project, kept turning it around in my head. Should we really stop here with the 22-acre parcel for the law school? Weren't there bigger possibilities lurking between the lines? Wasn't there something here that would not only profit the law school but the whole city of Albany?

The more I pondered the situation the more I realized that the chance of a lifetime was hiding here.

Why?

A few years ago we had started out this whole thing looking for three or four acres to squeeze in a few extra buildings to keep Albany Law afloat. Now, out of the blue, we had a chance to acquire twenty-two prime acres smack in the middle of Albany. If we got this land why not branch out to the other schools in the area? This twenty-two acre parcel doesn't just abut the law school. It's also adjacent to a medical school, a pharmacy school, and to a woman's college, Russell Sage.

What if we got hold of this twenty-two acres—that's a lot of land—and used it to expand *all four of Albany's major schools?* What if we then joined the schools together under one umbrella association, and made the community of colleges into a kind of hub, a center of education not only for Albany but for the entire country? Heck, for the entire world?

◆→ ◆→

The raw materials were already in place, I thought to myself: the land, the facilities, the colleges, the people. All we needed was the money. That was my department.

Why not go for the whole enchilada? I thought to myself. Why not take this thing up a few levels, above the local, above the national even, all the way to the world-wide?

Why not go for broke?

The University Heights Association

And so it began.

Before long we formed what is today known as the University Heights Association (UHA), a mutual education coalition consisting of the four neighboring Albany colleges, all of which are to share the twenty-two acres purchased from the Christian Brothers Academy. The schools involved include the Albany Law School, the Albany Medical College, the Albany College of Pharmacy, and Russell Sage.

At the heart of this project was the new construction to serve a variety of student and graduate needs.

What kind of construction? It was—and is—an amazing list. Let me name the proposed projects one at a time:

✔ A student union that will be shared by all four colleges
✔ An art museum and art facilities for Russell Sage
✔ New laboratories for the medical and pharmacy schools
✔ A wellness center that will be made available for all students, employees, and staff of the university

✔ A state-of-the-art computer center
✔ Day care facilities for staff members and married students
✔ A combined-use student union with a food court, copy center, bookstore, travel agent, and a retail outlet for banking
✔ A new combined-use dormitory
✔ A new library
✔ A combined classroom, office center, and legal clinic
✔ A conference center/ deluxe hotel for providing professional information services, continuing education support, and general networking capabilities between the four colleges and the Albany community at large.

The facilities of the four colleges, what's more, will be tied together via a networking communication system that not only reaches every classroom and office in the university but which has national and even international broadcast capabilities. Which means that a graduate law student in Omaha, Nebraska, say, can tune in to a lecture given at Albany Law School and share in the learning wealth.

Thomas Sponsler, who then was dean of the Law School, stated the mission and purpose of this new project in concise terms. "The collaboration with the other institutions that comprise the University Heights Association," he wrote in the *Albany Law School Magazine*, "will permit us to do things that none of us could do on our own, such as entering the market of long-distance learning and teleconferencing. We expect to be able to offer an increased level of student services and athletic facilities that none of us could provide alone. The UHA project very likely will offer opportunities we cannot even imagine yet. It has already brought the four institutions closer together, and that will undoubtedly result in joining activities in the areas of academic programs as well as student services and administration."

Provincial Thinking

Now all of this was, of course, tremendously exciting to me and to my family as we watched the pieces of the project fall into place, and as we saw construction begin on the first buildings.

Yet despite the magnitude of this proposal, the people involved from the universities and state government were still seeing things in local terms. By doing this, I believed, they were setting their sights too low. Such provincial thinking was summed up in an incident that occurred during the building of the Albany airport.

What's in a Name?

The city of Albany, it turned out, had just completed construction on a new airport. This rather impressive structure was staffed with facilities for large jets, and was slated, the Albany people hoped, to eventually become a hub airport for the entire East Coast.

After completion of the project the State brass decided to call it the "Albany County Airport."

Albany County Airport? The name sounded like a puddle jump for Piper Cubs more than a major skyway connection. The government wasn't even using the word *State* in the title. Just *county*!

In my role as cheerleader of the Albany renaissance, I'd by now made a number of crucial connections in New York

State government. In order to get this project off the ground I'd had to play local politics with everyone in town from the governor on down. In the process I'd gotten to know the important players in Albany. Indeed, the political subtext of the University Heights project was not simply better education; it was total urban renovation. The idea behind constructing such a massive college center was to create jobs, attract business, resuscitate civic pride, and make this colorless city into a major player on the East Coast.

When I learned that the wonderful new airport in Albany was going to be given a hick name like County Airport, I thus made a few calls and let my opinion be known.

"Don't call it the County Airport," I pleaded with them. "That makes it sound like a local stop-off."

"What should we call it?" they asked.

"Call it Albany *International* Airport," I said.

"But it's not international," they objected.

"Not yet," I replied. "It will be someday. And anyway, if you want to make something international start out by calling it international. The rest will follow."

After hemming and hawing, and after offering every excuse in the book, the pundits in the local government decided that giving it a more cosmopolitan name might just be the ticket. So today the name of the airport in Albany is—Albany International Airport.

(I recently heard they're now running international flights into Albany International Airport. The flights come from our neighbors in Canada, true. Not very exotic or international, granted. But it's a start!)

At any rate, this gives you an idea of how provincially the wheels of bureaucracy can grind, and how difficult it can be to get people to share a vision. Yet as it turns out good things attract good things, and there were to be several more fortuitous events following this project just around the corner.

A Few More Additions

It's always been my philosophy to let experts oversee the carry-through of any project. My role in charity work, and to some extent in business too, is as an initiator, a starter-upper, and (as both my friends and enemies like to call me), a dreamer.

It was no different with the University Heights enterprise. From the start I had taken pains not to let the people in Albany nominate me for any board, elect me to any office, dub me any kind of director or officer or financial consultant. My place in this drama of urban revival was to see the possibilities, arouse public interest, seed the project with leverage money, help structure the deal, then stand back and let the experts finish the job.

And so after the purchase of this land and the mapping out of the building projects my job seemed to be done. Not only were plans moving ahead that would profit all four colleges, but I was delighted to see that the Christian Brothers Academy had completed construction on its own school, and that they were now opening their door to hundreds of new students.

Though I had wrestled and parried with them for more than three years, and though there were times when I had to count to ten with these fellows and then count again, I couldn't help feeling a surge of pride the day they invited me up to the ribbon-cutting ceremony.

Their new school was located on 100 acres that a local construction company had donated, a gorgeous piece of work with huge playing fields, grassy lawns, a picture-perfect campus, and a group of administrative and educational buildings filled with up-to-date teaching facilities. Though it had not been my first priority to sponsor a new school for the Christian Brothers, it was a fine secondary benefit now to think that I'd played a part in helping a lot of kids get a better education. As with many things in life, when a project is founded on good intentions everyone tends to profit.

At any rate, after seeing the new school go up and helping launch the University Heights Association, I was ready to go on to greener pastures, and to leave the construction of the new campus to the four colleges themselves.

Yet each time I visited Albany I couldn't help noticing that several other spacious buildings near or contiguous to the new project were being underused or were lying entirely fallow.

One of these buildings was especially intriguing: the local National Guard armory, a looming, roomy structure with plenty of architectural character. I learned from the Albany grapevine that this building was receiving a minimum of use from the local community, and that most of its rooms were unused.

I also learned that the building was situated on nine acres directly adjacent to the twenty-two acres in the original parcel, and part of which abutted the Law School's tennis courts. Nine more acres, I don't have to tell you, would be a considerable packet of land in Wyoming, not to speak of in downtown Albany.

Indeed, during the entire time I'd been negotiating for the Academy land I'd had my eye on this tempting piece of real estate, but I'd been too busy to pursue it other than a few preliminary conversations with the Governor. As with any government building, there was a mountain of red tape involved in finding out who controlled the rights, and whether it was available for purchase. Nonetheless, we decided to go for it.

To make a long story short, after a great deal of negotiating, this time with the local and federal government, we managed to obtain the rights to the Armory and to do with it as we saw fit.

We now had nine acres to add to the original twenty-two. That made thirty-one acres.

And there was more.

Yet Another

If you stand somewhere between the armory and the Albany Medical College today you will see a large Y-shaped building known as the Albany Psychiatric Hospital. Architecturally this building is remarkably imposing with 150 large, sunny rooms, numbers of skylights all round, beautifully landscaped grounds and gardens, an adjoining 500-car garage, and lots of amenities. Constructed a few decades ago at a cost of more than $50 million, the state had high hopes that it would someday become a major psychiatric facility in the area.

But drops in state and federal funding plus a host of unforeseen political setbacks cut into these plans. Soon the hospital fell on hard times. By the mid 1990's Albany was spending $26 million a year to maintain the hospital staff of 600 doctors and its dwindling roster of 150 patients. The Albany Psychiatric hospital, in short, was on the ropes.

What if we acquired this building? I thought to myself. And yet another building nearby, the Veterans Hospital. This redoubtable structure sat on the edge of the University Heights property, contained 1,300 rooms, towered up 13 stories, and came with 22 more acres of its own land.

Like the Psychiatric Hospital, the Veterans Hospital was in decay. Most of the older veterans were dying off. The hospital's patient load was diminishing every year. The Veterans Administration was hurting financially.

Making a trip to Washington, I spoke with several key members at the VA, and it soon became clear that for the right price they would be more than willing to let us take this building off their hands.

And that's what we proceeded to negotiate for. Along with the psychiatric hospital and the armory.

●► ●►

And so as time goes by more and more opportunities present themselves on the Albany campus, and each day a new vision of the University Heights project swims into view. Indeed, with further land acquisitions it will become possible to transform all four Albany colleges into major world players: the law school into an international law school, Russell Sage into a topflight woman's college, and the medical and pharmacy colleges into a vast 21st century medical complex that will become larger and more technologically advanced than the Mayo Clinic itself.

The Albany campus can become more than a hub for New York State education. With the proper planning it is possible to remake this growing complex into one of the great educational centers of the world—indeed, to make it the gateway of international education.

This plan is mind-boggling. Yet it is within reach.

Meanwhile another building, the Harmanus Bleecker, also became available near the campus. A landmark structure built in the early 1920's by the famous architect William Robinson, this handsome two-story, full-block edifice once housed the city's public library. Now it's for sale; and once again, the vision expands.

Why not add it to the Law School's already expanding resources? The building can be used as a government law center and as a much-needed night school for the Law School. As I write these words, negotiations are underway.

As Many Stars as There Are in the Sky

How far can it all this go?

Hard to say. A famous astronomer once remarked that there are as many stars in the sky as you care to look for—the more you look, the more you find.

The same is true for the Albany renewal project. Its boundaries are limited only by the enthusiasm of the people who are creating it, and by the enthusiasm of the community that puts it to use. The more time and energy we invest in this enterprise, the greater it will grow—and the more we will see better possibilities presenting themselves for the education of our children.

As I write these words, in fact, plans are going ahead for the $200 million University Heights Association along with various side projects, the sum total of which, I most deeply hope, will end up creating a world-class learning hub in Albany that the whole country and the whole world can draw on.

And after that?

Who knows? How about a covered bridge spanning the Hudson River and connecting the residential community of Rensselaer to downtown Albany? How about a six-mile boardwalk that runs from Albany all the way to Troy?

Whatever the project happens to be, there's still work to be done here and everywhere.

I won't be through until I'm through.

●+ ●+ ●+

An aerial view of downtown Albany,
with the University Heights area in the center.

*"You ain't seen nothing yet.
The best is yet to come!"*

—**Marty Silverman**

July 16, 2003

DAYENU

If you ever had the privilege of attending a Passover Seder (dinner), you may recall hearing a prayer which is recited by everyone at the Seder Table, from the youngest to the oldest. They say in unison, "If you had only brought us forth from Egypt, it would have been sufficient!" We then go on to relate the additional blessings for all the things the good Lord did for us since he brought us forth from the land of Egypt.

At this time I would like to say my "DAYENU" and thank the good Lord for bringing me to this point in my life and giving me a wonderful wife and companion, my children, my grandchildren and my many friends all over the world, still leaving me with a couple of stepping stones to continue. I promise not to waste the new stepping stones and I promise that we will leave the world a better place than it was when we entered it.